American Film and Society since 1945

American Film and Society since 1945

LEONARD QUART

and

ALBERT AUSTER

Second Edition
Revised and Expanded by Leonard Quart

Westport, Connecticut
London

Library of Congress Cataloging-in-Publication Data

Quart, Leonard.
    American film and society since 1945 / Leonard Quart
and Albert Auster ; rev. and expanded by Leonard Quart. — 2nd ed.
        p.   cm.
    Previous ed. by Leonard Quart and Albert Auster.
    Includes bibliographical references and index.
    ISBN 0-275-93326-1 (alk. paper). — ISBN 0-275-93327-X (pbk. :
alk. paper)
    1. Motion pictures—Social aspects—United States. 2. Motion
pictures—United States—History.   I. Auster, Albert. American
film and society since 1945. II. Title.
PN1995.9.S6A87   1991
302.23′43′0973—dc20   90-24128

British Library Cataloguing in Publication Data is available.

Library of Congress Catalog Card Number: 90-24128
ISBN: 0-275-93326-1 (hb.)
        0-275-93327-X (pbk.)

First published in 1991

Praeger Publishers, 88 Post Road West, Westport, CT 06881
An imprint of Greenwood Publishing Group, Inc.

Printed in the United States of America

∞™

The paper used in this book complies with the
Permanent Paper Standard issued by the National
Information Standards Organization (Z39.48-1984).

10 9 8 7 6 5 4 3

Dedicated to our fathers:
Meyer Quart (1912–82) and Lazar Auster (1905–62)

CONTENTS

Photographs follow p. 70.

PREFACE TO THE
SECOND EDITION

My aim in writing a second edition of *American Film and Society since 1945* was to revise, expand, and update the original edition, which was first published in 1984. I took on this project alone, since my collaborator, Albert Auster, had other commitments.

This second edition basically adheres to the structure and critical premises of the original. However, I have made numerous stylistic changes, explored in greater depth the contested meanings and directorial style of a number of films, and dealt critically with films like Woody Allen's *Manhattan* and Martin Scorsese's *Taxi Driver* that were inadvertently left out of the first edition.

The most significant change was the updating of the book to include a complete chapter on the 1980s, concluding with 1989 films such as *Field of Dreams* and *Born on the Fourth of July*. The chapter explores the diverse ways in which Hollywood film in the eighties responded to Reaganite politics and the aggressively materialistic ethos that it ushered in. There is no single political and cultural current that films of the eighties evoke. The films analyzed include Vietnam films as ideologically antithetical as *Platoon* and *Rambo*, rural sagas like *Places in the Heart*, teen cult films committed to the crudest version of the success ethic such as *Risky Business*, feminist backlash films like *Fatal Attraction*, and films critical of American society like *Do the Right Thing* and *Silkwood*.

This book means to provide students, teachers, and the general public with an accessible, synthetic, intradisciplinary approach to American film. I hope it succeeds.

ACKNOWLEDGMENTS

Although the act of writing is often considered a solitary one, there are always people whose love, support, and assistance are invaluable in that lonely and isolated process. Therefore I wish to acknowledge my wife Barbara, who has shared a continued emotional and intellectual passion for film with me, and whose subtle critical insights have been consciously and unconsciously assimilated into my writing; and my daughter Alissa, who loves films and has begun to develop a unique take on them. I would also like to thank Albert Auster, my close friend and co-author of the first edition, who was always the most even-tempered and gracious of collaborators. I am grateful to the present and past editors of *Cineaste* magazine, who have been supportive of my writing career over the years. Finally, a special note of thanks to Chris Brookeman, who helped launch the first edition of this book almost a decade ago.

American Film and Society
since 1945

1

INTRODUCTION

From shadows and symbols into the truth.
                                     John Henry, Cardinal Newman

In 1981, John Huston's almost legendary World War II documentary about psychologically crippled veterans, Let There Be Light (1945), received its first commercial public showing, thirty-five years after it was produced. While the film had originally been suppressed by the U.S. Defense Department, which feared its possible pacifistic influence, interest in it was kept alive by film critics—most notably James Agee, who even included it on his best films list of 1946. Unfortunately time had not dealt too well with Let There Be Light, and most contemporary film critics found it ingenuous and naive to the point of simplemindedness.[1]

Despite the fact that Let There Be Light failed to live up to its critical reputation, it succeeded on another level. In fact, the showing of the film might be compared to lifting the lid on a time capsule—one that provided a clear insight into an era's cultural and social perspective and mood. By contemporary standards, a film that adheres to Let There Be Light's magical faith in the healing power of psychiatrists and Freudianism would be seen as innocent and overly sanguine. It's a vision of the human condition that would hardly be emulated by today's more cynical (albeit no more sophisticated) films. Let There Be Light may have left modern critics unimpressed with its moving portrayal of the plight of shell-shocked soldiers, but it does serve as a useful conduit to help understand the intellectual assumptions of the postwar period.

It is hardly an original point, though it bears repeating, that films have the ability to evoke the mood and tone of a society in a particular era. However, there was a time when a number of historians and social scientists were hesitant about accepting this truism. By films one does not mean merely documentaries, which obviously directly capture something of the reality of the way people live and feel, but also mainstream Hollywood commercial films. It is not only that these films sometimes convey and imitate the surfaces of day-to-day life, the way people talk, dress, and consume—though social realism is clearly not an aesthetic that Hollywood usually embraces or has seen as commercially viable. More importantly, fictional films reveal something of the dreams, desires, displacements, and, in some cases, social and political issues confronting American society.

Undeniably, films are a powerful and significant art form. As art historian and critic Erwin Panofsky has suggested, their absence from our lives would probably constitute a "social catastrophe."[2] He wrote: "If all the serious lyric poets, composers, painters and sculptors were forced by law to stop their activities, a rather small fraction of the general public would seriously regret it. If the same thing were to happen with the movies the social consequences would be catastrophic."[3] That sentiment obviously overstates the case, but films shown in theaters, on television, and on video cassettes are clearly one of the prime forms of entertainment for the general public, and one of the most democratic elements in the cultural fabric.

That films give a great deal of pleasure to a great many people does not necessarily mean that they are a significant form of cultural and historical evidence. But the fact that they reach a mass audience signifies that films do connect with some part of the conscious or unconscious experience of the general public or, at least, a large proportion of it. However, the attempt to define the specific relation of Hollywood film to popular consciousness is a difficult one. One problem is that the writers and directors of films—be they assembly-line products like *Risky Business* (1983) or works expressing a complex individual sensibility like Martin Scorsese's *Taxi Driver* (1976)—have no mystical access to the zeitgeist. There are no straight, clear lines to be drawn between the film industry and the popular mind. The industry is not a mirror of public feelings and habits, nor can one make the vulgar, mechanistic connection that implies that the industry is some evil empire conspiratorially shaping the social values and political opinions of a supine public. There is no question, however, that Hollywood's genius for manufacturing and publicizing seductive images like John Wayne's World War II heroes—icons who had a profound effect on the lives of countless young Vietnam enlistees—should not be minimized. These images often become a substitute for reality for their audiences.

The popular mind itself is no monolith. It is divided by age, social class, gender, region, ethnicity, and race, and is often fickle and change-able in its response. In a matter of four or five years, during the late 1960s and early 1970s, the movie audience shifted from sympathy to social outlawry in *Bonnie and Clyde* (1967) to law-and-order vigilantism in *Dirty Harry* (1971), and it's doubtful that that shift corresponded with some radical transformation of popular feeling. Still, it's possible that during that period both responses towards crime coexisted in American society, and that the films tapped different audiences. It's also hard to be certain why a film achieves popular success. For example, was the suc-cess of *Rambo* based on its political significance—its voicing populist, patriotic, and anticommunist sentiments—or on Stallone's muscle-headed charisma and the film's nonstop action and violence? The an-swer is that it is probably a combination of all these elements that helped garner a large audience for these films. And it's truly difficult to distin-guish which aspects of the film were the basis of its audience appeal.

All one can say with certainty is that American directors, like Altman or Coppola, most of whose films express powerful personal visions and styles, share some of the same dreams and cultural tensions and influ-ences other Americans do. Consequently, films like *Nashville* (1975) and *The Godfather*, parts I and II (1972 and 1974) cannot help but convey some of the cultural and social strains the directors hold in common with their audience. And for the rest of Hollywood's output—films that are much less personal in nature—the movie industry spends a great deal of time and money trying to divine popular values and trends, often succeeding in attracting an audience by knowing just how to package those concerns. For example, some of the biggest commercial hits of the summer of 1989 were films like *Field of Dreams*, which constructed a mythic American past by nostalgically conjuring up the Chicago Black Sox of 1919 playing on a pristine and bucolic baseball diamond, and the well-crafted sitcom *Parenthood*, which views the family as the foundation of American life and consecrates the act of having babies as if family planning had never existed. Both of these films lure audiences by shut-ting out much of the larger social world and being awash with nostalgia for an earlier America. Clearly film images rarely determine our values, but they are both suggestive signs of and reinforcers of popular feelings.

During the last twenty years a number of historians and culture critics have begun to give films their due as important social and cultural evi-dence. Noteworthy works in this vein include *American History/*

American Film, edited by Martin A. Jackson and John E. O'Connor, *Movie Made America* by Robert Sklar, *We're in the Money* by Andrew Bergman, *Film: The Democratic Art* by Garth Jowett, *America in the Movies* by Michael Wood, *From Reverence to Rape* by Molly Haskell, *A Certain Tendency of the Hollywood Cinema, 1930–1980* by Robert B. Ray, and *Camera Politica* by Michael Ryan and Douglas Kellner. In fact, the pendulum may have swung so far that for a number of historians films have come to be one of the most important clues to understanding the state of the American mind. As Arthur Schlesinger Jr. has said, albeit in an inflated manner,

> Strike the American contribution from drama, painting, music, sculpture and dance, and even possibly from poetry and the novel, and the world's achievement is only marginally diminished. But film without the American contribution is unimaginable. The fact that film has been the most potent vehicle for the American imagination suggests all the more strongly that movies have something to tell us not just about the surfaces but the mysteries of American life.[4]

Of course, stating this is much easier than defining precisely how we can penetrate those surfaces and reveal those mysteries. Obviously, the political and social significance of explicitly political films ranging from Abraham Polonsky's Marxist film noir *Force of Evil* (1948) through Stanley Kubrick's sardonic and apocalyptic *Dr. Strangelove* (1964) to Oliver Stone's mixture of social realism and Manichean melodrama in *Platoon* (1986) can easily be gleaned. But again the relation of the political and social perspectives of even these films to the public's social and cultural beliefs is never a seamless one.

All films, however, can be considered political—for films as varied as *On the Town* (1949) and *Batman* (1989) convey a point of view, an implicit ideological perspective, on the nature of American reality. Of course, it is more difficult to discover cultural and social meaning in ostensibly apolitical films like Michael Curtiz's *Mildred Pierce* (1945) and Steven Spielberg's *E.T.* (1982). These two works, like the great majority of American films, rarely attempt to consciously illuminate cultural and social patterns. They usually stylize, mythologize, and at times trivialize the social world—primarily aiming to provide glamor, escape, thrills, or a sense of emotional security to a mass audience. That these films, both the explicitly political and the nonpolitical, were and are often constrained by forces like the power of the studios to make final cuts, genre conventions, collective screenwriting and rewriting, censorship, and the star system, creates one more obstacle to gleaning the social and cultural perspective of the films. (The film's original intent is blurred by the number of people and industry controls that go into shaping the final product—inadvertently creating conflicted texts in some films.) Given all these variables, the effort to explore the link between these films and the basic premises, values, and problems of American society must be by its very nature tentative and touched with ambiguity. No absolutes or certainties underlie this relationship, and there are few films whose social meaning is not open to contesting and contradictory interpretations.

In the act, however, of either displacing or stylizing social reality Hollywood was able to create vital and reverberating images, characters, and dialogue that granted a great deal of insight into American culture. It succeeded in helping to shape the consciousness of its audience by creating mythic landscapes and urbanscapes—the transcendental West of John Ford's Monument Valley and the magical, neon-lit Broadway of countless musicals—and archetypal figures like the gangster, private eye, and femme fatale. The link between Hollywood and its audience, as stated previously, is a reciprocal one. Frank Capra's humane, harmonious small towns and the New York apartments and night clubs of screwball comedies of the thirties like *Holiday* (1938) and *The Awful Truth* (1937) were distinctive Hollywood creations that had resonance for audiences because they reinforced public fantasies and feelings.

The nature of cinematic archetypes and landscapes has changed through the years, but most Hollywood films still follow a set of narrative and stylistic conventions (though in the last two decades a number of major directors have played with and veered from them). The classic Hollywood film was committed to a linear narrative, to temporal and spatial coherence and closure, usually centering around a protagonist the audience could emotionally identify with, and through whose actions the narrative would be resolved. Implicitly this narrative tradition, with its emphasis on the patterned and predictable, usually reinforced the social status quo. The films were also built around either individual heroism or at least the centrality of the individual—a value that Hollywood has embraced since its beginnings. In fact, most American political films, from *Home of the Brave* (1949) to *Platoon* (1986), define political events in terms of an individual's fate and consciousness. The ideological and institutional context of Vietnam, for example, is left untouched by *Platoon*, the war being basically conceived as a murderous rite of passage and existential drama that one individual soldier experiences.

Hollywood films have also been firm believers in the American success ethic, almost never questioning the viability and virtue of our social and economic system. As a result, films have usually promoted the notion, in a wide variety of genres, that most white males have the ability and opportunity to succeed in America. In recent years, in films like *Working Girl* (1988), some women have been added to the host of Hollywood characters who easily overcome the obstacles of class, ethnicity, gender, and even race (at least in the case of a star like Eddie Murphy) and are able to achieve the American Dream.

Socially subversive and anarchic elements obviously exist in popular American films—like the psychopathic gangster and the detective who breaks all the police department's rules. However, despite their deviant behavior, characters like James Cagney's psycho gangster in *White Heat* (1949) or Clint Eastwood's vigilante cop, Harry Callahan, in *Dirty Harry* don't ultimately disrupt the social status quo. Still, despite the fact that classical Hollywood has usually restored the traditional order of things at the film's conclusion, a great many of its films contain camera set-ups, snatches of dialogue, elements in the mise-en-scène, and performances that counter the thrust of the narrative and call the conventional world and its values into question. Even amid the familial sweetness of a film like *Meet Me in St. Louis* (1944) there are dark and uneasy images that, for a moment, subvert the film's serene vision.

Hollywood has, however, made films that break ideologically with the status quo. In the thirties King Vidor's low-budget *Our Daily Bread* (1934) envisioned a collective farm, where unemployed people would work communally, as an alternative to the harshness of Depression poverty and capitalism. But American films that proffer alternative political and social visions are very rare. Far more common are films that see the world as dark and murderous—without political or social alternatives— and provide no concluding image of hope or reconciliation. However, for every film like Stanley Kubrick's *Full Metal Jacket* (1987), a black-comic, profoundly pessimistic, and genuinely critical vision of the American military and the human condition, there are innumerable *To Live and Die in L.A.*'s (1985) with their pop nihilism and gratuitous violence— conventional films that seemingly have merely inverted the classical Hollywood idea of closure and made the bleak, bloody climax their parallel to the happy ending.

Nevertheless, though American films can be politically radical and liberal or conservative, nihilistic, ambiguous, confused, and conflicted ideologically, the analysis of the relationship between them and society still remains problematic. For example, can one really link *E.T.*'s affirmation of innocence and distrust of adult authority to the nostalgia-drenched, anti–big government pieties of the early Reagan years? And what does the audience really perceive that film's ideological intent or, more importantly, that of a film like Spike Lee's *Do the Right Thing* (1989) to be? Despite my wariness about coming up with facile generalizations about the connection between film and society, it is as important to explore that relationship as to study the nature of directorial sensibility and style, the range of Hollywood genres, star biographies, and the history of the studios—not that any of these elements are mutually exclusive.

Clearly, any cultural and social analysis of Hollywood films would have to take into account a variety of theoretical and critical approaches. The auteur critics' origins go back to French critics-cum-directors like François Truffaut, Jean-Luc Godard, Jacques Rivette, and Claude Chabrol, who wrote for *Cahiers du Cinéma* about neglected commercial directors—mostly American—who needed to be explored in depth. They promoted the notion that the basic starting point of film is the personal sensibility, style, and especially the motifs of the director, which give him a "signature"—a coherent world view, and that the best films are those that most clearly bear the signature of their creator.

Though more interested in defending, even glorifying, the aesthetic value of the Hollywood studio films than in exploring their social and political meaning, American auteur critics like Andrew Sarris (writing in *Film Culture* and *The Village Voice*), who took their lead from the French, did chart how John Ford's vision of family and community had remained constant through such diverse films as *The Grapes of Wrath* (1940), *They Were Expendable* (1945), and *She Wore a Yellow Ribbon* (1949). Auteur critics were, however, in their unsystematic, polemical, (in their homages to individual auteurs they overrated their mediocre work and almost never mentioned how powerful a role the studios played in producing these films[5], sometimes defensive manner, primarily interested in demonstrating how a film's visual style was redolent with meaning. They loved to demonstrate just how the mise-en-scène of a Budd Boetticher B western had much greater aesthetic and even intellectual value than the liberal pieties pervading a Stanley Kramer or Richards Brooks social-problem film. As a result, they were able to redeem and sometimes create the critical reputations of directors such as Howard Hawks, Nicholas Ray, Douglas Sirk, and other less deserving figures.

In doing that, the auteur critics granted added luster and cultural importance to commercial Hollywood genres like the western, the thriller, the screwball comedy, and the woman's picture. These genres themselves were subject to a body of criticism that explored their themes, structures, and iconography. Genre criticism often traced the shifts in the form's conventions and themes (for example, the changes in the western from Tom Mix through John Ford to Sam Peckinpah) or examined the relation of the genre to its audience. Most genre critics were more interested in analyzing the films as self-contained forms, in dissecting the iconography of the musical, than in evoking its cultural and social significance. However, there were critics such as Robert Warshow and Leo Braudy who sought to analyze the relationship between a genre's popularity and the attitudes and needs that audiences bring to it. For example, Warshow's essay on the gangster film asserted that the vicious, avaricious behavior of the protagonist in films like *Little Caesar* (1930) appealed to the part of the American psyche that rejects official American culture.[6]

There have also been film critics who have directly sought to unravel, by using a psychoanalytic interpretation, the hidden social and psychological meaning of a film. A theorist like Siegfried Kracauer believed that films are never merely the product of an individual artist, but a collaborative expression of mass feelings.[7] For instance, his landmark work, *From Caligari to Hitler*, although marred by too heady a faith in German films' ability to reveal the secrets of the collective mind as well as predict the rise of Nazism, still yields interesting insight into film as a means of illuminating the "deepest psychological dispositions"[8] of a society. This, coupled with the Freudian notion that films, like dreams, have a latent and manifest content, has proved of some value in wringing social meaning from even the most escapist of films.

Nonetheless, these perceptions are weakened by the fact that they make the meaning of a film dependent on some kind of unconscious activity. It is impossible to demonstrate how the Jungian "collective unconscious" (even if we accept its existence) or the latent content of Freudianism manifests itself in the narrative and imagery of the film. A critic must maintain an almost mystical faith that it does, or more commonly see it as mere speculation and feel that to prove its existence is unnecessary. But in writing about notions such as the mass unconscious, there is a tendency to graft elaborate meanings onto the most commonplace of films. As a result, the work of art becomes something secondary, even insignificant; what becomes all-important is the analysis and interpretation, or else, as in the words of Paddy Whannel and Stuart Hall, art—or in this case film—becomes merely "sugar on the pill."[9]

In recent years a number of theoretical approaches to film, like structuralism and semiology, have held that film is "a system of conventions and codes, a set of structures dictating and circumscribing the ultimate possibilities of any individual film."[10] According to these theoretical perspectives, it is the underlying cultural patterns, not the individual artist, that create meaning in a film. The emphasis in semiology is on sign systems and in structuralism on broader organizing principles (e.g., the antinomy between civilization and the wilderness that runs through the western film) rather than on the individual artist's vision or the work's aesthetic virtues or weaknesses. As a result, the distinction between high art and popular art, and between art and artifact, becomes of little or no interest to the critic—all being equally open to structural and semiological analysis.

Probing beneath the surface of films to discover these patterns and codes can enlarge one's way of seeing. For example, the idea of the camera's gaze in classical Hollywood film as a male one—which sees women as objects of voyeuristic pleasure—alters one's way of thinking about familiar films. However, if on the one hand modernist theory leads to fresh insights into the role culture plays in determining films, on the other, it remains abstracted from the particularity of the individual film and its historical context. And in his contempt for subjectivity, the modernist theorist tends to be removed from the concrete act of viewing a film—an emotional experience that makes one see how the specific texture of a film can often contradict and even undermine those structures and codes that have become the lifeblood of academic film study.

In writing this book, however, although we have been influenced by genre, auteur, feminist, psychoanalytic, Marxist, structuralist, and other critical perspectives, we are not wedded to any one critical system. Our aim is to depict and evaluate, both politically and aesthetically, the way American films convey their social and cultural values and commitments. Given our belief in film's historical and social significance, it is the particular purpose of this study to look at American films from 1945 to the present and analyze how they perceived and conjured up the American social and cultural landscape. In addition, we have included a brief rendering of some of the major political events and social and cultural trends that dominated a decade and left a mark on its films.

To accomplish this our method is a simple one. For one thing, since almost 95 percent of the film time on the American screens, and a large percentage on foreign ones as well, is dominated by Hollywood films, we have treated Hollywood and American film as being synonymous. And for the purpose of this study we have left out avant-garde and most documentary films. We are also aware of the hazards of adopting a decade-by-decade approach, for clearly the culture and politics of the sixties did not end on December 31, 1969 – and the Cold War and the anticommunist crusade were not limited to one decade. The general tone, concerns, and values of one decade often overlap into the following one. Despite the somewhat arbitrary nature of our book's structure it has the advantage of convenience and popular acceptance – references to decades like the fifties and sixties continue to denote a particular set of social and cultural values and patterns.

One serious difficulty in writing the book was selecting films that best illuminated these trends. In order to accomplish this we have relied in the main on a large body of films that could be called "public classics"[11] – films whose box office grosses, awards, and critical reputation (which have either stood the test of time or grown with it) indicate that these films have a connection with the popular consciousness. Undoubtedly, there are many other films that may have pointed in different directions, dealt with the themes we have analyzed in a clearer, sharper manner, or been perhaps visionary in their ability to herald future trends and themes. Nevertheless, it does seem to us that some degree of consensus exists about the importance of specific films and their relation to the society of their times – for example, films like *The Best Years of Our Lives* and the forties, *Rebel Without a Cause* and the fifties, and *Bonnie and Clyde* and *Easy Rider* and the sixties. We have included in our study a number of films of this type. Also, since this book was intended as both an introduction and a guide to American film and culture for students, we have tried to include films that are accessible to them through video rental services and stores and available archives, although this was by no means the decisive factor in our choice.

Finally, as far as the theme of this study goes, it is important to return for a moment to *Let There Be Light*. When that film is placed alongside some films of the seventies dealing with similar problems and themes, like *The Deer Hunter* and *Coming Home* (1978), and a documentary like *Hearts and Minds* (1974), one cannot help but see what a different portrait the films of the seventies provide of American life and how that image has radically changed over time. In *Let There Be Light*, for example, the officer informs the just-discharged patients (without irony) that "On your shoulders falls much of the responsibility for the post-war world." It is the sort of uplifting sentiment that traumatized Vietnam war veterans, such as Nicky (*The Deer Hunter*) and Bob (*Coming Home*), would greet with the stony stare of suicidal despair. Throughout the book we have attempted to show how American films moved from the relatively self-confident affirmation of the American Dream in the late forties (Hollywood at its zenith) through the films of the sixties and seventies and the politically retrograde and nostalgic Reagan eighties, when, despite a continued dependence on big budgets, stars, and genre formulas, films grew increasingly more anxious, alienated, and nihilistic in tone. In constructing this pattern we have tried to avoid subsuming the contested meanings of individual films and the often contradictory history of cinematic cultural trends and cycles under reductive and rigid sociological categories. We have been conscious of the feelings of doubt and loss that began to appear beneath the buoyant surface of forties' films, and the preservation of American Dream imagery in the generally darker, more pessimistic work of the sixties, seventies, and eighties.

Ultimately, what we have written is only one more step in the ongoing and complex study of the multiple and diverse interactions of culture and society, and, more specifically, film and society. We have not conceived this book as a definitive work, but as one among a number of possible ways that help illuminate the nature of American society and culture. The book is based on the now anachronistic idea that a passion for and a personal commitment to the imaginative life of films can be an integral part of the critical process, and that the critique can be conveyed in a language that any intelligent person who cares about film can understand. This view is best summed up in the humanist perspective of Raymond Williams, which holds that art is a means to "learn, describe, to understand, to educate"[12] — a way of heightening one's perception of self, the social world, and much of human experience. We finally believe, as did James Agee on writing his first film review in *The Nation*, that the final function of any review or critical study is to aid those "who watch any given screen, where the proof is . . . available in proportion to the eye which sees it, and the mind which uses it."[13]

NOTES

1. Andrew Sarris, "Hobgoblins of Reality," *The Village Voice* (January 21–27, 1981), p. 45.

2. Erwin Panovsky, "Style and Medium in the Motion Pictures," in G. Mast and M. Cohen (eds.), *Film Theory and Criticism* (New York: Oxford University Press, 1974), p. 152.

3. Panovsky, "Style and Medium," p. 152.

4. John E. O'Connor and Martin A. Jackson (eds.), *American History/American Film: Interpreting the Hollywood Image* (New York: Frederick Ungar, 1979), p. x.

5. Thomas Schatz, *The Genius of the System: Hollywood Filmmaking in the Studio Era* (New York: Pantheon, 1988), pp. 3–12.

6. Robert Warshow, *The Immediate Experience* (Garden City, N.Y.: Anchor, 1964).

7. Tim Bywater and Thomas Sobchack, *Film Criticism: Major Critical Approaches to Narrative Film* (White Plains, N.Y.: Longman, 1989), p. 121.

8. Siegfried Kracauer, *From Caligari to Hitler: A Psychological History of the German Film*, 3rd ed. (Princeton, N.J.: Princeton University Press, 1970), p. 6.

9. Stuart Hall and Paddy Whannel, *The Popular Arts* (New York: Pantheon, 1965), p. 28.

10. Bywater and Sobchack, *Film Criticism*, p. 175.

11. Michael Wood, *America in the Movies: or, "Santa Maria, It Had Slipped My Mind!"* (New York: Basic Books, 1975), p. 11.

12. Raymond Williams, *Communications*, 3rd ed. (London: Pelican, 1976), p. 11.

13. James Agee, *Agee on Film: Reviews and Comments* (Boston: Beacon Press, 1966), p. 23.

2

THE FORTIES

In 1936 President Franklin D. Roosevelt announced that Americans had a "rendezvous with destiny." The war years turned that prophecy into a reality as America emerged from its traditional isolationism and became an imperialist, interventionist nation—the most powerful nation in the world. The political energy that had once gone into the struggle against the Depression was now concentrated on the war effort. And that undertaking granted to many people on the home front a sense of purpose, exhilaration, and community that was rare in American history.[1]

The same energy and optimism that helped bring about victory carried over into the postwar years. However, this optimism had more to do with people's material well-being (in the 1940s the average American enjoyed an income fifteen times greater than the average foreigner)[2] and national pride than with any new political and social commitments. In fact, most Americans had become weary of the long years of economic depression and foreign wars and, in general, bored with politics. Constricted by the enforced savings of World War II, Americans wanted to enjoy their newfound prosperity and victory. A new era seemed about to open, offering ordinary Americans not only increased income, but a chance for education and greater social and economic status.

One of the driving forces behind this new mood was the GI Bill of Rights, which became law in 1944, helping returning veterans to borrow money to set up businesses and attend universities that they had once viewed as preserves of the upper middle class. In addition, a baby boom gave evidence that Americans felt freed from the social anguish of the past decade and a half and had begun to feel that the future held infinite promise.[3]

Another key factor in this changing climate was the accession to the presidency, upon the death of FDR in 1945, of Vice President Harry S Truman, who was a moderate Democratic party organization stalwart from Missouri. At first, Truman's presidency suffered by comparison with the charismatic Roosevelt. In addition, he was beset by a resurgent conservative congressional coalition of Southern Democrats (Dixiecrats) and Republicans, who frustrated his attempts to extend the New Deal and forced him to watch helplessly as they overrode his veto of the anti-labor Taft–Hartley bill in 1947. However, even when he came into his own, after a startling come-from-behind victory in the presidential campaign of 1948, he merely introduced a Fair Deal program that was only a pale copy and codification of the New Deal. Thus, despite his political triumph, the Truman era was dominated by the profits and developing prestige and power of the corporations rather than by the forces of social reform.[4]

Nevertheless, although feelings of both material abundance and the irrelevance of social conflict were prime cultural themes of the forties, there were darker signs. A crippling strike wave, culminating in a coal strike led by FDR's nemesis John L. Lewis, served notice that labor was no longer willing to continue its rather unequal collaboration with business and wanted a larger share of the wealth generated by the war. The labor insurgency coupled with high inflation caused ripples of anxiety in the economy. Equally significant, though largely beneath the surface, were a pair of major demographic changes. One was the great migration of poor blacks to the North to work in defense plants during World War II. There they exchanged the certainties and oppression of southern rural life for the anxieties and higher wages of the northern cities. Paralleling this black migration was the movement of whites (aided by low-interest Federal Housing Administration and Veterans' Administration loans) to the suburbs. Hand in hand, the twin migrations would alter the entire social fabric of America.[5]

However severe these labor problems and demographic changes were, they were merely minor irritants compared to the turmoil caused by foreign affairs. Long used to neglecting foreign relationships, Americans were thrust by the war into a leading international position. It also moved the United States into an alliance with the Soviet Union—a nation considered in some prewar American circles as a greater menace than Germany, Italy, or Japan. Nonetheless, most Americans were little disturbed by the wartime alliance with the Soviets. In fact, many liberals saw that alliance (with the Soviet Union as the junior partner) as the basis of an enduring peace where postwar social reforms would become the prime commitment of both nations. Yet among conservatives there were always undercurrents of suspicion of the Soviet Union and towards the U.S.–Soviet alliance. And when Stalin, in quest of greater security, broke the 1945 Yalta agreements, conservative unease and anger toward the Soviet Union increased, a wariness that many liberals soon began to share.[6]

During the next few years, despite the dream of a new international order embodied in the United Nations, the Cold War (as it came to be known) escalated and relations between the United States and the Soviet Union were permeated with fear, suspicion, and distrust. As a result, the two ideologically expansionist powers, their wartime cooperation seemingly forgotten, confronted each other with neither side genuinely seeking peace or rapprochement. On their side the Americans continually evoked images of an "iron curtain" and the threat of Soviet expansion, while the Russians talked of "American imperialism" and the constant threat to their borders and security.[7]

The conflict was not solely confined to rhetoric. In 1947, breaking with a long-standing American tradition against peacetime military and political alliances, President Truman gained congressional approval for 400 million dollars in military and economic aid to Greece and Turkey to help them in their struggle against communist guerrillas. This action, soon to be dubbed the Truman doctrine, had broader implications— including the seeds for later American interventions—for, in the words of Truman, America was now committed "to support free people who are resisting attempted subjugation by armed minorities or by outside pressure."[8]

The crisis between the two former allies deepened as a Soviet-sponsored coup in Czechoslovakia in 1948 eliminated the last vestiges of democracy in eastern and central Europe, and the Marshall Plan and the North Atlantic Treaty Organization established an American-backed *cordon sanitaire* in western Europe. The *cordon sanitaire* was worked out by diplomat-scholar George F. Kennan and his State Department policy planning group and was given political sponsorship by Secretary of State George C. Marshall, based on the reasoning that an anticommunist foreign policy was not enough to impede the spread of communism in Europe. They believed that only with the recovery of the European economy (one that would also provide markets for the United States) could the Soviet threat be thwarted. Indeed, with the passage of the Marshall Plan in 1948 western Europe did take a giant step towards economic recovery and enhanced its capacity to resist communism.[9]

However, even with western Europe stabilized by 1949, American anxieties about communism hardly lessened. The fear of communist aggression from abroad was soon replaced by terror over a native communist fifth column whose task was seemingly to ferret out military secrets as they subverted America's will to resist. These feelings were reinforced by a succession of spy ring revelations—Igor Gouzenko, Judith Coplon, Elizabeth Bentley, and Whittaker Chambers being some of the prime participants. The explosion of a Soviet A-bomb, coupled with the fall of mainland China to the communists, transformed these fears into a full-fledged anticommunist hysteria. Angered by their sense of a growing visible and invisible communist menace and becoming anxious over their own survival, Americans sought facile explanations for what they saw as an imminent threat. Rather than confront the long-term economic and social causes that produced both wars of "national liberation" and communist takeovers (at the time they were neatly equated), Americans attributed the reasons for the success of the left to a supposed international communist conspiracy.[10]

In the vanguard of this search for traitors was the House Un-American Activities Committee (HUAC). Dormant during the war years, the committee saw its chance to regain the limelight in 1947 when it held hearings investigating communist influence in the motion picture industry. Drawn by the prestige and glamor of the film industry, the committee was more interested in the political affiliations of its ten "unfriendly" witnesses—some of whom were the most talented and politically active writers and directors in Hollywood (for example, Dalton Trumbo, Albert Maltz, and Ring Lardner Jr.)—than in the supposedly subversive content of their films.[11]

At first the moguls and liberals in the industry protested about the committee's actions, but seeing the witnesses take the first amendment regarding their politics they quickly succumbed to expediency, fearing their profits and careers might be threatened. In a meeting at the Waldorf–Astoria hotel soon after the "ten" appeared before the committee, the moguls issued their craven Waldorf Statement, which was in essence a tacit agreement to establish a blacklist refusing to reemploy either the "Hollywood Ten" or other members of the Communist party.[12]

Of course the HUAC investigations of Hollywood were just one element of the growing fear of and attack on the presumed communist conspiracy. In 1949 the leaders of the U.S. Communist party were convicted under the Smith Act for conspiracy and sent to prison. More significantly, the deeply symbolic Hiss–Chambers affair, which saw the former high-level New Deal bureaucrat Alger Hiss accused of espionage and convicted of perjury, brought the New Deal under attack for being soft on communism. The forties concluded with a portion of the American public, dominated by midwesterners, recent immigrants, and Catholics, holding that New Deal liberalism and communism were one and the same thing.[13]

Nevertheless, despite the growing fear of the "red menace," the forties were still essentially a time of optimism and consensus, and nowhere was this more evident than in American film. For, although they had a dark side touched with pessimism and self-doubt, the movies basically endorsed and reflected a feeling of national triumph. Moreover, for the industry itself the postwar era was a bloom time. From 1942 to 1944 Hollywood produced about 440 films a year, and 1946 was the most commercially successful year in its history. The forties were a time of big stars and big audiences when the studios, with their armies of talented technicians and performers, reigned supreme. The last years of the decade did see Hollywood beset by labor troubles, adverse Supreme Court decisions (the Paramount case), and the aftereffects of the HUAC hearings—leading to the blacklisting of a large number of major creative contributors to the industry. But the forties were still "the last great show of confidence and skill" by Hollywood before it became paralyzed by competition from television and the death of the studio system.[14]

Nowhere was this optimism more evident than in the war films that the studios churned out through the war years. The overriding purpose of these films was patriotic uplift, and, despite the fact that an occasional hero lapsed into *Casablanca* (1942)–like cynicism or malaise, they were all eventually aroused to a commitment to the collective struggle against fascism. With Hollywood helping to shoulder the wartime burden of maintaining morale, there were few films that dealt with the reality rather than the romance of combat, or with the psychological effects of the war. Those that did, like John Huston's pacifistic documentary, *Battle of San Pietro* (1945), which evoked haunting and harrowing images of the war with great immediacy and intensity, were prevented by the Pentagon from reaching the public. Neither the Pentagon nor Hollywood wanted films that filled the screens with images of exhausted soldiers, cemeteries of dog tags, and terrified peasants. They desired war films that exulted in America by creating mythical—ethnically, regionally, and occupationally heterogeneous—platoons to personify American democracy.

By the end of the war, however, with victory clearly in sight, self-righteous propagandistic films like *God Is My Co-Pilot* (1943) and *The Purple Heart* (1944) were replaced by more sophisticated and realistic films. Among the first of these was Lewis Milestone's *A Walk in the Sun* (1945), which provides a realistic treatment, through its subtle and moving use of close-ups and light and shadow, of an infantry unit's battle fear and anxiety. The soldiers are fallible human beings, not Hollywood heroes, though the film still contains the usual sentimentalized melting pot of "dogfaces" who engage in tiresome, colloquial banter, and even go in for self-conscious interior monologues. But if A Walk in the Sun indulges in anti-fascist and pseudo-democratic (Popular Front) clichés and rhetoric about the "mighty Joes" and the people's folksy wisdom and capacity for artistic feeling, its images of long lines of soldiers walking in the darkness are vivid and poignant. And its generally unromantic treatment of a war where men become frightened and die placed it far above the run-of-the-mill war films with their bloodthirsty and barbaric "Nips" and "Krauts" being put to rout by the derring-do of an Errol Flynn or a John Wayne.

William Wellman's The Story of G.I. Joe (1945) was a much leaner and more solemn film than A Walk in the Sun. Based on Ernie Pyle's Pulitzer Prize–winning dispatches, this dry, understated, quasi-documentary work avoids almost all the inflated political rhetoric, histrionics, and stereotyping that characterized most other World War II films. The film is constructed, without a driving narrative to propel it, as a series of abruptly terminated scenes that powerfully capture the pathos and tragedy of the war. Wellman's infantrymen are not clean shaven or well fed, and the war takes a palpable toll—all the men are exhausted by the day-to-day slogging and fighting; a tough sergeant, obsessed with home and his son's voice, has a breakdown; and the strong, quietly dignified captain of the platoon, Bill Walker (Robert Mitchum), who is a towering figure, dies. Watching this film, James Agee was sufficiently moved to compare it, especially its final, somber, dark moments, to a Whitman-esque war poem.[15]

In a far different mode was John Ford's romantic and leisurely They Were Expendable (1945). Ford's film displayed little interest in the psychology or sociology of his PT boat officers and crew but was deeply committed to paying homage to a community of men who were portrayed as gallant and heroic in defeat. The film was filled with epic long shots of almost painterly sea battles and of the men's ritualistic arrivals from and departures into battle. Ford believed in the virtues of the military, conceiving it as a community built on a hierarchic code of power, self-sacrifice, responsibility, and obligation. The film's officers are viewed as heroes, men free of any fear or anxiety about the war, best illustrated by the impetuous, tough Captain Rusty Ryan (John Wayne), who is unwilling to allow mere wounds to prevent him from going into battle. They also understand that leadership demands that they subordinate individual desires to the good of the squadron—to become "team players."

Ford's film was a celebration, not a critical portrait of the American war effort. *They Were Expendable* is filled with patriotic and elegiac senti-ments: a soundtrack playing "The Battle Hymn of the Republic" and "Red River Valley," an affecting montage of wounded men—one of them blind, smoking a cigarette with trembling hands—and a melancholy full shot of exhausted, courageous nurses seen in silhouette walking through a hospital corridor. Consequently, it should come as no surprise, from such a paean to the military, that the film's apotheosis is the appearance of an actor embodying Ford's personal deity, General MacArthur, ac-companied by a series of reaction shots of sailors with glowing faces standing in awe of this American icon.

In the hands of another director without the pictorial or narrative gifts of Ford these rituals and stereotypes might have become mere historical tableaux. However, Ford's treatment of military rituals and codes is so profoundly felt, and his images so grand and stately, that the conven-tional and sentimental emotions and characters are transformed into archetypes, and the clichés into myths.

No less important in raising morale and maintaining commitment to the war effort than some of the flag-waving combat films were the home-front melodramas. In fact, a film such as David O. Selznick's *Since You Went Away* (1944) actually opened with the announcement: "This is the story of an unconquerable fortress, the American home, 1943." What followed was Hollywood's sanitized version of American women's com-mitment to the war effort. The plot has a typical suburban housewife, played by a miscast Claudette Colbert, leaving her comfortable home for a job in a welding factory. There she becomes a mentor in American-ization for the immigrant women who work beside her, who see her as the embodiment of the American Dream. It's not only the immigrant women who view her in this manner, for the film itself idealizes Colbert's family and friends, portraying their world as clean, unruffled, and inno-cent. The dream is made complete by a black mammy cook (Hattie Mc-Daniel), who, though the family can no longer afford her, returns each night, after a full day's work, to provide free housework, comic relief, and consolation. It's an image of racial unity that provides a fitting cap-stone to this relentless celebration of home-front USA.

Nevertheless, despite its saccharine, wish-fantasy quality, *Since You Went Away* did touch on one very important home-front reality, the new role for women as workers in defense industries. There were over four million such women in 1943, with many more working in other industries. Mass circulation magazines reacted to this new development by creating the symbol of "Rosie the Riveter," and Hollywood responded by having its female stars play women who go to work (for example, Lucille Ball as a defense plant worker in *Meet the People*, 1944). Hollywood's casting its stars as workers beautifully encapsulated the fact that everything shot in Hollywood during the years 1942–45, be it combat films such as Raoul Walsh's *Objective Burma* (1945), the Tarzan series, or Donald Duck cartoons, reflected or was actively committed to the war effort.

However, as the war came to a close, Hollywood began to turn from making films about the war to those that would help ease the transition from war to peace. Here it was the symbol of the returned veteran who became the embodiment of those issues. As a matter of fact, as Dr. Franklin Fearing wrote in the first issue of the *Hollywood Quarterly* (predecessor of the present *Film Quarterly*),

> "When Johnny Comes Marching Home" is not only the title of a popular Civil War song, it is a symbol and a situation. It is a symbol with curiously ambivalent meanings, it signifies the return of heroes, or wars ended, of happy reunions after hardwon but glorious victories, and of peace after battle. It is also a sign of dissension, of nervous uncertainty lest, in truth, we have not prepared a "land fit for heroes," of anxiety regarding possible capacity to adjust and even curiously of fear and hostility. The laughter and tears which welcome Johnny home reflect honest joy and relief, but there is an undertone of nervous tension. Has he changed? How much have I changed? Can we get along together? What is ahead?[16]

It was this type of anxiety that a film such as *Pride of the Marines* (1945) was intended to assuage. The film itself was taken from the real-life experiences of marine hero Al Schmid (John Garfield), who was blinded at Guadalcanal. After detailing Al's early life and his being wounded, the film presents his subsequent withdrawal into a shell of rage and resentment. In the hospital ward other veterans with problems like Al's overcome them by believing that the country will take care of them with the GI Bill, or that just standing up for their rights will get them heard. Al, however, remains unconvinced that there is a place for him in civilian society, and it's made clear that that is his personal problem, not America's. With the issue defined in psychological terms and society absolved, the conventional Hollywood solution is easily achieved. His fiancée confronts his self-pity and tells Al she needs him; predictably his neurosis then quickly dissolves (as does our concern about the fate of the returned veteran).

The same theme of postwar adjustment was taken up by *Till the End of Time* (1946), where the crippled veteran has no girlfriend, but a mother and a friendly army officer who are able to rouse him from his anger and withdrawal so he can enter the world again. These films paled by comparison with Samuel Goldwyn and William Wyler's *The Best Years of Our Lives* (1946), which dealt with the return home of three World War II veterans from different social backgrounds, and with the psychological, economic, and physical problems of readjustment they confronted.

The Best Years of Our Lives swept the Academy Awards, was the top box office attraction of 1947, and garnered great critical praise. James Agee, for one, wrote that it was "one of the very few American studio made movies in years that seem to me profoundly pleasing, moving and encouraging."[17] The Marxist, soon-to-be-blacklisted writer-director Abraham Polonsky wrote that "the era of human character which *The Best Years* makes available to its audience is a landmark in the fog of escapism, meretricious violence and the gimmick plot attitude of the usual movie."[18]

Praise like this catapulted the film into the realm of an instant masterpiece. And though that judgment was probably inflated, for the film tended to take few intellectual risks and be somewhat sentimental, *The Best Years* still contained more truth and insight about the readjustment of veterans to peacetime than any other forties' film. Moreover, its subtle and eloquent use of deep focus, flowing camera movements, and moving reaction shots that caught the emotional nuances of the characters' behavior, made it an unselfconsciously beautiful and lyrical film as well.

The Best Years was an intelligent, humane, deeply felt attempt to deal with the problem of the readjustment of veterans in postwar American society. At the same time, it was a stately, carefully balanced, and shrewdly manipulated tribute to the American way of life. It paid homage to American institutions like the small town (the camera lovingly providing a montage of American icons like hot dog stands, ball parks, and Woolworth's) and the family, and to Hollywood's own belief in the redemptive power of love. And the film tended to obfuscate social issues, dismissing class as a factor in American life by constructing a world where the comradeship of veterans, who run the gamut from bank officers to soda jerks, could unselfconsciously carry over into civilian life. It also personalized social problems such as the difficulties that GIs without capital had when they wanted to own a business or some land. Of course, the answer the film offers is not built on any institutional or structural reform. In the Capra tradition (e.g., *American Madness*), it's politically sufficient that the film's liberal banker, Al Stephenson (Fredric March), grant small loans without any collateral to respectable and hard-working veterans. Implicit in that act is the film's belief that the system can be made to work by good-natured, "regular guy" bankers (Al tells a nervous applicant for a loan, "Don't sir me—I'm just a sergeant") and that in America anybody with enough drive can make it.

As in the other veterans' films, the family and a woman's love help Al adjust to civilian life. Al comes home to his comfortable apartment and to the warm embrace of an urbane, supportive wife, Millie (Myrna Loy), and two almost grown children who now have lives of their own. However, he feels generally uneasy about his familial role and sexually tense, drinking and bantering compulsively to avoid confronting his feelings of alienation from both family and job. Al's behavior suggests more complex and tortured emotions about job, family, marriage, and self than the film is willing to explore (feelings that cannot have all been caused by his war experience). By the film's conclusion, all is neatly righted, and though Al may still drink too much and have some genuine discontent with the way his life has evolved, the domestic warmth and love of his family will ease his return without too much difficulty.

What is true for Al holds true for both the other veterans, Fred and Homer. Fred Derry (Dana Andrews) returns home a war hero with ribbons, citations, and nightmares from living so close to death. He also comes back without any qualifications for a decent job (the ribbons doing nothing to help him) except for the soda jerk position he had left and feels degraded working at. Fred is sharp, cynical, tough, and filled with middle-class ambitions, but the good jobs don't seem available to him. He also carries the added burden of marriage to a brassy, sexy blonde, who is that particular symbol of anxiety that bedeviled so many GIs— the unfaithful wife. Too narcissistic and independent, Marie (Virginia Mayo) cannot offer Fred any support and only makes him feel worse about himself. However, a good woman's love ultimately suffices to rescue Fred from despair, as Al's pert and sensitive daughter Peggy (Theresa Wright) offers him female understanding and support.

Although Fred's rescue by Peggy and the offer of a job recycling old bombers into pre-fab housing is rather contrived, the subplot provides one of the best reasons why *The Best Years* has been assigned a niche in the pantheon of American films. In one of the film's most formally dazzling and powerful scenes, Fred walks into an airplane graveyard overrun with weeds, which contains rows of bombers that are going to be turned into scrap (a metaphor for the now obsolete Fred), and climbs into one of the cobwebbed planes. Camera movement, sound, and editing then work together to reconstruct the sensation of take-off and flight. There is a close-up of a sweating, feverish Fred, the sound of engines on the sound track, and a nightmarish shot of Fred through the blurred glass of the cockpit. It's a sequence that provides a profound insight into Fred's relationship to a war that gave him a sense of power, self-esteem, and pain. By reliving the war in this one scene, both Fred and the movie audience get a chance to exorcise the war experience.

The postwar adjustment of the third veteran, the inarticulate, vulnerable Homer (Harold Russell), is sensitively and honestly rendered. The poignancy of his story is heightened by the fact that Homer is played by a real amputee (an example of the care that Wyler took in casting the film), who exudes great naturalness in the role. Homer's problem is not his handicap—he has already achieved a great deal of good-humored self-sufficiency using his hooks—but the unwarranted fear that his passive, loving fiancée, Wilma (Cathy O'Donnell), will be unable to deal with him. Homer does not want to be pitied or treated as a freak; in turn, he rejects Wilma and, as a result, begins to feel isolated and angry. Of course, in the context of the film, all he needs to be happy is to be willing to accept Wilma's love. However, before this foreseeable conclusion is reached, there are tender, understated scenes where Homer's father undresses him and takes off his hooks, and one where Homer, sitting somberly in the shadows, puts Wilma to the test by removing his hooks and describing how helpless he is. Of course, maternal, caring Wilma comes through.

Despite its limitations, The Best Years's emotionally moving scenes, its formal luminosity, and its well-defined characters did provide a genuine glimpse of postwar American life. And though it ultimately allowed each of its characters a graceful, albeit predictable, reentry into postwar American society, it suggested there were genuinely real and traumatic problems inherent in returning home from the war. There were also hints that underneath the film's essentially optimistic surface there existed some feelings of doubt about America's future. (The film's brief portraits of the civilians who stayed home and prospered during the war are so repellent that one begins to wonder how benign American society could be if it was populated by people of this type.)

This anxiety about America was not merely confined to the returned veteran, it also extended to other areas of American life. Traces of it could even be found in the work of that apostle of Hollywood optimism, Frank Capra. In Capra's very first postwar film, It's a Wonderful Life (1946), he began to modify his normal optimism and belief in the "little people" with a vision of a nightmare world. Capra's usual mythic, tranquil small town, Bedford Falls, is destroyed by selfish materialism and turned into a raw, industrial, neon-lit Pottersville (a fantasy possibly inspired by the squalid boom towns that grew up across America in the wake of the wartime industrial explosion). Even his archetypical common man, George Bailey (James Stewart), is beset with feelings of self-doubt and resentment. Nevertheless, "Capracorn" and the spirit of Christmas eventually do triumph, the whole cast of characters ultimately singing in unison "Auld Lang Syne," and the significance of each man's life, no matter how ordinary, is reaffirmed. In this Capra film the act of affirmation becomes more difficult, and Capra must contrive the deus ex machina of a cute, folksy angel, Clarence (Henry Travers), to bring this film to its benign and joyous conclusion.

It's a Wonderful Life (1946) was Frank Capra's favorite film and probably his most personal.[19] Its hero, George Bailey, is the most individualized and psychologically complex of Capra's heroic everymen. George is decent, intelligent, caring, and doomed to living a life he finds constricting, devoid of adventure or great success. In fact, despite the good he does in town (he builds a subdivision of clean, inexpensive new homes), George sees himself as having no real identity, a failure.

Unlike some of Capra's earlier films, especially his populist trilogy (*Mr. Deeds Goes to Town, Mr. Smith Goes to Washington,* and *Meet John Doe*), this film is more meditative, less dependent on montage and more on lengthy close-ups of George Bailey isolated within a frame. Previously, Capra had questioned the value of his form of populist political vision in *Meet John Doe* (1941), and there were moments of anguish in his other films, but in *It's a Wonderful Life* the despair becomes more personal and deeply felt. And in the style of forties' films, the doubts expressed deal more with the nature of identity and self than with social or political abuses. As a result, there is no steely-eyed Edward Arnold to play a corrupt political boss or a forbidding fascist tycoon who in the film can ominously threaten Bailey and Capra's ethics and politics. Instead, there is only Mr. Potter (Lionel Barrymore), the "meanest man in town," a solitary Scrooge type who owns slum tenements. Potter is a Dickensian cartoon, a small-town tyrant in a wheelchair whose threats cannot really be taken too seriously. George's nightmare, though supposedly brought on by Potter's villainous machinations, comes from inside himself, carrying the sort of intense rage that has him cry out to his cloyingly sweet wife Mary (Donna Reed), "Why do we need all these kids!" George's anger is finally defused, but it takes all of Capra's genius at manipulating an audience to achieve it, and a trace of his anguish cannot be fully erased.

What is more, Capra's nightmare sequence, filled with flashing neon lights, gin mills, harsh, pained characters, and a dark shadowy ambiance, contained most of the elements that characterized a whole genre of forties' films. For many of Hollywood's films, especially those dealing with contemporary American life, conveyed, through their somber black-and-white photography, a tone of claustrophobia and entrapment. Obviously some of this dark, oppressive mood derived from the budgetary limits placed on wartime filmmaking, where lighting had to be cut down and sets substituted for location shooting. Nevertheless, the eerie menace inherent in the films' look was more than an adjustment to industry economics. It was a conscious choice made by the films' directors, many of them expatriates who had been at Germany's UFA (Universum Film Aktiengesellschaft, the largest single pre–World War II European studio) and received basic training in the German Expressionism of the 1920s, with its emphasis on the visual evocation of emotional and intellectual states (e.g., *The Cabinet of Dr. Caligari, Nosferatu*). Other significant influences were the murky atmospherics of French prewar poetic realist films (e.g., *Port of Shadows*), the Warner gangster films of the thirties, and a strain of nineteenth-century romanticism.

Some leading figures among these expatriate directors were Billy Wilder (*Double Indemnity*, 1944), Otto Preminger (*Laura*, 1945), Robert Siodmak (*The Killers*, 1945, and *Cry of the City*, 1948), and Fritz Lang (*Scarlet Street*, 1945, and *Woman in the Window*, 1945). They made films that tended, in stylistic terms, to deliberately disquieting editing, low-key lighting, night-for-night shooting, subjective view shots, voice-over and flashback and oblique camera setups. Their films were also characterized by images of rainswept, foggy-night streets, shadowy figures, seedy bars, flickering street lamps, isolated coast roads, and rooms dominated by mirrors. Postwar French critics identified the films containing many of these elements as a genre, which they dubbed "film noir."[20]

Many of these film noir works constructed worlds where paranoia was the dominant feeling, and almost nobody could be trusted. It was a world where women, often in the central role, were glamorous and dangerous—seductive sirens whose every action was marked by duplicity and aimed at satisfying a desire for wealth and power. The male protagonists were frequently weak, confused and morally equivocal, susceptible to temptation, and incapable of acting heroically. In turn the villains were often superficially sympathetic figures whose charm masked malevolence and perversity and on occasion operated as alter egos or doubles for the films' heroes. Film noir also contained bizarre and seedy minor characters, ritualized violence, sadomasochistic behavior, sexual alienation, and a general sense of the perverse, and when the good triumphed at the film's climax (for the genre was still dominated by Hollywood conventions), its triumph was usually ambiguous.[21]

The film noir style encompassed a wide range of works of varying quality. For example, there were films like Fritz Lang's visually powerful *Woman in the Window* (1944) and *Scarlet Street* (1945), where a lonely, repressed, conflicted male (Edward G. Robinson) is victimized by a beautiful temptress (Joan Bennett)—who is also a victim. Both films were especially striking in their elegant mise-en-scène—more interested in the precise projection of a pessimistic world view through high overhead shots, low-key lighting, and emotionally charged objects than in an evocation of visual beauty. Lang's cold, nightmarish films envisioned a corrupt world where people are trapped by abstract forces—fate, instincts, society—and nobody really escapes punishment. The films also had a special gift for both imagining sadomasochistic encounters and creating vicious, insidious villains like those played by Dan Duryea in the two films mentioned above.

There were also less successful films like Robert Siodmak's *Cry of the City* (1948), which had a pungent, quasi-documentary feeling for low-life locales: perennially wet streets, neon lights reflected in windows, sinister cocktail lounges, and decaying tenements. It also contained some imaginatively constructed noirish set pieces: a gross six-foot masseuse (Hope Emerson) seen both in close-up devouring her breakfast, and through a glass door, in full shot, ominously striding through a house switching on the lights in room after room; a police interview of a group of emigré abortionists, the scene enveloped in squalor and pathos; and a meticulously executed escape scene, accompanied by a swelling drumbeat on the soundtrack, as the film's corrupt and charming villain slips right past the police. However, the film turns out to be no more than the sum of its carefully constructed and calculated tensions, a work of strong surface effects and style based on a banal, cliché-ridden script, and dominated by characters devoid of internality or genuine interest.

Much of the same film noir style also dominates Michael Curtiz's *Mildred Pierce* (1945), adapted from a novel by James Cain. *Mildred Pierce* charts the rise, through hard work, of a housewife, Mildred (Joan Crawford), from a waitress to a wealthy owner of a chain of restaurants in Southern California. Elements of film noir—stylish low-key lighting, seedy, smoke-filled police stations, pools of shadows, and avaricious, venal characters—permeate the film. *Mildred Pierce* could also be seen as a women's picture, a genre of romantic films designed to offer women, especially housewives, a cathartic experience. Glamorous Hollywood stars like Bette Davis (*Deception*, 1946) and Joan Crawford (*Possessed*,

1948) portrayed women who had to lie, scheme, and even murder to get what they wanted from life. The films gave expression both to alluring wish fantasies about love and luxury and to the frustrations of housewives by dealing with women who led self-sacrificial lives, had ungrateful children, or had to deal with chronic and terminal illnesses. Though often hopelessly soap-operatic and melodramatic, the women's films frequently featured strong women fighting for their own identities in a world controlled by men.[22]

In many ways *Mildred Pierce* fit the women's film pattern. It carried a predictable narrative about a mother's self-destructive love for her daughter, tended towards overstatement and hysteria, and contained major characters who lacked even a hint of psychological nuance. A prime example was Zachary Scott's cardboard cutout Monte—an aristocratic, decadent heel recycled from innumerable Hollywood melodramas. For all its lack of subtlety, however, *Mildred Pierce* was a work that resonated culturally and socially beyond its conventional narrative.

Crawford's Mildred is supposedly an ordinary, lower-middle-class housewife (though Crawford can never quite convince audiences that she is anything but tough-minded and glamorous) who escapes household drudgery and an enervated husband to become a successful entrepreneur. Warned early that the pursuit of success (it would have been interesting if the film had really begun to question the whole American obsession with success) and the abdication of her maternal role will prove destructive, she is punished by seeing her sweet, perky, younger daughter die of pneumonia and by having a relationship with the feckless, parasitical Monte, who is unfaithful and lives off her money.

But her ultimate punishment for being a strong, independent woman is to be treated with contempt and betrayed by her monstrous eldest daughter Veda (Ann Blyth). Mildred has spoiled Veda, compulsively sacrificing herself so that Veda can be raised to become a lady. In fact, Veda becomes so absurdly pretentious that despite Mildred's success she continues to treat her mother as if her own life had been irrevocably tainted by Mildred's having to work for a living. Veda's contempt for Mildred's being merely a waitress, and in turn Mildred's own embarrassment about her job, feel emotionally true and convey some insight into the sort of status and class anxiety that the usual Hollywood mythology of a classless America rarely could recognize or deal with.

On another level, as mentioned before, the film's treatment of career women is the most powerfully suggestive aspect of the work. Hollywood films usually treated career women (especially in the post–World War II era) as people who had to be domesticated and made to see the error of their ways when they competed with men. Even Katharine Hepburn, Hollywood's most noted feminist, had to accept ritualistic degradation and defeat (*Adam's Rib*, 1949) in her classic bouts with Spencer Tracy.[23] In a similar fashion, Joan Crawford's Mildred is clearly superior to the men who surround her but is still supposedly enough of a traditional woman to allow herself to be manipulated by these same callow males. Nor does the film even allow Mildred to pursue a career for profit, power, or a sense of self—her career is conceived of as merely a means to acquire and hold Veda's love. And Veda's behavior itself can possibly be viewed as an extension of Mildred's success drive, or a demonic variation on it.

At the film's conclusion there is a tacked-on happy ending with Mildred now bravely facing the future with her passive, dull, chauvinistic husband, who looks even more inadequate when forced to stand next to her. But given Hollywood conventions, he is there to save her from being a single woman. To underline this chauvinistic point the film allows Ida (Eve Arden), Mildred's handsome, sarcastically witty friend and workmate, to be treated by men as if she were not a "real woman"— the moral being that aggressive, intelligent career women are usually doomed to lonely and asexual lives, and in Ida's case would trade all their independence for the right man.

Obviously, Joan Crawford's career woman owed more to the conventions of the women's picture than to film noir, but in both genres women often enjoyed a great deal of power over the imagination and will of men. There were a number of possible reasons for the diverse and powerful images of female menace, power, and maternal patience and sacrifice that pervaded these films. For one thing, female stars had a great deal of prestige in Hollywood of the forties, and the films reflected that fact. Another explanation for their taking on the image of murderous wives and lovers may have partially derived from the American soldiers' nightmare of infidelity at home during World War II. Of course, the narrative, no matter how much the camera focused on the predatory sexuality or the psychological strength of the female, always restored male dominance by the film's climax.[24]

It was Rita Hayworth, a pin-up favorite of American males in the forties and Columbia Pictures's only major film star and sex symbol, who became the apotheosis of these dangerous females. In fact, the effect of her role as the sensual nightclub singer in *Gilda* (1946) was so strong that it inspired the U.S. Air Force to place Gilda's name on the atomic bomb dropped on Bikini. That role was shortly followed by her playing the

character of a mysterious, seductive Circe, Elsa, in the intricately murderous plot of *The Lady from Shanghai* (1947).

The Lady from Shanghai, directed by her then-husband Orson Welles,
is a virtuoso piece of baroque filmmaking filled with striking and bizarre
aural and visual images and metaphors (for example, the symbolic intercutting between the film's characters and flamingos, crocodiles, and
snakes), unusual camera angles, and the rich use of depth of focus. The
world it depicts is an embodiment of film noir, a dark, nihilistic universe
of men and women who deceive and destroy each other—in this case, in
exotic settings such as the Caribbean and Acapulco. Although there are
moments when the film seems like nothing more than stylish nonsense—
all windy rhetoric and meaningless confusion—the bewitching Elsa's manipulation of Michael O'Hara (Welles himself), a romantic innocent and
aspiring novelist, is touched with interesting ambiguities. Elsa is motivated by both greed and a feeling of being utterly adrift in the world,
and while she cares for Michael she is also willing to use and destroy
him.

Throughout the film, Welles takes pleasure in his cinematic virtuosity
and creates original images and sequences to evoke Elsa's lethal charm.
For example, there is an overhead shot of Elsa languidly lying down and
singing on the deck of the yacht, luring O'Hara from the bowels of the
boat. In an aquarium scene, her face is juxtaposed with an octopus, a
metaphor for her predatoriness. For a grand finale, Welles constructs
a playland sequence with grotesque laughing dolls, chutes, masks, and a
house of mirrors—a labyrinth of refracted and reflected multiple selves.
Elsa is the incarnation of film noir's femme fatale, whose snares are difficult to escape. And though her image is figuratively and literally destroyed, Michael escaping her trap into the light of day, we know, as in
many other forties' films, that he is bound to her image for life. As he
states: "Maybe I'll live so long that I'll forget her. Maybe I'll die trying."

O'Hara's final lines were characteristic of the romantic despair and
angst that was so much a part of film noir. The films projected a world
that was almost universally corrupt and morally chaotic, but gave little
sense of how particular social values and institutions helped shape or
contribute to this vision (though there were exceptions like Abraham
Polonsky's *Force of Evil*, 1948). Corruption was defined primarily in
metaphysical and, at moments, psychological terms—though the mon-
strosity of characters, like Veda in *Mildred Pierce*, was too outsized for
the film's psychological explanations. Many characters in film noir were
impotent and helpless in the face of evil, bending to its force, which

seemed to reside in an inalterable human nature. Others struggled against it but in the process were tainted by evil even when they achieved a victory. And there were still other characters who acted as if they were the personification of that corruption.

But a writer like Barbara Deming could still suggest in her book *Running Away from Myself: A Dream Portrait of Americans Drawn from Film of the 40's* that forties' films (not only film noir) revealed a crisis of public faith: "A vision of hell in which we are bound."[25] Of course, she qualified that perception by stating that the theme and the audience's response to it were in the main unconscious. Other critics speculated that the bleak mood of film noir derived from the cumulative anxieties of the Depression, World War II, and the Cold War, though it was difficult to see, by a close analysis of these films, how public events may have directly influenced or shaped the perspective.

If we took a critical leap and suggested that these films may, on some level, have been a revelation of an unconscious public despair, they could just as easily be seen as works that were mere derivations from other popular arts such as the successful hard-boiled detective novels of Hammett (*Maltese Falcon*, 1941), Cain (*The Postman Always Rings Twice*, 1946), and Chandler (*The Big Sleep*, 1946). On yet another level, like many Hollywood film trends, they could be viewed as a popular genre that was adopted by the industry because it had made a profit at the box office. And though a number of film noir works may have expressed a genuine directorial sensibility, the look of them—lighting, sets, and camera angles—often seemed more significant than their perspective on the world. In fact, many of these films were potboilers that seemingly did no more than adopt a successful set of formal and narrative codes.

Even more interesting and ironic is that the existence of film noir served only to highlight the essential optimism of the 1940s. Despite the hopelessness, cynicism, and sense of universal decay that film noir projected, both the filmmakers and the audience were readily prepared, even desirous, to avoid their implications. As a result, even though the logic of the film's imagery demanded an opposite conclusion, the simple solution, the happy ending, and even justice often triumphed. Of course much of this had to do with Hollywood's system of self-censorship and genre conventions. On the other hand, it was possible to conclude the films in this manner because of the audience's willingness and desire to suspend belief, an attitude which was probably aided by the war-inspired conviction that sufficient energy and goodwill existed in the society to solve any problem and triumph over any evil. In fact, film noir's evocation of evil may have served only as a delicious contrast; making the victory of goodness that much more grand and satisfying. Consequently, though film noir portrayed the darker side of human nature, this portrayal was based as much on cinematic form and style as on the expression of a genuine moral or personal vision, and the films and the audience's response to them hardly affected the basic self-confidence of the era.[26]

Nowhere is the era's basic optimism better illustrated than in some of the forties' films that dealt with social problems, particularly discrimination and racism. In the postwar years a number of Hollywood producers, directors, and writers were determined to extend the democratic ideals that ostensibly underlay the war effort into an examination of and attack on racism and bigotry in America. Films like Edward Dmytryk's *Crossfire* (1947) and Elia Kazan's *Gentleman's Agreement* (1947) were probably two of the first Hollywood studio products to confront anti-Semitism as a serious social problem. For although almost all the Hollywood moguls were Jewish, they were Jews who craved assimilation and made films that "reinvented the country,"[27] creating their own myth of America. Except in films like *The Jazz Singer* (1927), Jews were usually seen as secondary characters—often comic ethnic types in films usually dominated by the moguls' upper-middle-class WASP ideal. (Warner Brothers thirties' films had many ethnic, working-class, but not Jewish protagonists.) So even when films like *Crossfire* and *Gentleman's Agreement* proved profitable, no other films dealing with the subject followed.

Crossfire was an edgy thriller, whose visual texture—its mise-en-scène—was much stronger than its script. The film is filled with film noir shadows, razors so gleamingly polished that characters can be reflected on them, and a number of ominous low-angle and overhead shots. There is also a psychopathic villain, Montgomery (Robert Ryan), who is a deceptively soft-spoken sadist, seething with feelings of inferiority, resentment, and anti-Semitism—"Jewish people live off the fat of the land."

The power of the film lies in Ryan's performance, and the evocation of a tense, seedy night world of smoky bars, all-night movie theaters, and cheap apartments, inhabited by characters such as Gloria Grahame's Ginny, a tough, exhausted woman, and her odd, pathological-liar boyfriend. The bitterness and venom that is exchanged between the two of them, and the feeling that most of the characters are living near the precipice, is much more striking than the film's attack on anti-Semitism.

Crossfire's social vision is timid and evasive. The anti-Semite is conceived of as an uneducated psychopath, which distances the situation from the audience's own experience and values and absolves them of any guilt. The Jewish victim, Samuels (Sam Levene), is a war hero and an empathetic good guy, the film seeming to suggest that an ordinary Jewish scapegoat would be unable to elicit audience sympathy, only the extraordinary Jew being capable of evoking moral or social concern. And by turning the homosexual victim of the novel into a Jew the film demonstrated Hollywood's basic timidity and fear during this period (homosexuals could not be dealt with in a sympathetic light in films of the 1940s). Finally, in its implicit belief that all problems of prejudice and racism are interchangeable, Hollywood manifested an unwillingness to deal with the particular historical and social experiences of different groups. The films expressed a faith that tolerance—a decent, liberal principle—was sufficient to encompass and solve a variety of complex social problems. Both compounding and illustrating this mixture of intellectual and political timorousness and vagueness was *Crossfire*'s tendency to be awkwardly and superficially didactic. Its liberal spokesman, pipe-smoking police Lieutenant Finley (Robert Young), stops the action and provides a vaporous sermon about standing up to prejudice. It's an editorial that safely invokes nineteenth-century discrimination against the Irish as a historical parallel to anti-Semitism, rather than addressing the more charged and contemporary issue of race.

In contrast to *Crossfire*, Elia Kazan's *Gentleman's Agreement* (which won the Oscar for best picture in 1947), though lacking the former's visual style and texture, examined and dramatized facets of anti-Semitism that *Crossfire* never touched on. In the film a WASP magazine writer, Phil Green (Gregory Peck), pretends to be a Jew for two months so he can write an exposé of bigotry. In his pursuit of his story a gallery of anti-Semites make their appearance, running the gamut from raging bigots to genteel WASPs ("nice people"), who indulge in polite prejudice, and to self-hating Jews who object to Jews who are too ethnic ("kikey").

Despite *Gentleman's Agreement*'s more complex perspective on anti-Semitism, it is characterized by the same political superficiality endemic to social-problem films. Its use of a Gentile journalist to confront anti-Semitism evaded the whole issue. It implied that the distinct social and cultural history and ethnic characteristics that distinguished Gentile from Jew had never existed. And a Gentile's being the victim gave the audience the chance to express anger without having to confront the moral wrongness of prejudice. They now could get upset because an innocent man—a non-Jew—had by mistake become a victim of prejudice.

It was not only Jews who got a touch of liberal optimism from Hollywood in the forties. Blacks from the time of *Birth of a Nation* (1915) had usually been seen by Hollywood either as brutal, savage bucks, or as good toms and mammies. In thirties' films two new black stereotypes began to appear—sympathetic victims who were symbols of general rather than racial oppression (the black janitor who is brutally questioned by the police in *They Won't Forget*, 1937) and "tragic mulattoes" (e.g., *Imitation of Life*, 1934), whose skin color allowed them to pass into white society. However, until the 1940s problem films blacks were mainly confined to minor roles, and racism was never explored as an issue.

By the end of the decade Hollywood began to address the issue and a number of films dealing with race prejudice were released. In one of these, *Home of the Brave* (1949), an educated, emotionally disturbed black GI, Peter Moss (James Edwards) is cured of a trauma (psychosomatic paralysis) by a white psychiatrist. Moss's character is in the tradition of the noble martyr (though the film deals directly with racism, not generalized oppression), a passive, self-effacing figure who embodies white values. He is the perfect black to exemplify the liberal ideals of the film, since he is a war hero and a successful professional. He can be viewed by the white audience as someone whose character and life-style are no different from any white's. Just as in *Gentleman's Agreement*, Hollywood again affirmed tolerance and integration, providing it was for blacks and Jews who behaved like or really were WASPs. *Home of the Brave* defined racism as a psychological problem—racists being pathological and blacks being oversensitive to prejudice. For forties' Hollywood there was no such thing as institutional racism—where racist practice permeated, consciously and especially unconsciously, the dominant political and economic institutions of the society—and almost no sense of how profound a role racism played in the daily life of blacks and of society as a whole. Racism was conceived of as a problem that neurotic individuals suffered from, and which could be resolved simply with a dose of shared sympathy and understanding between whites and blacks.

In films like *Lost Boundaries* (1949) and *Pinky* (1949) a somewhat similar social perspective was communicated. *Lost Boundaries* was produced by documentary filmmaker Louis de Rochemont (creator of the *March of Time* newsreels) and was shot on location in New Hampshire and Maine, with a largely nonprofessional cast. Based on a true story, the film deals with a dedicated black doctor, Scott Carter, and his family, who, in the tradition of Hollywood's tragic mulattoes, pass for white in an idyllic New England town. The only seeming legacy of Carter's racial past is his children's gift for music (the "natural rhythm" of blacks)—though he still guiltily goes to Boston once a week to practice at a ghetto clinic. Ultimately the family secret is revealed when Carter is rejected for a naval commission because he is black, and the family is forced to deal with the mild social prejudice of the town, and, more importantly, their sensitive son's confusion (the children were never told) over his racial identity.

Lost Boundaries is a well-intentioned film but is limited by a neat Hollywood formula that turns racism into a peripheral problem and totally blurs even that issue by having the black Carters played by white actors (Mel Ferrer and Beatrice Pearson) in the Hollywood tradition of Showboat and Imitation of Life. Hollywood was unwilling to take the risk that audience sympathy could be elicited for black actors passing for white, so it made it easy for viewers. It gave them white actors playing characters who by some imperceptible accident of fate might have some black blood.

The film concludes with the town's Episcopal minister giving a sermon affirming Christian principles ("I am my brother's keeper") and announcing that the navy has seen the light and has begun to grant officers' commissions to people of all races. The sermon has a magical effect, moving a number of townspeople to apologetically welcome the Carters back into the community. Liberal optimism triumphs, and though black social and economic conditions are alluded to in some affecting documentary footage of Harlem squalor and violence and there is a self-conscious speech by a black police officer on the pernicious effect of an impoverished environment on black lives, this problem is in no way the prime concern of the film. The political essence and hope of the film lies in the acceptance of one upper-middle-class, church-going, white-black family by white society.

In a similar fashion, Elia Kazan's Pinky (1949) also focused on a tragic mulatto passing for white (again played by a white actress, Jeanne Crain), but the film lacks even the surface realism of Lost Boundaries. Pinky takes place in a studio-set southern town, all wisteria and willows, and trades in racial stereotypes and clichés: an irascible but just and independent white matriarch (Ethel Barrymore); a traditional, strong, wise nanny (Ethel Waters); a hypocritical, fat clubwoman bigot; white-trash rapists; and a lazy, no-account black with his razor-carrying wife. At the film's conclusion Pinky has refused to pass for white any longer and has affirmed her racial identity by starting a nursery-hospital for blacks. In rediscovering her black roots Pinky triumphs on a personal rather than a social level. Her victory is achieved with the assistance of paternalistic whites and gives no sign that the South's repressive and segregated order will ever be confronted, much less changed.

Other social-problem films during the period dealt with subjects like mental illness—for instance, Anatol Litvak's The Snake Pit (1948), which did bring about reform of some state mental hospitals—and with juvenile delinquency (Nicholas Ray's *Knock on Any Door*, 1949). But none of them really broke from the Hollywood norm.

In retrospect, the intellectual faintheartedness of these forties' social-problem films seems even more blatant. Of course, the films were, as always, constrained politically by the industry's prime commitment to making a profit. These films, however, were not only pallid, evasive, and sentimental in their handling of social issues, but most of them also had little cinematic energy, style, or dramatic life of their own. The characters inhabiting these works were usually impersonal figures, lacking a semblance of internality or psychological nuance, and operating as mere representations or symbols of social problems. The films conceived of their characters' behavior as being shaped almost totally by external forces or problems, rather than belonging to people with genuine inner lives who reacted to the charged social situations they were in. The result was that the characters' existential or political choices never seemed to stem from their own reflections or feelings.

All the same, despite their shallowness, these films must be seen and evaluated within the context of their own times. For one thing, they strongly suggest how deeply a politically committed culture of liberalism had taken root in historically conservative Hollywood since the thirties (one shortly to be decimated by HUAC and the blacklist). They also attest to the economic security enjoyed by the industry, which enabled it to feel confident enough to touch on previously taboo themes. Indeed the very existence of these social-problem films testifies to a shift away from the conventional Hollywood wisdom about social issues, which was, "if you want to send a message, use Western Union," to an equally crude belief in the power of a vague form of liberalism to produce instant social change. In fact, the lack of subtlety and complexity in these films can in some ways be seen as yet another sign of the overwhelming optimism of the era—a sanguine belief that no problem was insoluble.[28]

A few films departed from this facile optimism. *Force of Evil* (1948), written and directed by Abraham Polonsky (who was soon to be a victim of the blacklist), was a sharp contrast to films like *Lost Boundaries* and *Gentleman's Agreement*. On the surface *Force of Evil* was a formula melodrama about the numbers racket—complete with a head racketeer and his femme fatale wife, whose violent confrontations were awkwardly edited and devoid of dramatic tension. However, there was much more to the film than the predictable tale of a corrupt lawyer, Joe Morse (John Garfield), who is ready to go straight at the film's climax. Polonsky crafted an ambiguous and imaginative work that uses Hollywood con-

ventions to evoke on one level a portrait of American society dominated
by greed and acquisitiveness. On another level, it's the story of a passionate, guilt-ridden, love-hate relationship between Joe and his older
brother, Leo (Thomas Gomez), who has given up going to college to
send Joe to law school. The brothers share both a profound resentment
of and love for each other.

Though Polonsky's characters are all caught in the coils of the social
system and its pernicious values, they are not simply symbols of a corrupt society. They have inner lives that are both shaped by and independent of social forces. The characters are people who choose the direction
of their lives. In this small, poetic near-masterpiece, Polonsky has successfully fused Marxist and Freudian strains. The film's protagonist, Joe
Morse (John Garfield), is a tough, perceptive lawyer who is aware of his
inability to resist being part of the rackets and becoming corrupt. But
Joe is adept at rationalizing his choices by asserting that everybody is
guilty—that they all hunger for "the ruby." And in Force of Evil all the
characters, including sweating, apoplectic, self-righteous Leo and even
Leo's naive, dreamy stenographer, Doris, are tainted by the seductions
of money and success.

Polonsky's direction is characterized by extremely long overheads of
minute, isolated figures dwarfed by Wall Street buildings (seemingly
based on a Paul Strand photo)—a metaphor for monolithic and alienating capitalist power—and by the film noir images of seedy numbers par-
lors, opulent winding staircases, and shadows auguring doom.

Much more original than the film's imagery is Polonsky's use of language—both dialogue and narration—which he strives to maintain in an
equal, sometimes dialectical, relationship with the visual images. And
though at moments the script becomes overly literary and self-conscious,
its Joycean repetitions, city argot and inflection and metaphors (e.g.,
"money spread over the city like perfume") convey a genuine street poetry and set the film apart from almost all other forties' films.

Force of Evil concludes with Joe Morse descending on a gray morning
to the "bottom of the world" to discover Leo's dead body left looking like
an "old dirty rag." Polonsky does not have Joe indulge in grand, heroic
gestures nor does he insert polemics for radical change. There is only a
solitary Joe, willing to make his own understated moral stand, ready to
help if he can. Polonsky's film offers no easy solutions. It knows how
powerful the capitalist ethos is: Polonsky holds that it is not only Wall
Street that pursues a capitalist-gangster ethic, but that the consciousness
of most Americans is suffused with capitalist dreams.

Besides Force of Evil, other films that dealt with some insight and intelligence with political and social themes were Robert Rossen's *All the King's Men* (1949) (he had directed a boxing film *Body and Soul*, 1947, for which Abraham Polonsky had written the script) and Billy Wilder's *A Foreign Affair* (1948). *All the King's Men* was based on a novel by Robert Penn Warren dealing with the career of populist demagogue and Louisiana governor Huey Long, here called Willie Stark (Broderick Crawford in a flamboyant, forceful, Academy Award–winning performance). Stark begins his political career as a man of the people but is thwarted by the political machine and adopts its corrupt tactics to achieve and sustain his power.

All the King's Men is an intellectually ambitious but clumsy film. Stark's transformation into a power-mad megalomaniac is too abrupt and extreme, the reasons for the alcoholic, drifting journalist-narrator Jack Burden's (John Ireland) continuing loyalty to Stark are never really illuminated, and the script tends to telegraph its point of view. But despite the melodramatic turns and the choppy continuity, the film trenchantly captures the perniciousness of political power and how the use of corrupt means in pursuit of social change can ultimately become an end in itself.

In *A Foreign Affair* Wilder displayed a talent for mordant, cynical comedy satirizing the foolishness and naiveté of an American congressional committee investigating the morale of American troops (who are entwined in black-market dealings and affairs with German women) in postwar occupied Germany. Wilder is particularly nasty about American provincialism and ethnocentrism and shows how easily the committee's self-righteousness is subverted when confronted by European cynicism and sophistication. The portrait of the Germans, who are interested only in self-preservation—personified by a ruthless, sensual, ex-Nazi collaborator played by Marlene Dietrich—is not a sympathetic one. However, as is Wilder's wont, by the climax he has thoroughly softened the film's bite, ostensibly endorsing the American values he at first so savagely poked fun at.

Clearly, the compromises inherent in *A Foreign Affair* were the Hollywood norm, since the industry rarely had the courage or the imagination to deal directly and complexly with controversial political and social themes. It was much easier for Hollywood to work in genres that provided comforting fantasy images, such as the musical—a genre that ever since its "All Talkin', All Dancin', All Singin' " days of the late twenties and early thirties had become one of Hollywood's glories. During the late thirties various studios vied for the honor of producing the best musicals, but by the forties undisputed leadership in the genre had fallen to MGM. There the Arthur Freed unit, with talents like Gene Kelly, Judy Garland, Fred Astaire, Vincente Minnelli, and others, turned out hit after hit.[29]

Though often considered the most escapist of the Hollywood genres, the musical nevertheless succeeded in striking emotional chords that few other films could match. Its tunes became the hallmark of particular eras. For example, Judy Garland's *Wizard of Oz* (1939) rendition of "Over the Rainbow" became a worldwide hymn of a hoped-for postwar world of peace and prosperity. The same film's "We're Off to See the Wizard" became the anthem of the British Army as it chased Rommel across the sands of North Africa, and "Ding Dong, the Witch Is Dead" was danced the world over on VE Day.

On another level, the film's singing and dancing intimated that a great deal of energy lurked beneath the everyday surface and seemed ready to burst forth at any moment. During the war years that energy seemed to nestle softly in a nostalgic evocation of a turn-of-the-century America — an idealized world that was perhaps never better realized than in Vincente Minnelli's vividly colored and stylized *Meet Me in St. Louis* (1944). Except for the momentary anxiety over the family's possible uprooting because of the father's new job in New York, some nervousness about whether or not the boy next door, John Truett (Tom Drake), loves Esther Smith (Judy Garland), and the strikingly visualized Halloween night terrors of little "Tootie" (Margaret O'Brien), the Smith family lived on the surface a warm, almost idyllic existence. The film constructed an Edenic past centering on home and family, topped by a vision of an ever-progressing future embodied in the 1903 St. Louis World's Fair.

This version of a bright, promising new world was fully realized in Gene Kelly and Stanley Donen's MGM film *On the Town* (1949). The tale of three sailors on a three-day pass in New York, the film uses real locations — the Brooklyn Bridge, the Statue of Liberty, and Washington Square — and artfully designed sets to turn the city into a magical place where all of one's dreams can be fulfilled.

The film begins serenely with a long crane shot of a longshoreman lazily on his way to work at dawn, singing "I feel like I'm not out of bed yet," and then cuts to three animated sailors (Kelly, Sinatra, and Jules Munshin) bounding off their ship ready to take on New York. The sailors are "ordinary Joes" — innocents filled with a sense of wonder and exhilaration as they move naturally from everyday speech to sing "New York, New York, it's a wonderful town." There is nothing serene or simple about the city they're hungry to experience. But they are filled with confidence that all of New York can be absorbed, the camera tracking

after them as they sing "We're really living, we're going on the town."
Their energy is so infectious that it allows them to liberate three young
women—an overworked taxi driver (Betty Garrett), an oversexed social-
ite (Anne Miller) (class differences are no obstacle), and a pert ballerina
reduced for financial reasons to kootch dancing at Coney Island (Vera
Ellen). As they romp through New York, the city becomes a metropolis
of grandeur, romance, vitality, and sentiment (even the cops are soft-
hearted), the exuberant center of an even more buoyant America.[30]

It is this inexhaustible sense of energy, joy, and confidence that more
than anything else characterizes the forties and their films. Certainly
there were dark clouds looming, such as the HUAC threat, to sap Hollywood's vitality. In addition, film noir had raised the curtain on a darker
side of the American psyche and character. Nevertheless, for most
Americans the forties—particularly the late forties—were the first relatively unruffled period of peace and prosperity that they had enjoyed in
almost two decades. Despite fears of the Soviet Union and a native communist fifth column, there was also the faith that America had both the
material and the moral capacity to deal with the "red menace" and any
other problem it confronted. For example, films like Howard Hawks's
epic western about the first cattle drive up the Chisholm Trail, *Red River*
(1948), conveyed great confidence in the strength of the American character. The film's monomaniacal, forbidding hero, Tom Dunson (John
Wayne), easily masters the land, cattle stampedes, and Indian attacks.
And this exemplar of American individualism even learns to temper his
rigidity and rage and reconcile himself with his more flexible, feelingful
(but still tough) stepson, Matt Garth (Montgomery Clift).

Hollywood had emerged from the war with its coffers, audience, and
prestige at an all-time peak. As a result, the forties' films were perhaps
the last time that Hollywood had sufficient self-confidence to create an
insulated, coherent world, which could unselfconsciously endorse the
American Dream. For most Americans and for Hollywood the forties
were truly "The Best Years of Our Lives."

NOTES

1. Godfrey Hodgson, *America in Our Time: From World War II to Nixon,
What Happened and Why* (New York: Vintage, 1978), pp. 17–64.

2. Hodgson, *America in Our Time*, p. 20.

3. Hodgson, *America in Our Time*, p. 54.

4. Eric F. Goldman, *The Crucial Decade—and After, America 1945–1960*
(New York: Vintage, 1960).

5. Goldman, *The Crucial Decade*, pp. 46–70.

6. Stephen E. Ambrose, *Rise to Globalism: American Foreign Policy 1938–1970* (Baltimore, Md.: Penguin, 1971), pp. 102–35.

7. Ambrose, *Rise to Globalism*, pp. 136–66.

8. Dean Acheson, *Present at the Creation* (New York: W. W. Norton, 1969), p. 297.

9. Ambrose, *Rise to Globalism*, pp. 136–66.

10. Alistair Cooke, *A Generation on Trial* (Baltimore, Md.: Penguin, 1952).

11. Walter Goodman, *The Committee: The Extraordinary Career of the House Committee on Un-American Activities* (Baltimore, Md.: Penguin, 1969), pp. 207–25.

12. Goodman, *The Committee*, p. 300.

13. Cooke, *A Generation on Trial*, pp. 337–41.

14. Charles Higham and Joel Greenberg, *Hollywood in the Forties* (New York: Paperback Library, 1970), p. 18.

15. James Agee, *Agee on Film: Reviews and Comments* (Boston: Beacon Press, 1966), p. 173.

16. Franklin Fearing, "Warriors Return: Normal or Neurotic," *Hollywood Quarterly* (October 1945), pp. 91–109.

17. Agee, *Agee on Film*, p. 229.

18. Abe Polonsky, "*The Best Years of Our Lives:* A Review," *Hollywood Quarterly* (April 1947), pp. 91–2.

19. Frank Capra, *The Name above the Title* (New York: Bantam, 1972), pp. 418–26.

20. Higham and Greenberg, *Hollywood in the Forties*, pp. 19–39.

21. *Ibid.*

22. Molly Haskell, *From Reverence to Rape: The Treatment of Women in the Movies* (Baltimore, Md.: Penguin, 1974), pp. 153–88.

23. Haskell, *From Reverence to Rape*, pp. 189–230.

24. *Ibid.*

25. Barbara Deming, *Running Away from Myself: A Dream Portrait of America Drawn from the Films of the Forties* (New York: Grossman Publishers, 1969), p. 6.

26. Joseph G. Goulden, *The Best Years, 1945–1950* (New York: Atheneum, 1976).

27. Neal Gabler, *An Empire of Their Own: How the Jews Invented Hollywood* (New York: Crown, 1988), p. 7.

28. Peter Roffman and Jim Purdy, *The Hollywood Social Problem Film* (Bloomington, Ind.: Indiana University Press, 1981).

29. Hugh Fordin, *The World of Entertainment: Hollywood's Greatest Musicals* (Garden City, N.Y.: Doubleday, 1975).

30. Richard Dyer, "Entertainment and Utopia," in R. Altman (ed.), *Genre: The Musical* (London: Routledge & Kegan Paul, 1981), pp. 175–89.

3

THE FIFTIES

The fifties began on an ominous note with America, as part of a nominally United Nations–led force, becoming involved in a war in Korea, and the repressive and paranoid investigations of Senator McCarthy and company in full throttle. The decade, however, ultimately evolved into one permeated by a broad political and cultural consensus.[1]

The first years of the decade were dominated by the stalemated Korean War, where the Truman administration was willing to eschew military victory for a limited war and a negotiated settlement. Truman's military policies were challenged by World War II hero General Douglas MacArthur, who was then commander of the United Nations forces. Cloaking himself in his own sense of omniscience and nineteenth-century patriotic pieties, MacArthur saw Truman's policies as the appeasement of communism and committed himself to total victory in Korea. Truman, in turn, responded by firing MacArthur for insubordination and subsequently discovered himself the object of intense public rage.[2]

That rage soon found a home in the McCarthy, HUAC, and Senate Internal Security Subcommittee investigations of a domestic communist conspiracy. This conspiracy was seen as a threat to take over a number of American institutions, like the church, universities, private industry, and Hollywood. During the fifties the anticommunist crusade elicited the involvement, whether out of fear, political self-interest, or conviction, of a number of liberal groups and individuals. It included the American Civil Liberties Union, which from 1953 to 1959 refused to defend communists who were under attack or lost jobs, and Hubert Humphrey, who as a senator proposed a bill to outlaw the Communist party.[3] Interestingly enough, many liberal intellectuals placed the blame for men like McCarthy on the actions of the left rather than on the right, at times even supporting the general public's view that the rights of communists and communist sympathizers should be denied.

The leading and most brazen figure in the anticommunist crusade was Senator Joseph McCarthy, a crude Wisconsin Republican who opportunistically manipulated the issue to promote his own power and career. For four years he successfully used smears, innuendos, and lies to trample on individual rights and helped create a climate of political fear and conformity, which even had establishment institutions on the defensive. But in 1954, when McCarthy went after the army and even dropped hints that President Eisenhower was soft on communism, he overreached himself and initiated his own rapid fall from power and celebrity. McCarthy's decline did not signify a turn to the left. It caused no sudden opening of public discussion on such issues as the admission of China to the United Nations or talk of a social commitment to the poor, but it did mean a moderation of the repressive and divisive impulses that had dominated the early fifties.[4]

The prime American political symbol of the fifties, however, was not Joe McCarthy but General Dwight Eisenhower, the Republican president from 1952 to 1960. Ike was a World War II military hero, whose calm, avuncular, optimistic public presence helped create a nonideological political mood that muted controversy and offered something both to liberals and to conservatives. Though disliking the welfare state, Ike accepted the reforms of the New Deal without extending them and was prepared to use fiscal and monetary measures to maintain full employment. Despite believing in the Cold War, and unable to see the differences between communist and nationalist revolutions (e.g., CIA interventions in Iran and Guatemala occurred during his administration), he believed in a nuclear truce, refusing to engage in an arms race with the Soviets, and studiously avoided getting the United States involved in a war.[5]

Eisenhower was a cautious president who, though unsympathetic to the growing civil rights movement, reluctantly sent troops to Little Rock to ensure school desegregation in 1957 and in crisis after crisis kept political tensions beneath the surface. By dint of his confident cautiousness and political skills, Eisenhower was able to preside over a national political consensus that excluded only paranoid right elements, southern reactionaries, segments of the old left, and the few independent radicals who were still functioning as critics.[6]

This political consensus was built on and reinforced by an intellectual consensus shared by most American intellectuals. Some, like John Kenneth Galbraith, believed in a theory of "countervailing power" where big business power would be balanced by the power of big labor and government.[7] Others held that the age of ideology was over (e.g., Daniel Bell, *The End of Ideology*) and in its place substituted an optimistic faith in capitalism, political pluralism, and the uniqueness and perfectibility of American society. These tough-minded anti-ideologues had constructed their own ideology, building it on a belief that economic growth and the practical application of social science principles would provide social justice and solve social problems. In their social vision there would be no need for economic redistribution (many of them were ex-radicals and leftists who out of a complex of motives rejected their own political past), for the American people were supposedly becoming more economically equal. And poverty, during the rare times it was acknowledged to exist, was seen as gradually disappearing. In turn they also read the idea of class conflict, and even the significance of class, out of the American social and political landscape, promoting their own liberal mythology that in a totally middle-class society everybody had an equal opportunity to succeed. The other prime element of this ideological consensus was the aforementioned rise of liberal anticommunism (e.g., *The Partisan Review*, once a critical, sophisticated Marxist journal, became an avid defender of the West), which viewed Cold War politics as far more significant than domestic affairs. This commitment was so potent that even the newly merged American Federation of Labor and Congress of Industrial Organizations (AFL-CIO) gave more attention to the anticommunist struggle than to organizing the mass of workers who remained outside the unions.[8]

However, though most intellectuals either were utterly at home with the direction of American politics or turned to contemplating existential and religious questions emphasizing the limitations of human nature, simply ceasing to be political dissenters and critics, there were still a number of them who preserved their critical skills by analyzing and attacking the character of American mass culture. In the fifties the economy of abundance helped create a powerful suburban and consumer culture where the pursuit of success and an emphasis on social conformity became the dominant values of the era. As novelist Edmund White wrote about growing up in the Midwest in the fifties: "That was a time and place where there was little consumption of culture and no dissent. . . . It felt, at least to me, like a big gray country of families on drowsy holiday, all stuffed in one oversized car and discussing the mileage they were getting."[9]

College students were in harmony with this mood and were for the most part apolitical ("a silent generation"), interested in a fraternity-sorority-based social life and in preparing for future careers. The Reverend Norman Vincent Peale, with his message of "positive thinking," became the country's most popular moralist and preacher, and the country's growing religious interest seemed built on sociability rather than spirituality.

The mass media of the fifties reflected and reinforced these values. Television was dominated by entertainers like the droning, folksy Arthur Godfrey, who became one of its most powerful personalities, by the skilled slapstick of *I Love Lucy*, and by the naked greed of quiz shows such as *Twenty-one*. And though there were imaginative comedy programs like *Your Show of Shows* and original television drama on *Playhouse 90*, the most popular programs were often built on the most inane premises and on the marketing of personal comfort and instant gratification. One interesting statistic that conveyed something of the anti-intellectual taste of the times was that "about four times the expenditures on public libraries were paid out for comic books."[10]

In books like William H. Whyte's *The Organization Man* (1956) and David Riesman's more scholarly and complex *The Lonely Crowd* (1950), American middle-class life was criticized for its penchant for uniformity, social role-playing, and privatism. Other critics, both liberal and conservative, poked fun at the mass media, advertising, the automobile culture, and the anxiety-laden drive for social status and material goods. However, though the banality and tastelessness of much of what appeared on television and the blandness of suburban life were criticized, there was no attempt by these critics to break from the political and social consensus of the fifties. For the most part, they accepted the political and social system that helped shape the culture, and most of the targets they attacked were not particularly controversial ones.[11]

Nevertheless, despite the serene and confident veneer of the Eisenhower years, there were subversive currents that, though barely recognized, coexisted with the dominant mood of stability and complacency. The threat of nuclear war shadowed the period, creating among a number of people a sense of fatalism and despair and leading to protests in the late 1950s against the civil defense program. The program was seen as treating nuclear war as an acceptable military alternative which people had to prepare themselves to survive.

The fifties also saw the civil rights movement begin to take shape. Whites may have been content with the political and social world of the fifties, but black needs and problems were clearly left unmet by an indifferent Republican administration and a Congress paralyzed by the southern Democratic bloc. The only arm of government responsive to black grievances was the Supreme Court led by Chief Justice Earl Warren. In 1954 the Court came to a monumental decision. In *Brown v. Board of Education of Topeka* it outlawed segregation in the public schools. There were violent reactions in the South, but de jure segregation of the schools (de facto segregation is a continuing and deepening reality) was at the beginning of its end.

The Court decision led to the 1955 Montgomery bus boycott – a grassroots black protest against segregation in public transportation. The boycott was followed by protest movements in other southern cities and, most importantly, marked the ascent to national black leadership of Martin Luther King Jr.

The movement to the suburbs by urban whites also carried a critical, even dark, undercurrent. For though it was viewed either satirically – as a flight to a sterile, tedious, and vulgar world – or sympathetically – ordinary Americans achieving their small portion of the American Dream – the radical consequences of this flight (by 1950, 40 to 50 million Americans lived in the suburbs) for the inner city of the 1960s and 1970s were not foreseen. The departure of a white middle and lower middle class from the cities and their replacement by black and Hispanic poor led in the following decades to the erosion of the urban tax base (built on the sales and property taxes of its inhabitants), the escalation of often insoluble urban problems, and even greater residential segregation than had existed in the past.[12]

There were also other fifties' currents that indicated resistance to the conservatism of the decade. The Beat movement, which was an attack on both the middle-class conformity and hypocrisy of the Eisenhower years and the elite literary culture of the universities, came of age in the 1950s. Led by serious poets like Allen Ginsberg and Gregory Corso and novelists like Jack Kerouac (*On the Road*), the Beats modeled their writing on poets like Walt Whitman and novelists like Henry Miller and on the improvisation of jazz musicians like Charlie Parker. In their writing and lives they emphasized spontaneity, personal freedom, a contempt for authority, and spiritual exploration. The Beat movement did not consist only of artists; there were other young people – beatniks – who, taking their lead from the Kerouacs and Ginsbergs, adopted or mimicked a more natural, antibourgeois life-style (symbolized by pot, jazz, and free sex). And, though the Beats were never a part of a political or social movement, their writings rejected racism and the nuclear arms race and treated homosexuality without contempt or condescension.[13]

The fifties also saw the development of a distinctive youth culture accompanied by a new (though derived from black rhythm-and-blues music) form of music—rock and roll. For many older Americans rock music was too loud and overtly sexual, and sounded to them like aimless noise. However, at its best and most innovative (e.g., the rock of Chuck Berry and Elvis Presley) the music had an energy, freedom, and earthiness that offered the possibility of an undefined new life-style, which strongly contrasted with 1950s conventionality. Of course, by the late 1950s much of rock music's class and regional identity had been bleached out and transformed into the mass-produced, soporific sound of Frankie Avalon and his clones.[14]

Clearly these deviant currents and dark strains were not the preeminent ones in fifties' America. It is important, however, to recognize that the era was more complex than is implied by the usual images and descriptive phrases evoking a time supposedly dominated by a passive "silent generation."

Similarly, the films produced in Hollywood defied facile labels and categories. In the early 1950s, as in the late 1940s, HUAC garnered publicity by investigating the film industry. Its hearings helped buttress the already powerful blacklist of actors, writers, and directors, and created in its wake a "clearance"[15] industry that passed judgment on the political purity and future employment of the people who worked in Hollywood. And, just as in the late 1940s (*I Married a Communist*, 1949), cheap genre films were produced to purge the Hollywood image of any taint of radicalism. A film like *Big Jim McLain* (1952) used a documentary style, including an authoritative narrator, to exalt the FBI and HUAC while condemning communists more for their character traits (they were criminals, idealistic dupes, nymphomaniacs, or disturbed fanatics) than for their ideology. In fact, the ideology was never defined or explored. Communists were reduced to caricatures who saw human life as dispensable, had no room for private feelings, and were even in opposition to God and motherhood.

The most hysterical of these films, and probably the one least bound by genre conventions, was *My Son John* (1952). Its director was Leo McCarey (e.g., *The Awful Truth*, 1937), who had distinguished himself during the 1947 HUAC hearing by replying to a question about why the Soviets had banned his last film (*Going My Way*, 1944): "Because it had God in it." In addition, in 1950 he joined Cecil B. deMille in urging all members of the Directors' Guild to take a loyalty oath. *My Son John* differed from other anticommunist films by focusing on the conflict between father and son rather than the usual exposé of communist crimes and conspiracies. The film operated most powerfully on a barely ac-knowledged Oedipal level where both father and son struggle for the wife-mother's time and respect. However, it is clear that what McCarey tried to do in My Son John was to pit the all-American Jefferson family's communist son John, an unathletic, sexually ambiguous intellectual, played in his insidious, contemptuous Strangers on a Train (1951) style by Robert Walker, against his modest, down-to-earth parents (Helen Hayes and Dean Jagger), who believe in football, the Bible, the American na-tion, and the flag.

It is obviously an unequal struggle since the sullen, slick John is seen by McCarey as a monster, and since, though the overpossessive mother is a mass of neurotic tics—rolling eyes, tense smile, and flapping hands—and the father is a rigid, banal Legionnaire, they are totally vindicated at the film's conclusion. In an unbelievable final scene the dead John (killed by communist agents) leaves a tape recording of a commencement speech, which, enveloped in almost divine light, plays from the lectern to his former university's graduating class. The tape affirms his faith in his father and mother and informs the students how the communist serpent numbed his brain and led him to become a traitor.

In McCarey's feverish world, being an intellectual was clearly a dan-gerous, un-American vocation, and redemption could be found only in the moralisms of John's elementary school principal father and the hys-terical religiosity of his mother. For McCarey it is the heart and emo-tions, no matter how pathological, that won't lie or lead you astray. But the intellect is dangerous—it makes you question and doubt and leaves you open to subversive ideas and the rejection of commonsense wisdom.

Nor was McCarey alone in this view of the perfidy of the intellectual. This perspective was shared, albeit with greater subtlety and complexity, by Elia Kazan, who also played a leading role before HUAC. Kazan had joined the Communist party in the 1930s but had resigned, feeling in-tense bitterness and hostility towards it. However, he continued to see himself as a man of the left.[16] And in 1951, at the height of the Cold War, and close to the time he delivered his infamous cooperative testi-mony before HUAC, he made Viva Zapata, a film dealing with the he-roic leader of the Mexican Revolution. It was Kazan's first truly personal and structurally cinematic work—an intense film characterized by highly stylized and powerful imagery and lighting and a political per-spective open to a variety of conflicting interpretations. That was a sign either of its profound ambiguity or of its intellectual confusion.

Nevertheless, at the HUAC hearings Viva Zapata was viewed as a sus-tained anticommunist film, and Kazan himself promoted it as an anticommunist work. What could be considered anticommunist in the film was evoked most vividly by the character of Fernando (Joseph Wiseman), a Machiavellian professional revolutionary and intellectual. Kazan conceived him as a sterile, cold man – an anti-life force – dangerous not only because of his political opportunism, but because of his lack of capacity for human connection. In fact, Fernando is portrayed as a revolutionary devoid of any political ideology except a commitment to power – a common stereotype that Hollywood used to provide a negative portrait for revolutionaries. He is willing to shift from the political left to the right without a moment's hesitation or reflection. It is clear that Kazan wanted Fernando to be seen, despite the vagueness of his ideology, as the apotheosis of the Communist party commissar – a man who could use and betray both the people's demands and his personal relationships and loyalties to achieve power.

Kazan's evocation of the intellectual's power hunger is, however, only one example of the film's primary theme: the oppressiveness and meaninglessness of political power. For example, in a key scene Zapata (Marlon Brando) is depicted occupying the presidential palace and continuing both to temporize and to intimidate the peasants as the tyrant Diaz had done before him. Obviously, in this somewhat abstract, schematic sequence, Kazan wished to demonstrate to the audience that power corrupts and that revolutionary regimes have sustained the tyrannical patterns of their right-wing predecessors.

However, *Viva Zapata* cannot be reduced to an anticommunist polemic on the lines of *My Son John*, since it is filled with diverse (sometimes half-developed) strains that lead to often contradictory interpretations. Given this fact, it is understandable that the *Daily Worker* would have attacked the film for being Trotskyist,[17] that a number of film critics could condemn it for its Cold War anticommunism, and that a great many people in the 1960s New Left could love and embrace it.[18]

For *Viva Zapata* conveyed both populist and anarchist sentiments along with its anticommunism. The film was filled with images of peasants acting heroically and collectively to promote the revolution. For the most part Kazan tended to romanticize them, portraying them in static, archetypal images and in silhouette as models of innocence and solemn dignity. But Kazan's populism also had an underside in the person of Eufemio (Anthony Quinn), Zapata's brother, who is a barbarian desiring the fruits of the revolution – booty, women, and the land – without any other commitment beyond self-gratification. And the power of the people is often undermined by the charismatic figure of Zapata. Though Zapata is able to inform the people that "there is no leader but yourselves," he is depicted as a mythic figure whose instinctive nobility and life energy dwarf the noble peasants that surround and follow him. The mixture of Brando's larger-than-life performance and Kazan's conception of Zapata make it difficult to believe that with Zapata's death the peasants have become a populist force—the "strong people that don't need a strong man."

If Kazan's populism is bound by contradictions, his anarchism exists much more as a personal response, a belief in acting spontaneously and passionately, than as a politically coherent idea of state and society. There are no hints of Peter Kropotkin, Mikhail Bakunin, or some other form of anarcho-syndicalism inherent in the film. There is just Kazan's personal disdain for bourgeois repression and respectability and his ambivalence about the quest for middle-class success. And if in *Viva Zapata* there exists a genuine antagonism to political structures and hierarchies, it is more out of a commitment to the revolutionary image and emotion than to the political and social ends of revolution. Kazan is finally more interested in heroic myth (Zapata heroically astride his white horse) and the act of rebellion than in history or politics.

Clearly, *Viva Zapata* was not the unequivocal anticommunist polemic some critics perceived it to be. But Kazan did pay his dues to HUAC with his next film, *Man on a Tightrope* (1953). The film was neither a commercial success nor a personal favorite of Kazan's. Filled with Cold War speeches and stereotyped characters, it deals with a Czech circus fleeing to the West. It pits communist thugs and bureaucrats against the cosmopolitan life force and artistry of the circus performers. The communists are seen as stupid, petty, and anti-intellectual, committed to stifling all individuality and shaping it to fit the party line. *Man on a Tightrope* was a conventional melodrama, devoid of real people, whose main aim was to propagate an anticommunist line and help Kazan escape the committee's hook.

In 1954, however, Kazan's craft revived with his Academy Award–winning direction of *On the Waterfront*—on one level an emotionally charged and moving melodrama dealing with both one man's personal redemption and the nature of union corruption on the New York waterfront. On another level, Kazan used the film to justify being an informer before HUAC, with his protagonist, Terry Malloy (Marlon Brando), acting as a heroic stand-in for himself. Malloy becomes an informer in an extremely difficult situation—where he could be dubbed a Judas for breaking the neighborhood code of silence. But it is also a situation where the decent and virtuous characters (along with the audience) would view his unwillingness to talk as an act of moral cowardice.

In fact, Kazan stated: "Terry Malloy felt as I did. He felt ashamed and proud of himself at the same time. . . . He felt it was a necessary act."[19] In addition, Kazan partially sanitized the HUAC investigations by having their film counterpart, the crime commission, represent all that was benign and honest in governmental action.

However, in *On the Waterfront* the parallels to Kazan's experience with HUAC and the social significance of the film are overshadowed by the powerful and complex portrait of Terry Malloy that Brando and Kazan created. Malloy is a mumbling, shoulder-shrugging boy-man who raises pigeons, pals around with adolescents who worship him, and survives as the condescended-to pet of the egotistical and vicious union boss Johnny Friendly (played in a roaring, larger-than-life style by Lee J. Cobb), on the periphery of the longshoremen's community. He is also a gum-chewing, alienated, tough, urban wise guy with scar tissue over his eyes from his earlier stint as a prizefighter, who masks his vulnerability by upholding a code that is based on the notion that the world is a jungle where your first obligation is to look out for yourself.

As the film evolves, Kazan turns Terry from a comic-reading bum into a moral and social hero. It's a change seen most poignantly and concretely in his relationships with the fragile, protected "good girl" Edie (Eva Marie Saint), the morally tough Father Barry (Karl Malden), and his opportunistic, shyster, brother Charlie (Rod Steiger). Terry is barely articulate, but Brando is able to totally inhabit the role and with every gesture and word grants the character a complex inner life. Malloy is composed of a variety of parts: a profound sense of personal failure and lost dignity; a powerful loyalty to his brother and corrupt union boss; and a mixture of tenderness and brutality in his character. It all comes together in such a manner that the change in Terry is utterly believable.

On the Waterfront is also a film that deals with the world of the longshoremen and their corrupt union. The film's cinematography, though self-consciously pictorial, does evoke the physical surface of a world of heavy mist, haunting boat whistles, seedy pocket parks, garbage-ridden backyards, tenements covered with clotheslines, television antennas and pigeon coops, and an omnipresent river filled with boats. There are also painful glimpses of longshoreman rituals such as the soul-destroying shape-up, where the men scramble on the ground for tokens which provide them a day's work. But it is all an expression more of Kazan's sharp eye for dramatic detail than his interest in the social texture and dynamics of the docks. Kazan's longshoremen are never really particularized, they are "more social masks than people."[20] They are seen as a mass, first intimidated and submerged by the union boss and his goons, and, by the film's conclusion, following a bruised and martyred (though Kazan denies it, there is more than a hint of Christian symbolism in the film) Malloy back to work.

Aside from trying to vindicate the role of the informer, *On the Waterfront* is a much less political film than *Viva Zapata*. Kazan is not really interested in exploring the politics of one type of American unionism. The relationship of the longshoremen's union to the shipping interests and the political machine is barely touched on. The populist strain that is found in *Zapata* doesn't exist here. The workers are docile and cowed by the union—incapable of generating any collective political action on their own. It's the character and redemption of Terry Malloy that is the film's centerpiece, and although, in the film's operatic climax, Malloy leads the workers against Johnny Friendly, there is no political dimension to his victory. (There is even a note of warning about the nature of the triumph inserted, with a beaten but still defiant Johnny Friendly screaming, "I'll be back." And in the real world, his counterparts still control the docks.)

The heroic attack against corrupt power and repression of *Zapata* has become a purely personal and moral act. There is no suggestion that Malloy has developed a political and social vision like Zapata's; he is merely a more alienated and resentful version of that classic American hero, the courageous individual who stands up for the good against those who would degrade and threaten our lives (although this time there is an upright government to be of some help to the hero).

On the Waterfront can be seen as a conventional Hollywood film, filled with stock villains, overly theatrical sequences (e.g., Father Barry's speech in the hold attacking the mob), and a manipulative and intrusive score. However, a listing of the film's weaknesses does not convey Kazan's characteristic driving energy and passion. And in Brando's Malloy the film successfully brought to life one of the most striking manifestations of an anti-hero, who began to appear frequently in the films of the 1950s.

Kazan was hardly alone among fifties' directors who dealt either directly with communism or indirectly with the ideology and psychology surrounding the anticommunist crusade. Even Alfred Hitchcock in his commercially successful, charming, chase film *North by Northwest* (1959) added a Cold War spy story to its stylish mix of romance, wit, and suspense.

Early in the decade, with the advent of the Korean War, Samuel Fuller made *The Steel Helmet* (1951), a crude, earnest, low-budget film that on one level seemed determined to be second to none in its portrayal of communists as the last word in bestiality and savagery. Fuller has the North Koreans leaving booby-trapped corpses of dead GIs around, killing innocent children, and indulging in human-wave attacks that give clear evidence of their contempt for the value of human life. Nonetheless, Fuller, in his primitive anarchic fashion, gave ample hints that he was wary of all ideologies, finding fault with his American GIs' racial and cultural blindness and depicting his alienated hero Sergeant Zack (Gene Evans) as a cynical, sadistic, cigar-chomping figure, interested only in survival and untouched by the slightest hint of humanitarian impulse (except for his love for his South Korean ward). *The Steel Helmet*, despite its tabloid script and cartoon-like characters, had a great deal of bite and reality. It also showed that the war film could simultaneously mouth and subvert patriotic platitudes, and convey that the anticommunist side was no community of saints.[21]

To a degree, this flexibility allowed some directors and writers to use genres as a means of commenting on American politics. In 1952 director Fred Zinnemann (*The Search*, 1948; *From Here to Eternity*, 1953) and scriptwriter Carl Foreman (who had been cited by HUAC in 1951, had refused to cooperate, and was subsequently blacklisted) made *High Noon*, a popular western which was clearly a left-liberal parable about HUAC's attack on Hollywood. *High Noon* was a mature western about an aging, weary marshal (Gary Cooper in an Academy Award–winning performance) who has a deeply lined face and sagging flesh, and admits to being scared. Uncharacteristically for a western hero, he asks for the assistance of the townspeople, but is deserted by them and left alone to confront a murderous psychopath and his henchman. The craven townspeople find a variety of reasons why they cannot stand up to this threat to law and liberty: The parson cannot commit himself to killing; the old sheriff is paralyzed by despair; the judge is a smooth careerist whose only loyalty is to self-preservation; and others just hide or flee from the confrontation. We are left with the lone American hero who must face and, of course (for some of the genre conventions are maintained), defeat the villains.

High Noon is a skillfully directed, gripping, and intelligent film which uses incisive cross-cutting and an exciting sound track—an Academy Award–winning score by Dmitri Tiomkin and the rhythmic ticking of a clock (the film's running time runs parallel to this time of crisis in the marshal's life)—to successfully build narrative tension. However, it is a film whose images are merely functional and whose characters are intelligently conceived types without any genuine individuality. The film's moral heroism does not quite translate into political terms, for the hero has no politics and the villains have no institutional connections. Nevertheless, in its commitment to individual moral responsibility and courage, the film did convey to a portion of its audience that evils such as McCarthyism could no longer be rationalized or evaded and must be resisted.

Given the political mood of the period, *High Noon* was a bold film, but its use of metaphor and allegory, and its emphasis on moral rather than political courage, made it a relatively oblique one.[22] A film that dared to criticize American capitalism directly stood the risk of having its production disrupted by vigilantes and, even if completed, would find few distributors or theaters willing to exhibit it. Such a film was *Salt of the Earth* (1954), which was independently made by blacklisted writers Herbert Biberman (who also directed it), Michael Wilson, and Paul Jarrico, and was sponsored by the Mine, Mill and Smelter Workers, a union that had been expelled from the CIO in 1950 for its communist ties. The film focuses on the strike of a group of primarily Mexican-American zinc miners against a racist, exploitative, and repressive mining company. There are moments when the film is crudely polemical and stilted, with more socialist than social realism, particularly in its use of militant music, heavy-handed cross-cutting, and stereotyped villains; a clownishly crude and violent sheriff and his deputies; a callous pipe-smoking superintendent; and a company president who goes on African safaris. Of course, the Mexican workers are seen as spontaneous and brave, and the film's heroine Esperanza (Rosaura Revueltas, who was deported three times during the film's shooting) is a shy, glowing beauty who conveys great warmth and courage.

On the other hand, *Salt of the Earth* projects a feminist consciousness unique either on the left or on the right during the fifties. For the film centers on the conflict between the sexes on the workers' side, as well as on class oppression. The miners have never thought about the feelings and lives of their wives, who are taken for granted, traditionally bound to home and children. But as the strike develops, the women, who are forced to take the men's place on the picket line, assert themselves, asking to be treated as equals. The men's pride and machismo are hurt, but eventually they begin to accept the change in traditional patterns, and not only do they win the strike but they transcend their chauvinist notions of sexual identity. The conclusion is a pat one, but the images of women gathering on a hill to join the picket line and of some men struggling with the laundry are moving ones and predate anything Hollywood was to conjure up until the feminism-conscious 1970s and 1980s.[23]

With its unabashed left perspective, *Salt of the Earth* was an aberration in the fifties. A film more in tune with the spirit of the decade was Don Siegel's *Invasion of the Body Snatchers* (1956), a low-budget, witty science fiction film dealing with the subject of alien infiltration and mind control that pervaded so many of the science fiction films of the decade.

In *The Thing* (1951), a U.S. scientific expedition is threatened by a ferocious monster thawed out of a spaceship. In William Cameron Menzies's *Invaders from Mars* (1951), a small boy is unable to convince adults that Martians are kidnapping important figures and placing crystals in their brains that will force them to commit brutal acts. Of all these films, however, *Invasion of the Body Snatchers* was the most subtle. Its most distinctive quality stems from its director Don Siegel's matter-of-fact, realistic style, which eschews violence for still, silent, ominous images. The film projects a world where ordinary objects are strangely illuminated and people's faces remain unlit, where light signifies safety and hope and darkness and shadow mean danger. The paranoid plot focuses on an invasion by alien pods (a product of atomic mutation) of a small, neighborly town where everybody knows each other's first name. As the pods possess the people in the town, they turn them not into violent monsters but into bland, expressionless vegetables, who are incapable of love, rage, pleasure, or pain.

It is the depiction of the pods that opens *Invasion of the Body Snatchers* to a variety of interpretations. In one interpretation the pods can be seen as a symbol of a society where alienated people flee their individuality and seek refuge in mindless mass conformity — an exaggerated version of Riesman's *Lonely Crowd*. In another, more probable interpretation, the pods can be seen as communists, the omnipresent aliens of the fifties, who are everywhere conspiring to turn people into robots. Of course, it is doubtful whether *Invasion of the Body Snatchers* was perceived by its audience as anything more than a conventional entertainment film. Nonetheless, the anxiety, hysteria, and paranoia it tapped about the threat of communist totalitarianism made it a perfect expression of some of the decade's obsessions.[24]

Undoubtedly, a direct or even an oblique commitment to dealing with political issues was far from the dominant force in the Hollywood of the fifties. Given decreasing movie theater attendance and the competition from television, Hollywood gave a great deal of thought to recapturing its audience. Using color more heavily and then seeking out new technological processes, the studios attempted by overwhelming the viewer to attract him back to moviegoing. Processes such as Cinemascope, Vista-Vision, Cinerama, and 3-D were introduced, exploiting the size of the film image and experimenting (unsuccessfully) with the creation of the illusion of depth.[25]

Ultimately, the widescreen processes led to a number of expensive, lengthy blockbuster films like *The Robe* (1953), *The Ten Commandments* — which cost thirteen and a half million dollars to make — (1956), and *Ben Hur* (1959). These epics were on one level part of the religious revival of the fifties — cartoons of religious piety — and, more importantly, with their color, crowds, chariot races, and crucifixions they were the last great flings of studio excess (where "only too much is really sufficient"),[26] which allowed these films to fully exploit the vastness of the new screen.

The new Hollywood could be glimpsed in Billy Wilder's smart *Sunset Boulevard* (1950). The plot centers on an aging, once famous and glamorous silent screen actress, Norma Desmond (Gloria Swanson), who lives in a decaying mansion as if time had stood still. She fantasizes about making a comeback film with the aid of a decent, weary, and hungry screenwriter, Joe Gillis (William Holden), who becomes first her collaborator, then her lover and kept man. *Sunset Boulevard* follows a number of the conventions of film noir, using voice-over narration and flashback and centering on a possessive, hysterical, sexually devouring heroine and a morally ambiguous hero. However, the film's prime focus is not on the corruption of Joe Gillis but on the contrast between the old Hollywood and the new — not necessarily to the latter's advantage.

Though Billy Wilder and his cowriter Charles Bracket depict Norma Desmond as something of a wild-eyed, campy grotesque, the film is still an idiosyncratic homage to the absurdity, excess, and graciousness of the flamboyant old Hollywood. Luminaries of the old Hollywood like Buster Keaton, Cecil B. deMille, and Erich von Stroheim (who plays Max, Norma's first director, ex-husband, and present-day protector and servant) are treated sympathetically, while the plainer, sharp-tongued, grasping new Hollywood producers dismiss the "message kids," want to make Betty Hutton musicals out of baseball stories, and have no time for truth or art. For Wilder, the old Hollywood had style, if nothing else, which made the more pragmatic, businesslike Hollywood of the fifties (which he was an integral part of) pale in comparison.

Contrary to *Sunset Boulevard*'s sour view of the contemporary Hollywood scene, many producers still felt optimism about the future. Some of that hopefulness was based on the success of big-screen musical comedies, particularly adaptations of Broadway hits like *Oklahoma* (1955) and *Guys and Dolls* (1955).[27] However, these musicals, though commercially successful, suffered from ponderous and inflated production values. It also began to seem ridiculous for characters to break into song and dance at the slightest provocation. The best musicals of the decade appeared in the early fifties and came from the illustrious Freed unit at MGM. These medium-budget original musicals included Vincente Minnelli's decorative and stylized *An American in Paris* (1951), with an athletic Gene Kelly; his somber and witty *The Bandwagon* (1953), with the elegant and feathery Fred Astaire; and Stanley Donen and Gene Kelly's classic show-business musical *Singin' in the Rain* (1952).

Singin' in the Rain is a breezy, good-natured satire of Hollywood's Busby Berkeley musicals, film premieres, star biographies, and the introduction of sound, written by the urbane Betty Comden and Adolph Green and starring Gene Kelly as an earthy, dynamic, ordinary American Hollywood star, Don Lockwood. Kelly is, as always, brashly self-confident and jaunty, and in the film's title number he wistfully stamps around in rain puddles, and, holding his sole prop, an umbrella, exultingly embraces the studio rain. With its pastel colors, cheerful songs ("Good Morning"), and acrobatic pratfalls (Donald O'Connor energetically dancing through cardboard sets), *Singin' in the Rain* created a world where any action could spontaneously, calmly, and naturally be turned into music and dance. It was a world where despair and doubt do not exist and where the happy ending continues to survive. And if *Singin' in the Rain*'s plot about the transition to sound is a metaphor of the challenge that Hollywood faced from TV, it is also an indicator of just how much carefully honed optimism still dominated the studio product.[28]

A few years later, a much more melancholy and despairing note was conveyed in Donen and Kelly's final collaboration, *It's Always Fair Weather* (1955), in many ways a successor to *On the Town*. Here three GI buddies (Dan Dailey and Michael Kidd recreating the Jules Munshin and Frank Sinatra roles) decide to get together ten years after the war is over. It is a measure of the sour mood of the film that the three find they have very little in common and do not really like one another. Although both Dailey and Kidd are better dancers than Munshin and Sinatra, there is very little chemistry between the three—even their bravura garbage-can dance together, though clever, has none of the inspired warmth of the numbers in *On the Town*. Also indicative of the darkening Hollywood mood is the film's negative response to the world of media and TV. It takes satiric potshots at advertising—Dan Dailey as an ad executive singing the drunken "Situationwise"—and at TV shows like *This Is Your Life*.[29]

Even if *It's Always Fair Weather* did sound a despondent chord and if few fifties' films had *Singin' in the Rain*'s charming airiness and feeling of being at home in the world, the era still contained many genre films that upheld traditional virtues and values and were commercially successful. In George Stevens's carefully composed, beautiful *Shane* (1955), a blond, mysterious stranger in white named Shane (Alan Ladd) is befriended by a group of homesteaders and protects them in turn from a predatory rancher and his psychopathic hired killer dressed in black (Jack Palance). *Shane* tries hard not to be an ordinary western: It is a self-conscious attempt to create a mythic West populated by archetypes—with the enigmatic, perfect-featured, sententious Shane seen continually from the perspective of a hero-worshipping young boy (Brandon de Wilde).[30] However, despite its portentousness, it was a more conventional film (for all his grandiosity, Shane is not that much different from the more pedestrian radio and TV hero, the Lone Ranger) than the 1950s westerns of Anthony Mann (*The Naked Spur*, 1953), austere, bleak films built around a revenge motif, or John Ford's epic western *The Searchers* (1956), with John Wayne as the most ambiguous of Fordian heroes.

Ford's later films like *The Searchers* depicted a darker, less morally defined world than earlier works like *Stagecoach* (1939) and *My Darling Clementine* (1946). The plot of *The Searchers* revolves around a driven ex-Confederate soldier named Ethan Edwards (Wayne) who searches for years for his niece Debbie (Natalie Wood). Debbie has been kidnapped by Indians—who for the most part are treated here as savages or child-like, comic foils—whose way of life she has adopted. Edwards still has enough left of the character of the old Wayne–Ford hero to display indomitable courage, rescuing Debbie from the Indians he passionately hates and returning her to Ford's ideal world of family and community—the garden in the wilderness.

But nothing is quite the same in Ford's world in this film. Everything has become grimmer: The landscape is more threatening; Ford's beloved cavalry both less noble and more absurd; and his sullen, violent hero consumed by murderous rage. Ford's heroes can usually reconcile their individuality with community—nature with civilization. But Ethan is the "man who wanders" who is unable to enter the door of the hearth again. The stirring long shot of him riding away, framed by the doorway of the house, is not an affirmation of the romance and freedom of a Shane-like hero who can never be domesticated, but a tragic, desolate image of a man doomed to solitude. (In the 1980s *The Searchers* became a model for films like *Rambo: First Blood Part II*, where the freeing of MIAs from the barbaric captivity of the North Vietnamese followed the pattern of Ethan's quest to free Debbie from the Indians.)

Despite the sense of unease that began to creep into fifties' film, neither Hollywood nor the public were particularly open to films that took formal or intellectual risks. Exemplifying this attitude was the popular comedy team of the fifties, Martin and Lewis (*Artists and Models*, 1955), whose slapstick routines, and Jerry Lewis's twitchy, idiotic victim's persona, did not differ much from the style of earlier B-film comic teams like Abbott and Costello.

Just as indicative of the basic conservatism of popular taste and values were films dealing with women's consciousness and identity. During the decade not only were there fewer films about independent women than in the thirties or forties, but there were fewer films dealing with women at all. In the literate, epigrammatic Academy Award–winning *All About Eve* (1950), a temperamental, sarcastic, ambitious star of the theater, Margo Channing (Bette Davis), is also a vulnerable, insecure woman underneath all her wit and drive. She ultimately sees her career as insufficient, as something separate from being a real woman, and opts for marriage, children, and retirement. Her mousy and devoted protégé Eve (Anne Baxter) turns out to be a predatory and manipulative actress who wants to be a star and is willing to use any means to supplant Margo. In *All About Eve* successful women are either unhappy or so distorted by their ambition that they lose their humanity in the process.

In a minor role in the same film, Marilyn Monroe, the sex symbol of the fifties, plays another of her dumb blondes, a woman-object, whose sexuality is unthreatening, guileless, and childlike. Towards the end of the decade, in films such as Billy Wilder's frenetically paced, transvestite sex farce, *Some Like It Hot* (1959), she added vulnerability to her victim's persona.

While Monroe was more a male fantasy figure than a woman that other women could identify with, the freckled, eternally sunny Doris Day was one female star capable of eliciting both male and female sympathy. In a period where being popular had become a prime cultural value, Day's persona in battle-of-the-sexes comedies such as *Pillow Talk* (1958), with Rock Hudson, conveyed a super-hygienic, wholesome cheerfulness. However, though these comedies were built on an extremely puritanical, timorous form of sexiness, with Day remaining always the virgin, her supposed sexual innocence was less significant than her drive, ambition, and spunkiness. In fact, so potent were those qualities that as a tailored-suited journalism professor in *Teacher's Pet* (1958) she is tough enough even to put to rout Hollywood studs (albeit in this case an aging one) like Clark Gable. Despite Day's girl-next-door looks and behavior, her characters often had jobs and projected a tougher, more independent persona than most of the other major female stars (e.g., Grace Kelly, Audrey Hepburn) of the decade.[31]

But though the characters Doris Day played may have held down jobs, most women in the 1950s' films were housewives or women seeking to avoid spinsterhood, who found salvation in marriage. In one traditional genre, however—the soap opera—German-born director Douglas Sirk made films that used the genre's conventions to make oblique criticisms of traditional female roles and middle-class conformity.

Backed by one of the most commercial Hollywood producers, Ross Hunter, Sirk's *All That Heaven Allows* (1955) was characterized by artificial studio landscapes and townscapes, melodramatic, fortuitous accidents, a saccharine score, and a predictable, neat conclusion. Despite the clichés that permeated the film, Sirk was a consummate stylist who could use color, light, clothes, and furniture to express his sensibility and capture his heroine's state of mind. Throughout the film Sirk uses reflections on TV screens, mirrors, and piano tops and ubiquitous screens and doors both to evoke a middle-class world dominated by gleaming surfaces and appearances and to catch the heroine's feelings of imprisonment. It's an eloquent use of cinematic form to comment on content[32] and, at moments, transcends the lack of subtlety and soap-operatic quality of the script.

The film presents the world from the point of view of an older heroine, Carrie (Jane Wyman)—an upper-middle-class widow with few interests, little emotional connection between herself and her unpleasant, grownup children, and a number of stolid, acceptable men desiring to marry her. She breaks from the mores of her country club set and arouses the disapproval of her children by becoming involved with a young, passive, handsome hero, Ron Kirby (Rock Hudson). He is not only much younger than her, but a landscaper who lives a comfortably bohemian life dimly committed to simplicity, love of nature, an uncompromising belief in being autonomous, and a disdain for snobbery and status-seeking. But he's also college-educated and refined, and his home and friends look more like models for a Norman Rockwell magazine cover—cute and unnaturally wholesome—than some bohemian enclave.

For all that, Kirby is not the usual alternative for heroines in fifties' and women's pictures. Carrie chooses to fulfill her own emotional and sexual needs, and not only rejects her friends but decides she won't be a Stella Dallas (the heroine in Vidor's film of the same name in 1937) or Mildred Pierce and sacrifice her life for her children. Sirk's film, however, was clearly no feminist work. Carrie's choice of a new way of life is predicated on the existence of a man to provide her with an alternate set of values and a refuge in marriage—in terms of the narrative a very safe sort of rebellion. But its criticism of middle-class materialism, hypocrisy, and emptiness (more telling in the film's mise-en-scène than its narrative) was symptomatic of much less oblique works that rebelled against the complacency and conformity of Eisenhower America. In these films, male stars such as the aforementioned virile, angry Brando (*On the Waterfront*), the brooding, vulnerable Montgomery Clift (*A Place in the Sun*, 1951; *From Here to Eternity*, 1953), and James Dean (Kazan's *East of Eden*, 1955) played anti-heroic heroes who in different ways were at odds with the prevailing social order.

In *A Place in the Sun* (1951) Clift plays a haunted, sensitive outsider in a dark, romantic version — all dramatic tight close-ups, shadows, superimpositions, and dissolves — of Dreiser's naturalistic novel *American Tragedy*. George Eastman (Clift) is a quietly ambitious, uneducated young man who wants to escape his street missionary boyhood and enter the world of his wealthy relatives. However, the film's emphasis is much less on the nature of social class and the hunger for success in America than on Eastman's doomed relationships with a clinging, drab, working-class woman (given texture and poignancy in Shelley Winters's performance) and with Angela Vickers (Elizabeth Taylor), who is the embodiment of glamor and wealth. In the Oscar-winning *From Here to Eternity* (1953) Clift played another vulnerable, doomed outsider (Prewitt), brutalized by a corrupt army on the eve of Pearl Harbor. Prewitt is here a man of courage and integrity who is unwilling to bend to the dictates of an institution he loves.

The rebellion expressed by three actors was, however, neither political nor social in nature, nor were the characters they played artists, beats, or bohemians. They were just sensitive, sensual, and often anguished young men seeking to discover and define their identities. In the process they raised doubts about the values and behavior that dominated American culture and society, and indirectly conveyed some of the undercurrent of dissatisfaction that existed during the decade.

Of the three stars, James Dean had the most profound effect on the consciousness of the young in the fifties. Dean had an aura — a mythic presence — and with his abrupt and tragic death in a car crash in 1955 generated a cult and became a legend. His film career was a brief one, but in Nicholas Ray's extremely popular *Rebel Without a Cause* (1955) he left his unique mark on the fifties.

Rebel Without a Cause was less about rebellion than about the anger of Jim Stark (James Dean) towards his middle-class parents and the world. Jim is a brooding, suffering, isolated high school student who hates his apron-wearing father's (Jim Backus) flaccid amiability and weak submission to his self-involved, backbiting wife. Mumbling, slouching, hunching his shoulders, curling up in a fetal position, cigarette dangling from his mouth, the tormented Jim is like a coiled spring ready to cry and rage. Surrounding Jim are two other pained, rejected adolescents, Judy (Natalie Wood), stunned and emotionally thrown by her father's sudden rejection, and Plato (Sal Mineo), a morbid, friendless boy who lives alone with a black maid because his divorced parents have deserted him.

Rebel Without a Cause's uniqueness rests more in its cinematic style and Dean's performance than in its script. Ray uses a variety of camera angles, a dislocated mise-en-scène, tight close-ups, point-of-view shots, intense color, and rapid, turbulent cutting to successfully project the tension, anger, and sense of almost metaphysical alienation that permeates the film. There are also luminous, metaphoric sequences: the "chicken run," with a pinkish-white specter, Judy, signaling the beginning of the race in the center of a pitch-black runway lit by car headlights— an initiation rite or journey confronting death; and the scene shot in the vastness of the planetarium (which is located on a precipice) with its apocalyptic, end-of-the-world images of the galaxy exploding as the three alienated kids sit alone in the dark watching—all providing a powerful metaphor for the insecurity and isolation of adolescence.

Rebel Without a Cause's dialogue and narrative are much more pedestrian than its imagery. In terms of the narrative, the film sees the causes of adolescent turmoil as solely psychological—caused both by the instability and conflict within families and by their failure to communicate and provide understanding. There is an implicit critique of upper-middle-class status striving and conformity, but the script's emphasis is not on social or class reality. In fact, the film even introduces an understanding detective who acts as a social worker (the helping professions, such as psychologists and social workers, became commonplace in fifties' films) and surrogate father to Jim.

The film's conclusion is both clichéd and sexist, the submerged father taking off his apron, asserting his authority and embracing Jim, and reconciliation and love triumphing over fragmentation. However, what is most memorable is not Jim's opting for a 1950s affirmation of domesticity—shedding his asocial self for a responsible familial one—but those powerful existential images of lostness, of being a romantic outcast alone in the world.[33]

Dean departed from this image in his third and last film, George Stevens's *Giant* (1956), which was adapted from Edna Ferber's novel. He plays Jett Rink, a sullen, inarticulate ranch hand who becomes an oil millionaire. Rink is the only character in the film with the suggestion of an internal life—a tribute to Dean's gift for giving nuance and complexity to even this most seemingly stereotypical of characters. Although in

Giant Dean continues to mumble and slouch, he is transformed from a hostile, arrogant outsider, filled with resentment of those who have power, to a wealthy but pathetic power-wielder consumed by alcoholic self-pity, racism, and the resentments of youth. Dean's Jett is not a particularly sympathetic figure, but the tension and energy he conveys in the role are among the few vital elements in this inflated and trite epic about Texas culture and society.

However, in contrast to Dean's earlier films, *Giant* does make some interesting social points, albeit they are built on a sentimental, liberal point of view characteristic of the Hollywood social films of the mid-1950s. For *Giant* is both a ponderous soap-operatic chronicle about a wealthy ranching family and a critique and a bit of a satire of Texas materialism, anti-intellectualism, machismo, and racism. Unfortunately, the critique is subverted both by the long shots exalting an almost mythic Texas landscape and by the beautiful and somewhat progressive eastern heroine's, Leslie's (Elizabeth Taylor), ultimate embrace of Texas and its ethos. And her acceptance of that world after years of ambivalence only occurs when her stolid rancher husband Vic (Rock Hudson) displays his humanness and manliness by brawling for the rights of his half-Mexican grandchild. *Giant* contains no real political critique; Leslie does not want to give up her privileges or make changes in the political and economic structure, she merely wants the elite to be more paternalistic (to sustain the values of her Maryland adolescence) and demonstrate some kindness to the poor Mexicans who work for them. However, she is bold enough to accept intermarriage, and the film clumsily suggests, through its final shots of Leslie and Vic's white and copper-skinned grandchildren sitting together in their playpen, that the answer to racism may lie in the coupling of the races—the traditional Hollywood embrace of personal rather than political solutions.

Richard Brooks's *Blackboard Jungle* (1955) was a fifties' film carrying more social bite and tension than *Rebel Without a Cause* or *Giant* and dealing with similar issues—delinquency and racism. In fact, when the film was screened at the Venice Film Festival it elicited a diplomatic protest from Claire Booth Luce (ambassador to the Vatican) because she felt it exported a squalid, unfavorable image of American life.[34]

Blackboard Jungle centers around a tough, crew-cut idealistic teacher, Mr. Dadier (Glenn Ford), who believes in education and democracy and must tame a group of violent young hoods. In true 1950s style the actions of the hoods are given no social roots or explanation, merely psychological chatter about permissive childrearing. Nevertheless, these hoods are no Bowery Boy cream puffs, but alienated, resentful, and vicious, especially their leader, West (played with an imitation Brando–Dean posture by Vic Morrow). *Blackboard Jungle* is a perfect example of what in Hollywood passes for social realism and social exposé. New York is reduced to a studio set devoid of any sense of texture or place, and the teachers in the main are stereotypes, ranging from Murdoch (Louis Calhern), a cynic who calls the school a "garbage can," to the frustrated Miss Hammond, who wears tight, sexy clothes and is almost raped by one of the students. The plot is also built on a series of contrived, mechanical twists featuring sudden shifts of destructive or cynical characters to the side of virtue, and of course offering Hollywood's usual solution to complex social problems: the concern and commitment of one courageous, caring individual – Dadier.

Despite these discordant elements, the film was still capable of capturing some of the difficulties involved in teaching tough, disruptive adolescents (it uses the dissonant sounds of a machine shop class and the passing elevated subway train to help evoke feelings of oppression). The potent use of one of the first rock hits, "Rock Around the Clock," conveys a strong feeling of the unbridled energy and antagonism of 1950s' youth culture. The issue of racism is also raised with the introduction of the character of Miller (Sidney Poitier in one of his early, more complex roles). Miller is a sensitive, strong, intelligent underachiever, who at first, angry and resentful of what he perceives to be a white education system, baits and torments Dadier. But by the film's climax he turns into a noble hero joining Dadier against West and his brutish allies.

Blackboard Jungle is filled with embarrassing clichés about the promises of equal opportunity in America – Dadier attempts to get Miller to continue to go to school by invoking the careers of black success stories like Joe Louis and Ralph Bunche. Nevertheless, the film does touch on the reality of black anger, and that is a positive step in a decade where, excepting *No Way Out* (1950) – Poitier as a middle-class doctor – there were no other films dealing with black consciousness and problems until Martin Ritt's *Edge of the City* (1957). However, in *Edge of the City* Poitier plays a longshoreman-saint who sacrifices his life for a confused, neurotic white friend, played by John Cassavetes, and no real feeling of black life or problems is conveyed.

In Stanley Kramer's *The Defiant Ones* (1958), Poitier plays an escaped convict (Cullen) in the South whose character is given enough pungency and reality to directly express his anger at southern racism. Because Poitier is a symbol of virtue, his rage is balanced by qualities like intelligence, tenderness, loyalty, and courage. *The Defiant Ones* is a conventional, contrived work of liberal poster art whose key image – a close-up of two hands, black and white, manacled together—is an obvious metaphor for Kramer's view that blacks and whites are inescapably linked to each other in America. Cullen has escaped chained to a white convict, Jackson (Tony Curtis), who is morally and physically much weaker than he. Jackson is an insecure, petty criminal, who dreams of the big money and lives by the southern racist code. But it is predictable from the very beginning that Jackson will be transformed and the hate between him and Cullen will turn into concern and love.

The Defiant Ones, like *Blackboard Jungle*, has a great deal of surface excitement and even some dramatic punch—the cross-cutting between the convicts on the run and the liberal sheriff (Theodore Bikel) in pursuit is especially effective. However, like *Jungle* it offers a simplistic social answer—the achievement of racial solidarity through the commitment of individual blacks and whites to each other. And there is no attempt in the film to depict or even suggest the complex economic, political, and cultural dimensions of the race problem. Of course, integration is made easy for whites, because the black character is Sidney Poitier, a charismatic, seductive, and superior presence, who at the film's climax even sacrifices his freedom for his white friend (invoking jeers from the blacks in the audience). Indeed, it was this dignity and transcendent humanness that made Poitier the one black star who was consistently successful and acceptable to white audiences. Poitier never bowed or scraped to whites, but he was so reasonable and humane that the white audience knew that his anger would always stay within acceptable bounds and that there was nothing to fear from the characters he portrayed. They were men who could arouse the hatred or abuse only of the most ignorant or reactionary of whites.

Later on, during the more militant sixties, blacks often put down Poitier's persona as middle-class, masochistic, and liberal.[35] Nevertheless, he was one black actor who no longer had to sing, dance, and roll his eyes to have his image appear on the screen. And though Hollywood's handling of the race problem was neither bold nor imaginative, given the conformist political tenor of the time the emergence of a token black star could still be viewed as a minor triumph.

Ultimately it was this lack of political and artistic ferment or originality in 1950s Hollywood that allowed an opening for a group of independently produced films such as the Academy Award–winning *Marty* (1955). Ironically, it was Hollywood's bête noir, TV, that was the inspiration for *Marty* and other films of this type. For along with the hours of dross that dominated 1950s TV there were some moments that broke the mold. Under the inspiration of innovative spirits such as NBC's

Sylvester "Pat" Weaver new forms like the magazine concept show ("Today"), talk shows ("Tonight"), and spectaculars ("Peter Pan") were produced on TV. Producers such as Fred Coe and Worthington Minor created original live drama shows such as "Studio One" and "Philco Playhouse," featuring the talents of new writers (Paddy Chayefsky, Rod Serling, Horton Foote), directors (Sidney Lumet, John Frankenheimer), and actors (Paul Newman, Kim Stanley, Rod Steiger).

Marty was the first and most commercially successful of these films adapted from live television. Written by Paddy Chayefsky and made on location in the East Bronx in low-budget black and white, it dealt with the daily lives of ordinary people. *Marty's* major achievement was in evoking the tedium and loneliness that permeates the life of an unattractive Bronx butcher (Ernest Borgnine), who ultimately finds happiness by going out with a shy, homely teacher.[36] Although Chayefsky claimed that his work opened up the "marvellous world of the ordinary," *Marty* was a dialogue-bound, formally inexpressive film, whose camera did not probe deeply into the faces and behavior of lower-middle-class life. It was merely a quietly sentimental story, touched with a fine ear for Bronx dialogue and syntax—for instance, answering a question with a question (e.g., "What do you feel like doing tonight?" "I dunno, what do you feel like doing?")—and offering Hollywood's predictable, all-purpose solution—love—to give Marty's life some purpose.

Marty's commercial success led to other "small" films, the most distinctive being Sidney Lumet's *Twelve Angry Men* (1957), adapted from a television play by Reginald Rose. *Twelve Angry Men* is an account of a jury's deliberations over a murder case where the defendant is a Puerto Rican boy. Using a single set of a New York City jury room on the hottest day of the year, Lumet succeeded in adapting most of the conventions of the television play—tight close-ups, medium group shots, panning, and fluid and precise cutting from sweating face to face—to build a dramatically effective film. He was especially gifted directing actors, and a cast that included a combination of New York character actors (Lee J. Cobb, Jack Klugman, E. G. Marshall) and a Hollywood star, Henry Fonda, as the jury gave a seamless illustration of ensemble playing.

Twelve Angry Men was a socially committed work which raised questions about the nature of the jury system and, by extension, the nature of American democracy itself. The jury is a gallery of social types: bigots, a shallow, spineless advertising man, a decent working man, an immigrant deeply committed to the democratic process, a cold, logical stockbroker, and the hero, an intelligent, decent, liberal architect (Henry Fonda) who must convince the rest of the jury members that what seems like an open-and-shut case is liable to reasonable doubt. He is a resolute man with a soft, cultivated voice, who ingeniously and logically succeeds in convincing the other jury members that the prosecution's case has holes. Despite the doubts the film raises about a system where bigotry, complacency, and convenience (one juror wants to resolve the case quickly so he can get to a Yankee game) become the sole basis for deciding the guilt or innocence of a defendant, the film ends on a positive note, with the defendant allowed to go free and the American system of justice affirmed.

Twelve Angry Men's strength lies in its dramatic fireworks and its well-drawn social types rather than in the depth of its social critique or the psychological complexity of its characters. It is a film where the villains sweat, rage, and bellow a great deal, and whose hero is a totally admirable and reasonable man. Every scene in the film is neatly choreographed and calculated for dramatic impact, with each of the characters given a single note—the old man on the jury is observant and notices details—to define themselves, and a significant moment where they shift their vote. And though the film does not gloss over the fact of how ambiguous and complex the meting out of guilt and innocence in a criminal case can be, it still holds that for our institutions to be just they merely need one good man who will tap the basic virtues of other ordinary Americans. It is the type of Hollywood political fantasy that such vastly different directorial sensibilities as Frank Capra and Sidney Lumet could share.

Besides Marty and Twelve Angry Men there were other small films that elicited critical attention during the late fifties, such as Richard Brooks's Catered Affair (1956) and Delbert Mann's Middle of the Night (1959). But the production of these small films began to decrease at the same time as live drama was replaced on television by filmed series. And although good, small, realistic films were still produced during the next three decades—The Luck of Ginger Coffey (1964), Hester Street (1974), El Norte (1984)—after the fifties there never again was a time where the small film seemed capable of becoming one of the dominant cinematic forms in Hollywood.

The small, realistic films did not attempt to subvert either Hollywood conventions or the dominant political and cultural values of the fifties. However, in the late fifties two films were made which were critical of the military mind and of the development of nuclear weapons—Paths of Glory (1957) and On the Beach (1959).

Of the two, the more formally distinctive and politically subversive was Stanley Kubrick's independently produced Paths of Glory. Despite the fact that the film takes place within the confines of the French Army of World War I rather than in the more charged and contemporary setting of the U.S. Army of the Korean War, *Paths of Glory* trenchantly conveys the cynicism, hypocrisy, and careerism of the French officer class and provides a powerful indictment of war.

In what was to become his characteristically cool, dazzling, and original style, Kubrick evokes an unjust and death-saturated world through sound (drum beats, whistles), camera movement, lighting, and vivid imagery rather than through antiwar sermonizing. The two prime villains of the film are the calculating, subtle, and insidious General Broulard (Adolphe Menjou) and the neurotic, murderously ambitious General Mireau (George Macready), who live in opulent châteaux and hold glittering formal-dress balls. They are totally contemptuous of their men, treating them like chess pieces to be manipulated or ants to be casually slaughtered—"scum" who can be sacrificed to their own career ambitions. Mireau watches the battle through binoculars (one of Kubrick's many devices conveying war as a voyeur's sport of the officer class) and hysterically rages at the soldiers' retreat.

Though the film puts greater emphasis on the class structure and inequity of the war machine than on the horrors of the war, Kubrick still evokes the advance and retreat of the soldiers in nightmarish, richly textured battlefield scenes. The battlefield is a lunar landscape of craters, mud, and puddles, littered with bodies, barbed wire, and the wreckage of a plane, punctuated by whistling shells and enveloped by a flare-lit sky. The camera relentlessly tracks the men as they scramble to their anonymous deaths through the debris and smoke.

The hero of *Paths of Glory* is the granite-faced, courageous, and compassionate Colonel Dax (Kirk Douglas), who is at one with the men. Dax is an uncomplicated idealist who can openly say to Mireau that "patriotism is the last refuge of scoundrels." He also defends three innocent, court-martialed soldiers—he is a defense lawyer in civilian life—who have been chosen arbitrarily from the mass of soldiers to be punished for their supposed cowardice (in reality to cover the general's mistakes) in battle. Though Dax is a jut-jawed hero and idealist, the three soldiers are fallible, frightened men who cry and rage and whose death is absolutely barbaric and meaningless. Kubrick concludes the film without a glimmer of hope: Dax not only fails to prevent their deaths but, almost immediately after the court martial, is forced to lead his exhausted troops, who are longing for home, back to the murderous trenches. The system has him in its hands, and there is no escape.

Stanley Kubrick went on to make much more mordant and outrageous films, where strong, noble figures like Dax not only rarely appear but would be parodied and undermined if they did (e.g., *Dr. Strangelove*, 1963; *A Clockwork Orange*, 1971). For the smug fifties, a film that portrayed the military hierarchy as moral monsters and maintained such a bleak view of the human condition was a radical work and, of course, doomed to commercial failure. *Paths of Glory* did not offer the facile, personal, and liberal solutions of *Blackboard Jungle* and the *Defiant Ones* or the leftist optimism of *Salt of the Earth*. It was a profoundly pessimistic work that offered only contempt for the conduct of war and the corruptions of power and privilege, and nothing more.[37]

In contrast, Stanley Kramer's disaster movie *On the Beach* (1959), although it is built around the notion that the world is on the verge of extinction by nuclear war, ends on a curious note of hope. Based on Australian novelist Nevil Shute's best-selling book, the film was seen in some ways as a small step towards the easing of Cold War tensions because it was screened almost simultaneously in Moscow and Washington. But despite its political pretensions, this tale about the aftermath of World War III, and a last surviving American submarine arriving in Australia just ahead of a postnuclear exterminating cloud, seems nothing more than a backdrop for a doomed love affair between Ava Gardner, an alcoholic war widow, and Gregory Peck, the submarine commander.

Stanley Kramer's aim to make a star-laden film (Fred Astaire also had a role in it) that would act as a warning about the consequences of the nuclear arms race had good intentions. In fact, few people could take exception to the film's decent instincts, but only in Hollywood would bromides like the need to preserve the wonder of life be seen as socially significant. There is also something bland and antiseptic about the images of the nuclear holocaust that the film projects. However, there are moments when the film captures the kind of despair that might become an integral part of the lives of the doomed survivors, particularly in a car race in which the drivers drive with a consciously suicidal recklessness and abandon. These scenes are rare, and *On the Beach*'s real purpose is revealed in its final image of a Salvation Army banner proclaiming the message that "there is still time, brother!"[38]

Though the film was intended as a cautionary message about the apocalyptic consequences of the arms race and nuclear war, the implications of this message might also serve as a convenient summary of Hollywood's passage from the optimism of the forties to the anxiety of the sixties. On the one hand the film evokes the complacency of an industry that despite economic decline and political problems still went on churning out films built on the ersatz emotions, melodramatic conventions, and evasive political and social formulas of previous decades. On the other hand, however, a number of these films managed to contain a deeper sense of uneasiness and urgency, and a greater sense of the imperfections of American society, than in the past. Of course, the fifties ended with Eisenhower in the White House and Doris Day starring in *Pillow Talk* (1958), but inherent in all that manufactured calm and good cheer was a sense of disquiet, perhaps even of time running out on a period of stability and consensus.

NOTES

1. Eric F. Goldman, *The Crucial Decade—and After, America 1945–1960* (New York: Vintage, 1960).

2. Goldman, *The Crucial Decade*, pp. 292–311.

3. Richard Rovere, *Senator Joseph McCarthy*, rev. ed. (New York: Harper and Row, 1973).

4. *Ibid.*

5. Ronald Steel, "Two Cheers for Ike," *The New York Review of Books* (September 24, 1981), pp. 10–12.

6. Richard Rovere, "Eisenhower Over the Shoulder," *The American Scholar* XXI (Spring 1962), pp. 34–44.

7. Frederick F. Siegel, *Troubled Journey: From Pearl Harbor to Ronald Reagan* (New York: Hill and Wang, 1984), p. 99.

8. William L. O'Neill, *Coming Apart: An Informal History of America in the 1960s* (New York: Quadrangle, 1971), pp. 3–24.

9. Edmund White, *The Beautiful Room Is Empty* (New York: Ballantine, 1988), pp. 7–8.

10. Eric Goldman, *The Crucial Decade*, p. 291.

11. O'Neill, *Coming Apart*, p. 4.

12. Godfrey Hodgson, *America in Our Time: From World War II to Nixon, What Happened and Why* (New York: Vintage, 1978), pp. 54–64.

13. Morris Dickstein, *Gates of Eden: American Culture in the Sixties* (New York: Basic Books, 1977), pp. 3–12.

14. Charlie Gillett, *The Sound of the City: The Rise of Rock and Roll*, rev. ed. (New York: Pantheon, 1984).

15. Victor S. Navasky, *Naming Names* (New York: Viking, 1980).

16. Michel Ciment, *Kazan on Kazan* (New York: Viking, 1973).

17. Ciment, *Kazan on Kazan*, p. 94.

18. Peter Biskind and Dan Georgakas, "An Exchange on Viva Zapata," *Cineaste* VII, 2 (Spring 1976), pp. 10–17.

19. Ciment, *Kazan on Kazan*, p. 110.

20. Ciment, *Kazan on Kazan*, p. 108.

21. Nicholas Garnham, *Samuel Fuller* (New York: Viking, 1971).

22. Nora Sayre, *Running Time: Films of the Cold War* (New York: Dial Press, 1982), p. 176.

23. Deborah Silverton Rosenfelt (ed.), *Salt of the Earth* (Old Westbury, N.Y.: Feminist Press, 1978).

24. Stuart Samuels, "The Age of Conspiracy and Conformity: Invasion of the Body Snatchers," in John E. O'Connor and Martin A. Jackson (eds.), *American History/American Film* (New York: Frederick Ungar, 1979), pp. 203–17.

25. Pauline Kael, *Kiss, Kiss, Bang, Bang* (New York: Bantam, 1969), pp. 446–47.

26. Michael Wood, *America in the Movies: or, "Santa Maria, It Had Slipped My Mind!"* (New York: Basic Books, 1975), pp. 180–81.

27. Robert Sklar, *Movie Made America: A Cultural History of American Movies* (New York: Vintage, 1975), pp. 283–84.

28. Wood, *America in the Movies*, pp. 146–64.

29. *Ibid.*

30. Phillip French, *Westerns* (New York: Oxford University Press, 1977), p. 70.

31. Molly Haskell, *From Reverence to Rape: The Treatment of Women in the Movies* (Baltimore, Md.: Penguin, 1974), pp. 231–76.

32. Jon Halliday, *Sirk on Sirk* (New York: Viking, 1972), pp. 97–98.

33. Venable Herndon, *James Dean: A Short Life* (New York: Signet, 1974).

34. Garth Jowett, *Film: The Democratic Art* (Boston: Little, Brown, 1976), p. 385.

35. Sidney Poitier, *This Life* (New York: Ballantine, 1980), pp. 331–41.

36. Eric Barnouw, *Tube of Plenty: The Evolution of American Television* (New York: Oxford University Press, 1977), pp. 154–65.

37. Norman Kagan, *The Cinema of Stanley Kubrick* (New York: Grove Press, 1972), pp. 47–67.

38. Donald Spoto, *Stanley Kramer: Filmmaker* (New York: G. P. Putnam's Sons, 1978), pp. 207–15.

The Best Years of Our Lives (William Wyler, 1945). Courtesy of the Museum of Modern Art.

Rebel Without a Cause (Nicholas Ray, 1955). *Courtesy of the Museum of Modern Art.*

Easy Rider (Dennis Hopper, 1969). *Courtesy of the Museum of Modern Art.*

The Godfather II (Francis Ford Coppola, 1974). *Courtesy of the Museum of Modern Art.*

Platoon (Oliver Stone, 1986). *Courtesy of the Museum of Modern Art.*

4

THE SIXTIES

In 1848 revolutions broke out almost simultaneously in Paris, Berlin, Vienna, and Milan that toppled long-established reactionary regimes and attempted to institute political and social reforms. Historians referring to this period call it the "springtime of the nations." These revolutions were ultimately crushed or gave way to even more sophisticated autocratic governments which were in many ways more repressive than the ones they replaced. Nevertheless, in their brief moment of triumph these revolutions exposed some of the most glaring contradictions of their societies—most notably the growing, almost unbridgeable gulf between the bourgeoisie and the newly emergent industrial working class—laying to rest the myth that Europe was moving towards a harmonious era of the golden mean.[1]

If the events of 1848 sound familiar to modern ears it is because a somewhat similar pattern of events took place during and after 1968. That year saw concurrent riots, insurrections, and near-rebellions in the streets of New York, Chicago, Detroit, Paris, Mexico City, and Prague. This " '68 Spring" was also crushed in successive waves of assassinations, Soviet tank invasions, and police and army tear gas and bullets. However, like their 1848 predecessors, these revolts also exposed a number of the contradictions inherent in their societies.[2]

In America, 1968 was merely the most apocalyptic year of a momentous decade. During that period the myths underlying the foreign policy of containment, the belief that domestic affluence ensured social peace, and the basic optimism that had dominated American life and spirit since World War II were buried forever. For many Americans their image of themselves, their society, and their place in the world underwent a painful transformation. Despite the fact that the upheaval ultimately ushered in a period of intense social and political conservatism (whose force and grip on power has clearly still not abated), it left hope that this was no permanent state of things—that some form of social and cultural rebellion could arise again.[3]

The decade was ushered in with a growing sense of possibility for political change. Symbolic of that hope was the presidency of the handsome, youthful John F. Kennedy, who projected an image of great energy and eloquence. That persona veiled his militant Cold War postures and other political commitments he shared with his Republican opponent in the 1960 election, Richard Nixon. Kennedy was elected on his promise to "get the country moving again" and his vision of a "New Frontier." The public had become a bit tired of the malaise and apathy of the last years of the Eisenhower administration: the constant economic dislocations (recessions and unemployment); foreign policy disarray (the U-2 incident, Japanese student riots, the Cuban revolution) and missile gap myths. Still, the reaction to the cool, stylish senator from Massachusetts was not overwhelming—he won the presidency with the slim mandate of only 118,000 votes.[4]

In his inaugural address, Kennedy neglected to mention domestic issues but promised a renewed dedication to world leadership and proceeded to convert his mandate into a foreign policy of constant challenge to the Soviet Union and its allies. Kennedy and his crisis-management teams ranged worldwide confronting the communists in Laos, Berlin, and Cuba until they almost brought the world to the brink of nuclear disaster with the 1962 Cuban missile crisis.

Sobered by this flirtation with the apocalypse, Kennedy negotiated a long-awaited nuclear test ban treaty and raised hopes for further détente with a thoughtful foreign policy address at American University in Washington, D.C., in June 1963. His assassination, however, tragically cut short more concerted attempts to bring about disarmament and disengagement.[5]

Kennedy's capacity for exciting the public's expectation of a breakthrough in the Cold War was paralleled by his seeming encouragement of black American hopes for some form of civil rights legislation. Hardly a radical on the issue during his senatorial career, and barely mentioning it in his Churchillian inaugural address (one brief sentence), Kennedy did not initially view race as a major concern. However, equality for black Americans was "an idea," in the words of Victor Hugo, "whose time had come."[6]

Ever since the forties blacks had almost imperceptibly made significant social and economic gains, and had become more critical of racist and discriminatory policies and practices. Their migration to the urban North led them to become one of the mainstays of the Democratic party's political coalition and provided the margin of victory for both Truman and Kennedy. In the 1950s, the leading black civil rights organization, the National Association for the Advancement of Colored People (NAACP), which had diligently struggled in the courts against segregation and discrimination in education and voting, won the aforementioned landmark decision in the Supreme Court against segregation in the schools (the 1954 *Brown* decision) and established racial equality as one of the prime and unavoidable political and moral issues facing the United States.[7]

What is more, the black community had produced leaders in the 1950s and 1960s such as Martin Luther King Jr., James Farmer, Roy Wilkins, Whitney Young Jr., Bayard Rustin, and the younger "new abolitionists" of the Student Non-Violent Co-ordinating Committee (SNCC). Beginning with the successful Montgomery bus boycott, through sit-ins, freedom rides, and voter registration drives, blacks made clear their demand for integration and equal rights. It was a demand that peaked during the Kennedy administration in the 1963 "March on Washington," where blacks made a highly visible, well-organized, and disciplined bid for their demands to be heard, culminating in Martin Luther King's eloquent and evangelical speech, "I have a dream."

Though the march was probably the apotheosis of liberal optimism and self-confidence, in its midst there were the seeds of discord symptomatic of tactical, ideological, and programmatic differences within the black leadership and community. The most fully reported of these episodes was the radical speech attacking the Democratic party leadership that John Lewis, executive secretary of SNCC, intended to make, which was so objectionable to other members of the march coalition that it almost caused their withdrawal.[8]

However, even if the march maintained its facade of harmony, it did not prevent a northern black leader, scornfully dismissing the march's goals of civil rights legislation, from commenting: "What difference does it make if you can sit at a lunch counter with whites if you didn't have the money to order a hamburger?" This remark neatly summarized the feelings of many northern blacks who for years had had de jure civil rights but were deprived of jobs, adequate education, and housing, and imprisoned in a psychology and ethos shaped by racism, one that no amount of civil rights could allay or transform.[9]

This oppressive and alienating environment propelled blacks into a series of violent ghetto riots that engulfed numerous major cities in the 1960s. The riots resulted in a diminution of white liberal support for (and in some cases a backlash against) the civil rights movement—edging the movement further away from its integrationist philosophy. The move away from both nonviolent resistance and a commitment to integration had already begun to take place. Continued violent southern resistance—the murder of three civil rights workers in Mississippi in 1964—and a feeling that institutions such as the Democratic party and the labor unions were hesitant about dedicating themselves to social change helped bring about this shift. As a consequence, there emerged a number of militant, angry black leaders like Malcolm X and Stokely Carmichael who repudiated acceptance by and integration into white America for an ideology of black nationalism and separatism.[10]

The task of Kennedy's successor, Lyndon B. Johnson, was to respond to demands that went beyond mere civil rights. Johnson was a complex man of immense energy, virtuoso political skills, and genuine compassion, whose crudely manipulative and abrasive personality and ideology of globalism were ill suited to the demands of the time. A southern moderate, who in his senatorial career had been more conservative than Kennedy, he nonetheless fully committed himself to the task of civil rights legislation. He succeeded in winning the passage of laws, like the Voting Rights Act, that assured blacks of their rights as no other political figure, including Kennedy, could have accomplished. In an attempt to deal with black as well as white economic and social deprivation he updated the New Deal and fashioned a program (including aid to community-action groups and minority businesses), which he called the "War on Poverty," intended to be a link in creating for all Americans what he dreamed would be a "Great Society."[11]

Unfortunately, from its inception, Johnson's war fell victim to underfunding, administrative chaos, ripoffs, and an insufficient understanding of how complex and profound were many of the social problems confronting the war against poverty. The program also caused resentment and anger among white working-class and lower-middle-class people who felt that the government was neglecting their needs in favor of blacks—a problem that still confronts almost any social program that seems exclusively aimed at helping minorities. This set of circumstances ultimately became terminal as the United States became more and more enmeshed in a futile ten-year war to stop "Communist aggression" in South Vietnam, and the poverty program in turn began to lose both funding and the President's attention and commitment.[12]

The Vietnam war dominated political debate and policy making during the second half of the sixties, and the assumptions that guided this struggle were the same as those that had directed American policy in Europe since 1945. We continued to believe that Soviet-controlled communist movements were seeking to expand at the expense of weak liberal-democratic regimes and must be contained by the military and economic power of the United States. The corollary of that notion was that if one nation fell, all would collapse—the "domino effect."

However, the principles of containment did not apply to Southeast Asia and particularly South Vietnam. Here the communist monolith had long been stalled on the shoals of divergent Moscow–Peking versions of communism, ancient distrusts, and even ethnic and racial hostility. There was no evidence that Ho Chi Minh had any desire to do more than create a unified Vietnam. And the governments that the United States tried to support were never democratic and hardly liberal. Finally, the war was also not quite a naked communist power grab, but at first largely the result of indigenous communists' and nationalists' attempting to wrest power from the hands of increasingly isolated, dictatorial, and corrupt neo-colonialists.[13]

Instead of confronting communist expansionism the United States self-destructively thrust itself into a civil war. This meant little to the policy planners of the State Department and the Pentagon, who saw the war as both a way of extending the Pax Americana to Asia and an opportunity to test their new military tactics against the post–World War II "wars of national liberation."[14]

To accomplish this policy the government had to hide its purposes behind carefully built up subterfuges, such as claiming that the United States was helping the Vietnamese to help themselves, and by instigating provocations that inflamed American patriotic feeling (the Tonkin Gulf and Pleiku incidents) as a pretext for a military buildup. Indeed, as a consequence of this policy the government had over 500,000 troops in South Vietnam by 1968 and was spending upwards of 27 billion dollars a year on the war.

The inconsistencies and contradictions of this well-orchestrated escalation were not lost on a growing number of middle-class, white American youth whose commitment to activism and social change had been inspired by the early idealism evoked by the rhetoric and style of the Kennedy administration and the actions of the civil rights movement. In the early sixties a group of college students formed Students for a Democratic Society (SDS), elaborating and attempting to implement a program of political and social reform based at first on non-violence and participatory democracy. This "New Left," as it was called, took the lead in recruiting and politicizing an effective and dynamic antiwar movement numbering thousands of Americans (most of whom were far from being new leftists) repelled by the U.S. conduct of the war, the growing number of American casualties, and the rising draft calls.[15]

The New Left was the most politically conscious section of a larger movement of students, young and not so young men and women, who were not only estranged by the war but also were alienated from what they perceived as American culture's spiritual emptiness and puritanical repressiveness. A product of the baby boom of the postwar era, the expansion of education, and the growing suburban affluence of American life, the "hippies" or "flower children" (most accurately the counter- or adversary culture, since most of its most influential spokesmen were well over the dread age of thirty) gained intellectual awareness and legitimacy from the writings of 1950s intellectual radicals such as Norman Mailer, Paul Goodman, C. Wright Mills, and the novelists and poets of the "beat generation." Nonetheless, the basis of the counterculture's ethos was not intellectual (indeed, many were aggressively anti-intellectual) but the shared experience of: drugs like marijuana and LSD; personal style—long hair, cast-off army clothes; folk and rock music—the Beatles, Bob Dylan, The Rolling Stones; and a burgeoning, assertive underground press, including the *Los Angeles Free Press*, the *Berkeley Barb*, and the *East Village Other*.[16]

Although there were some stylistic and many intellectual differences between the amorphous counterculture and the chaotic but more self-conscious and organized New Left, they existed in uneasy coalition with each other. The coalition reached its apogee of political power and influence when their shared antagonism to the war helped lead to President Johnson's dropping out of the 1968 presidential race. They were also able to join together in the demonstrations and riots that engulfed Columbia University in the spring of that year and the Democratic Convention in Chicago that summer. A similar public expression of the communal spirit of the sixties, though much more affected by the values of the counterculture, was the Woodstock music festival in the summer of 1969.[17]

However, both the New Left and the counterculture quickly splintered when Martin Luther King Jr. and Robert Kennedy were assassinated and demonstrations did not bring the instant collapse of the Pentagon or the war effort. Revolution-intoxicated leaders turned from community building and constructing a resistance to the war to nihilistic terrorism or sterile neo-Stalinist and Maoist dogmatism. At the same time, the counterculture found itself usurped by hip capitalists and a sensation-hungry media, who marketed and trivialized some of its more innovative and original elements. And the simplistic counterculture ethic of "doing your thing" was used by criminal elements to penetrate the milieu and exploit its ingenuousness. In addition, the anti-work, anti-family, anti-patriotic, and anti–white-working-class rhetoric and image of the New Left and the counterculture aroused an aggressive backlash which first manifested itself in the populist racism of the Wallace movement and then became an integral part of the conservative coalition that elected Richard Nixon to the presidency in 1968.[18]

The last years of the decade saw what was left of these movements destroy themselves and most of their appeal in a paroxysm of violent "Weatherman" demonstrations, the bloody Rolling Stones concert at Altamont, and the paranoid and murderous destruction of the Manson family (which could be seen as a pathological parody of the counterculture). Also helping to bring it to the ground were the cunning policies of the Nixon administration. Nixon manipulated Vietnam troop withdrawals and began an end to the draft, while at the same time intensifying the air war in Vietnam and expanding the ground war into Laos and Cambodia. It was all done to give the public the impression that the war was gradually winding down, and to lead to its removal as a prime element in the national consciousness.[19]

Despite ending on such discordant notes, the 1960s nevertheless had positive results. Among the most permanent of these was a revisionist impulse that stimulated many Americans to look critically at themselves, their history, and social and political ideas and institutions. Of course this did not guarantee that real change would come about, but it did make political and social nonconformity more difficult to repress and the simplistic political and cultural pieties of the past harder to sustain.

Nowhere was this tendency to ignore reality or bend it to its will more firmly entrenched than in Hollywood at the beginning of the sixties. Nonetheless, even in Hollywood the 1960s were a force for renewal and transformation. The spirit of optimism may have marked the opening of the decade for the rest of the country, but the film industry was at its nadir. The most startling victim of that decline was the vaunted studio system, whose final demise was symbolized in the 1970 MGM auction of artifacts like Judy Garland's *Wizard of Oz* ruby slippers.

Taken over by financier Kirk Kerkorian in 1969, the studio (which had once boasted "more stars than in heaven") was promptly turned into a hotel-gambling enterprise with only incidental filmmaking interests.

MGM was only one (albeit the most prominent) of a number of studios that went completely out of the filmmaking business (RKO) or became part of the leisure-time divisions of conglomerates like Gulf and Western (Paramount), Transamerican (United Artists), MCA (Universal), and Warner Communications (Warner Brothers).

Gone forever were the dream factories with their armies of contract actors and actresses, writers, directors, craftspeople, technicians, and publicists. Instead the new studio head, who operated under the logo of the old studio, was likely to be a former talent agent (Ted Ashley, Barry Diller) who could put together talented packages of superstar actors, actresses, and directors. By the end of the decade the studios were no longer interested in making films; they had assumed merely the marketing and financial end of the process.[20]

Nevertheless, not every change during the sixties was an unmitigated disaster. Indeed, as a result of relaxing societal sexual standards and court rulings overturning rigid obscenity laws, the sexual taboos long governing Hollywood began to fall by the wayside. Gone were the twin beds and in to replace them came full frontal nudity. Although this freedom was used by some filmmakers as an excuse for sexual titillation and spawned a successful independent cottage industry of hard- and soft-core film pornography, it did permit a widening of the range of permissible film topics. American films now had a greater chance to convey aspects of human relationships that they previously had had little freedom to depict.[21]

In addition to sex, other Hollywood blind spots were breached by the protest movements of the 1960s. Blacks could no longer be either totally ignored or merely cast in subservient and stereotypical roles—though no great breakthrough for films dealing with black life took place. And the deviant life styles and political ideas of the young, though often exploited and adulterated by Hollywood, still had to be dealt with, especially since the young had begun to make up the largest portion of the cinema audience.[22]

One of the first intimations of a new mood in Hollywood was Hitchcock's extremely successful *Psycho* (1960). It was a formally dazzling and brilliantly perverse film, oriented to a new generation of filmgoers, and more erotic, violent, and macabre than any of Hitchcock's previous work. In this bleak black-and-white film, Hitchcock, working with his usual obsessions (i.e., guilt, voyeurism, Oedipal complexes, and misogyny), utilizes the iconography of the horror film—an isolated motel, an old, forbidding Victorian house, a sensational murder sequence (using an Eisenstein-like montage) that arouses feelings of terror, a chilling musical score, and a murderer who is a transvestite and psychotic. *Psycho* marked the introduction of the formula thriller "which redefined the limits of sex and violence in films,"[23] and would in a decade or more overrun the theaters with mediocre slasher films.

An early sixties' film that both prefigured the style of other films during the decade and had an almost prophetic quality was John Frankenheimer's *The Manchurian Candidate* (1962). *The Manchurian Candidate* was based on the fifties' liberal conceit that suggested that "If Joe McCarthy were working for the communists, he couldn't be doing a better job."[24] In a rather intricate, ironic script, adapted by George Axelrod from the novel by Richard Condon, chilling, odious Sergeant Raymond Shaw (Laurence Harvey) comes back from the Korean war a Medal of Honor winner. However, it turns out that the incident for which he was awarded the medal is a fabricated one, and Shaw is really a programmed communist assassin (the brainwashing done in Manchuria by murderous Soviet and Chinese Pavlovian psychologists) controlled by his communist agent mother (Angela Lansbury). This monstrous manipulator of a mother turns out to be merely using him as a weapon to put her buffoonish, McCarthy-like senator husband into the White House and acquire absolute power for herself. *The Manchurian Candidate* allows Frankenheimer to succeed in constructing a neat liberal balancing act, condemning McCarthy while simultaneously invoking the specter of a vicious "red menace" and conspiracy.[25]

Within this inventive but somewhat hysterical thriller framework, Frankenheimer sought to create the ultimate send-up of McCarthy (a bit belated since McCarthy was already dead and his power long since curbed), with war heroes, senators, and even the ne plus ultra of American virtue—Mom—revealed as communist agents. He also succeeded in creating an almost absurdist sense of American politics, where irrationality is the norm, plots abound, mother-dominated sons are turned into robot-like assassins, overwrought liberals denounce right-wingers as "fascists," right-wingers parade around at costume parties in Abraham Lincoln outfits, and most figures of authority and power are never what they seem to be. Frankenheimer may have succeeded beyond his own expectations in creating a film of political prophecy. In it he augured not only the media politics of the 1960s, with scene after scene dominated by the almost baleful gleam of the TV screen, but—most ominous of all— the decade's political assassinations, particularly with the Oedipal and vengeful Madison Square Garden shootings of Raymond's parents, linking private pathology with public and political action.

Unfortunately, Frankenheimer's skillful, flashy, sometimes gratuitous blending of fifties' political issues with prefigurings of the late sixties' "put-on" style—the use of bizarre effects and outrageous overstatement to make a point and get a laugh—did not inspire a host of films that struggled to illuminate American politics. Instead the key issue in films such as Otto Preminger's *Advise and Consent* (1962) and Franklin Schaffner's version of Gore Vidal's cynical, literate novel *The Best Man* (1964), with its political convention-battling between Stevensonian and Nixonian candidates, was homosexuality.

However, there was more to *Advise and Consent* than its melodramatic, prurient treatment of homosexuality. With his cool, objective and lucid style—characterized by long takes, deep focus, and fluid tracks and pans—Preminger was able to successfully evoke the atmosphere of the Senate and its procedures—pages, the gallery, quorum calls, and the workings of the committee system. Preminger endorsed the American system's gift for compromise and flexibility—the film's hero being the honorable, decent majority leader, Senator Munson (Walter Pigeon), who is committed to the civilities and rules of "the Club" (the Senate). Munson affirms the system of checks and balances and is repelled by the behavior of the film's villain—a tactless, vile, left-liberal opportunist who respects nothing but his own drive for power. Preminger's idea of a left-wing senator is a crude caricature, but the film tries to balance him off with florid, manipulative, reactionary southern Senator Seab Cooley, played with such flair by Charles Laughton that he is able to elicit audience sympathy. However, *Advise and Consent* was not interested in either senator's ideological stance—the film never really explores the rights and wrongs of the issues. Its concern was with honorable behavior, and for Preminger such conduct came from understanding that the political world is not built on moral purity but on a sense of ambiguity and compromise.

Advise and Consent was a generally intelligent film, which, like much less sophisticated Hollywood products, saw political conflict as primarily a struggle between personalities. However, its personal dynamics were more complex than the usual heroes versus villains. But in its affirmation of political flexibility the film never questioned the truism that the system serves all segments of the American population, nor asked about the nature of the social ends that the governmental process is geared to serve. In fact, Preminger's complacency smacked of fifties' consensus thinking about the effectiveness of American democracy.

Nevertheless, Preminger's satisfaction with the workings of the government was supplanted by films dealing with the apocalyptic terror aroused by the possibility of nuclear attack and annihilation. In *Seven Days in May* (1964) a statesmanlike, peace-oriented president (Fredric

March) signs a nuclear nonproliferation treaty with the Soviet Union, prompting a group of right-wing generals led by a megalomaniacal zealot, General Scott (Burt Lancaster), to plot a coup. The villain is no longer a communist fifth columnist, as in early fifties' films, but a charismatic general who believes the country can only be saved from the Soviets by a man on a white horse. The coup is predictably subverted by decent men who believe in the democratic process and the Constitution.

Seven Days in May was a much less imaginative work than films made in the same year about the actual threat of nuclear destruction. In the words of Susan Sontag, films about nuclear war struck the audience's "imagination of disaster, [their sense of participation] in the fantasy of living through one's own death and more the death of cities, the destruction of humanity itself,"[26] and gained wide popularity. It was a vision of the world that certainly contributed to the success of two films with radically different styles, *Fail Safe* (1964) and *Dr. Strangelove: Or, How I Learned to Stop Worrying and Love the Bomb* (1964).

Unlike *Dr. Strangelove*, released earlier that year, *Fail Safe*, adapted from a best-seller by Eugene Burdick and Harvey Wheeler, saw nuclear disaster as resulting from the probable malfunctioning of nuclear weaponry's safeguarding technology, rather than from the actions of paranoid generals. In *Fail Safe* it is a technological breakdown that launches American bombers on a full-scale attack of the Soviet Union. Hoping to avert a catastrophe, the decent American president (Henry Fonda) negotiates with the Soviet premier over the hot line. However, the bomber does get through to bomb Moscow, and the American president, to save the world, winds up having to trade the destruction of New York for the obliteration of the Soviet capital. Despite this rather far-fetched conclusion, Sidney Lumet's semi-documentary approach and his powerful and horrifying final montage of the destruction of New York and Moscow give the film a chilling measure of reality.

The most compelling moments of the film are the image of Fonda framed in almost total isolation, trying in his characteristic dry, almost laconic tones to assure the Soviets that it was all a mistake; and his shedding a tear after hearing the shrill sound of the telephone that signals the bomb exploding in Moscow. These scenes capture a sense of the unbearable tragedy that hangs in the balance as men representing very different power structures and interests try, against imponderable odds, to reason with each other about the dire consequences of both nations' nuclear arms policy. An audience viewing these scenes would be hard pressed to avoid feeling how close to the brink we were, and what slender resources existed to avert such a disaster.

Fail Safe is a cautionary film about an out-of-control technology that makes men its pawns and disciples. It is not particularly subtle, turning most of its characters into ciphers who merely serve its theme. In Walter Matthau's overstated, Dr. Strangelove–like political science professor (Groteschele), the film has a character who conveys genuine political substance. Matthau represents the 1960s Cold War intellectuals (e.g., Kahn, Teller) who expressed their vision of realpolitik and their machismo fantasies by indulging in "thinking about the unthinkable." These were men who could talk casually and obsessively about building advanced weaponry and about the possibilities and necessary risks of nuclear warfare, without any moral or humane qualms about the consequences of these policies.[27]

This assault on murderous realpolitik was one of the prime themes of Stanley Kubrick's sardonic black comedy *Dr. Strangelove*. The director of one critically acclaimed antiwar film, *Paths of Glory* (1957), Kubrick had long been interested in the problem of nuclear war and its effects. At first he tried to do a faithful adaptation of Peter George's novel *Red Alert*. However, each time he attempted to write it the whole notion seemed more and more "ridiculous" and he decided to do a black-comic film instead.

Kubrick was able to enlist the mimic and comic talents of Peter Sellers, who played three roles (the stiff-upper-lipped British Group Captain Mandrake, the balding, literally egg-headed President Merkin Muffley, and the bizarre, Nazi-refugee scientist Dr. Strangelove). He also blended the talents of George C. Scott as the General Curtis Lemay–like, adolescent, gravelly-voiced, platitude-spouting Air Force Chief of Staff Buck Turgidson, and the deadpan of Sterling Hayden's mad, grim General Jack D. Ripper, the man who initiates the unauthorized bomber raid.

Complementing this ensemble acting was Kubrick's genius for creating striking images and settings. This talent is maintained from the opening scene where the B-52 is seen copulating with its refueling plane (to "Try a Little Tenderness" on the sound track), to the black-comic finale where the doomsday mechanism has exploded, resulting in a void with only mushroom clouds filling it, and on the sound track English popular singer Vera Lynn can be heard singing the World War II favorite "We'll Meet Again." Kubrick also constructs three imaginative settings, cutting from one to another throughout the film: the extremely realistic and intricate-looking technology of the B-52 cockpit; the war room in Washington whose flashing lights, big board, large circular table, and vast empty space skirt the line between realism and surrealism; and Burpleson Air Force Base, where the psychopathic General Ripper is shot in tight close-up from a low angle, and his troops' violent defense of the base against other American troops is shot with a handheld camera in grainy cinéma vérité style.

These elements came together in a narrative that describes the destruction of the world by a Soviet-constructed doomsday machine ignited by a nuclear attack launched by General Jack D. Ripper. He initiates the attack because he absurdly fears that the nation's sexual potency is on the brink of being undermined by a communist-inspired plot to fluoridate the American water supply. Terry Southern's antic screenplay served Kubrick brilliantly in satirizing a world of well-meaning but ineffectual liberal politicians, war-mongering generals, espionage-obsessed Soviet ambassadors, and demonic nuclear-war strategists.

Dr. Strangelove went beyond satire of the foibles of the power structure and its thinking about nuclear war, linking their behavior to the primal instincts of sex and death—eros and thanatos. There are scenes of the president talking over the hot line from his crypt-like war room to a drunken Soviet Premier Kissoff, who can't comprehend what's being said because he's dallying with his mistress; of Turgidson in turn getting calls from his mistress in the midst of a war-room discussion; and of Colonel Kong (Slim Pickens) astride the B-52's nuclear bomb (looking like a monstrous phallus) as it descends to penetrate and destroy the Soviet Union and the world.

Of course the humanistic tradition presumes that the forces that kindle these passions can be held in check by reason. However, *Dr. Strangelove*'s most caustic barbs are aimed not only at the deadly logic of thinking about the unthinkable, but at sweet, humane reason itself. Time after time, we hear President Muffley's bland, decent conversations with the Soviet premier ("Now Dimitri, you know how we've always talked about the possibility of something going wrong with the bomb—the bomb, Dimitri, the hydrogen bomb") or his shouting "you can't fight here, this is the war room" as the Soviet ambassador and Air Force chief of staff wrestle on the floor, and we are reminded of the futility and impotence of reason as men try to cope with the enormity of the forces that they have unleashed.[28]

Kubrick posits no alternative to an insane world whose leaders are either ineffectual, stupid, infantile, or obsessional personalities. There is no plea for sanity or belief in social change inherent here. There is only the monstrous Dr. Strangelove, who is the personification of scientific reason gone amuck. Strangelove with his self-propelled Nazi-saluting arm, his belief in the divinity of computers, and his gleeful plans for a postnuclear holocaust society of subterranean polygamy (the ultimate expression of America's obsession with macho potency and power) emerges as a brilliant parody of the worst strains in American politics and culture.

In allowing us to take this black-comic peek at the apocalypse, Kubrick succeeded more in creating an inoculation against the fear of annihilation (laughter providing a means for coping in a world perched on the edge of the abyss) than in providing even a hint of some sane strategy for dealing with nuclear weapons. Kubrick's world is a mad, hopeless one, and as Pauline Kael wrote in her review of Dr. Strangelove, "What may have been laughed to death was not war, but some action about it."[29]

Despite this sort of criticism, Kubrick's film was able to sum up the anxieties about nuclear disaster that haunted the fifties and, with the Cuban missile crisis, almost turned into reality in the sixties. And by making both sides responsible for the state of affairs it cut through the Gordian knot of Cold War mythology.[30] As social philosopher Lewis Mumford noted, it was "the first break in the cold war trance that has so long held this country in its rigid grip."[31]

Dr. Strangelove's breakthrough may not have changed the nature of nuclear policy, but it allowed film directors to use black comedy and irony to make social and political points. (The use of black humor reflected the influence of savagely satiric novelists like Joseph Heller, Thomas Pynchon, and Kurt Vonnegut.) It gave directors and the industry the opportunity to critically confront controversial issues without alienating an audience.

Besides films like the aforementioned Manchurian Candidate, there were works like The Americanization of Emily (1964), which ironically celebrated cowardice. It was a film clearly ahead of its time. The only stir it initially created was by virtue of Julie Andrews's post-Poppins dramatic debut. However, when it appeared again in 1967 its attacks on war and heroism fit nicely into the spirit of the sixties. There was a ready-made audience for its cynical, wheeler-dealer anti-hero, Naval Lieutenant Commander Charles Madison (James Garner), whose credo was that cowardice does more for humanity than courage.

The film doesn't just pay homage to cowardice; it takes potshots at the madness of war, especially Madison's superior officer, who wants the first dead man on Omaha Beach to be a navy man. This sort of satire may not have been profound or radical, but it broke from the conventions that had dominated films about the military in the preceding decades.

Nevertheless, the industry preferred, in the main, to grind out its usual quota of genre films, led by the Cold War–inspired superspy ex-

ploits of James Bond and his imitators like *Our Man Flint* (1966) and the
Matt Helm series *(The Silencers*, 1966; *Murderer's Row*, 1966; *The Am-
bushers*, 1967). Occasionally, these films were buttressed by a prestige
picture like the nominally anti-Nazi but essentially Grand Hotelish *Ship
of Fools* (1965), the theatrical, message-bloated *A Man for All Seasons*
(1966), or Sidney Lumet's *The Pawnbroker* (1965), a self-conscious, over-
emphatic but at times moving work.

The Pawnbroker centers on a haunted, emotionally frozen concentration camp survivor, Sol Nazerman (Rod Steiger), who owns a pawnshop
among the violent, broken, and defeated in New York's East Harlem.
The film's emphasis is on the isolated Nazerman's anguish and his catharsis, but there are also some vivid, unsentimental portraits of customers whose lives are also bound by suffering. However, influenced by
Alain Resnais's *Hiroshima, Mon Amour*, the film indulges in a great deal
of parallel cutting from the garbage-laden ghetto streets and lots to harrowing memory images of the concentration camp. But the attempt to
equate the camps with East Harlem blurs and dilutes the social and historical reality of both experiences.

If *The Pawnbroker* failed to get to the heart of urban reality, its images
of street thugs, overcrowded tenement apartments, and stoops lined
with worn people were more in touch with some aspects of life in sixties'
America than most of Hollywood's product. Just how far out of step
Hollywood was could be seen in the films that focused on black life, for
despite the civil rights movement there had been no great surge in the
direction of making films about blacks or black life either in the late
fifties or early sixties. However, in films like *The Defiant Ones* (1958) and
Raisin in the Sun (1962) there was an attempt at least to portray blacks in
a positive manner and to wrestle with some social and economic issues
(especially in *Raisin in the Sun)* – but all within the context of an optimistic, integrationist philosophy. These were films that suggested that the
American Dream was open to blacks if white attitudes shifted and
blacks pursued their ambitions more relentlessly.

Despite the fact that the fantasy of equity and integration was being
destroyed no further away from Hollywood than the streets of Watts,
the film industry still clung tenaciously to its sentimental and reductive
vision of black-white relations. In the Oscar-winning crime melodrama
In the Heat of the Night (1967), a stiff, dignified black Philadelphia homi-
cide detective, Virgil Tibbs (Sidney Poitier), solves a murder case in a
Mississippi town and predictably wins the respect of the bigoted, bellow-
ing, lonely police chief (Rod Steiger). Tibbs, of course, is smarter and
more professional than any of the local cops – a man towards whom only

the most benighted could display any racist feelings. What is distinctive about the film is not the script or performances, but Haskell Wexler's cinematography, which captures the oppressive heat and tension of summer nights in a racist, rural southern town.

Nowhere was the faith that social change could be brought about through personal understanding and affection between blacks and whites more evident than in Stanley Kramer's *Guess Who's Coming to Dinner?* (1967). Kramer's liberal credentials were already well established with his portentous, social-problem productions of anti-racial prejudice, such as *Home of the Brave* (1949), the anti-Nazi *Judgment at Nuremberg* (1961), *On the Beach,* and *The Defiant Ones.* In the glossy *Guess Who's Coming to Dinner?* Kramer and scriptwriter William Rose decided to tackle the subject of interracial marriage.

However, "tackle" is hardly the right word since there rarely has been such a field of straw men and women. The black male lead was again Sidney Poitier, who had already established himself as a worthy and successful missionary to white folks in a great many films (e.g., *Lilies of the Field,* 1963; *A Patch of Blue,* 1965) and in this film portrays a handsome, chaste, and charming doctor well on his way to someday winning a Nobel prize. In fact, he is too good a catch for the innocent, simpering daughter (Katharine Houghton) of liberal millionaire presslord Matt Drayton (Spencer Tracy) and his feisty, gallery-owning wife, Christina (Katharine Hepburn).

Although there are objections to the marriage, ranging from the bigoted snobbishness of one of Christina's art gallery employees to the comic protests of the Draytons' cute black maid ("civil rights is one thing, but this here's another!"), they are easily brushed aside. More difficult to sweep away are the more serious doubts expressed by Matt Drayton about the social problems the young couple will have to face. However, even his reasonable concerns are effectively bypassed by Beah Richard's (Poitier's mother in the film) suggestion that it is not race that is preventing the marriage, but the fact that Drayton and her husband (who also opposes the match) have forgotten what it was like to be young.

As a result, what ostensibly emerges as a prime issue in *Guess Who's Coming to Dinner?* is not race but the clash of generations. Of course, it's a situation that is immediately rectified in Tracy's valedictory to Christina, about love conquering all, which is as much a commentary on his own twenty-seven-year relationship with Hepburn as it is an address to his fictional wife, since Tracy was to die within weeks of the conclusion of filming.[32]

And though the issue of the generation gap feels totally bogus, especially in a film ostensibly dealing with the complex issue of intermarriage
(not to mention the total blindness and irrelevance of the film's liberal,
integrationist impulses to the rage and despair of the black community),
it nevertheless superficially touched on something significant: the growing polarization between generations. This polarization—resulting from
the Vietnam War and the rise of the New Left and counterculture—
intensified and helped divide America in the late 1960s.

Already the coming of the young into American politics had been
celebrated in the prose of authors such as Norman Mailer who saw them
as "those mad middle-class children with their lobotomies from sin . . .
their innocence, their lust for the apocalypse."[33] However, their image
had still not been forged in film, nor would it until Arthur Penn's *Bonnie
and Clyde* (1967).

Bonnie and Clyde not only shifted the focus of film to the young, it also
defined a unique sixties' cinema and sensibility in ways that *The Manchurian Candidate* and *Dr. Strangelove* had only hinted at. The best indicator of how far the film went in accomplishing this was the vehemence
of the attacks on it by the critical establishment, led by *New York Times*
critic Bosley Crowther. Nevertheless, audiences flocked to it, copied its
clothing styles, and made it one of the year's top grossers.

Vindicating the judgment of audiences over film critics is only one of
the film's minor achievements. Its greatest success was in both introduc-
ing the ideas and techniques of the French "New Wave" into the Hollywood mainstream, and in firmly fixing the gaze of American filmmakers
on the lives and styles of the alienated and discontented.

Written by two young *Esquire* writers, David Newman and Robert
Benton, it was originally seen by them as a possible project for either
François Truffaut or Jean-Luc Godard, a hope based on their appreciation of the French New Wave's understanding of the poetry and mythic
nature of the American genre film. However, neither director was available, and the film was ultimately produced by Warren Beatty and directed
by Arthur Penn.

Penn had also been influenced by the New Wave, so little was really
lost by the change, and he was able to incorporate many of their techniques into the film. Along with free intercutting of time and space, the
use of slow and accelerated motion, he also used little vignettes ending
in visual and verbal puns à la Truffaut, and alternation of comic and
violent moments apropos of Goddard. In fact, it was the irony and humor of *Bonnie and Clyde* (for instance, the chase scene where careening
and zigzagging cars comically pursue each other accompanied by a

wildly twanging banjo sound track, or the gang's picnic with a middle-class couple, who, though at first terrified, ultimately refuse to leave them) which helped prevent the film from turning into conventional social melodrama.

These techniques updated a story that had been done before by Hollywood in Fritz Lang's *You Only Live Once* (1937) and Nicholas Ray's *They Drive by Night* (1949). Yet this timeworn tale of two youthful outsiders who choose a life of crime held a powerful attraction for an audience who felt they were living cut off from the channels of power and incapable of bringing about social and political change.

This restless quality is caught right from the opening Depression-era scene in which the beautiful and bored Bonnie (Faye Dunaway) sees the limping, toothpick-chewing, handsome Clyde (Warren Beatty) attempting to steal her mother's car. Attracted by his bravado, she becomes involved in a life of crime. It takes them on a number of botched and bumbling robbery attempts, and after the addition of Clyde's crude, guffawing brother Buck (Gene Hackman), his bovine, pathetic wife Blanche (Estelle Parsons), and a nose-picking, hero-worshipping rustic driver named C. W. Moss (Michael J. Pollard), they go on a bank-robbing rampage that makes them celebrated and notorious figures.

Despite their violent and criminal acts, Penn never allows the audience's sympathy to leave Bonnie and Clyde. On the one hand, they are seen as outlaw-rebels (though never social victims) against an unjust social order represented here by the banks and police; on the other hand, they are innocent, awkward clowns, who in one robbery can't get the attention of their victims. Penn also attempts to reinforce our positive feelings for them through his use of shallow Freudianism. Clyde is sexually impotent, which supposedly provides the character with a measure of vulnerability and gives his gun a crude, symbolic significance.

In depicting Bonnie and Clyde as ordinary folk, seeking to be immortalized, Penn sometimes catches the pathos underneath their posturing and bravado. For the sheepish, slow, inarticulate Clyde—match in mouth and permanent limp—and the slatternly, poetess-manqué Bonnie—constantly looking at her image in a blurred mirror—are nothing more than a yokel sharecropper and a waitress who hunger for the American dream of glamor and success. No matter how often Bonnie may dress in expensive clothes and obsess about her image and making the headlines, she still longs for her mother and dreams of settling down with a man in a home. And though the scene where Bonnie returns to the family picnic is overly stylized and filled with soft-focused, sentimentalized, pastoral imagery (e.g., an almost too picturesquely weathered and stark-looking farm-woman mother), it succeeds in evoking the rural and church-bound social world both outlaws come from.

Most striking in the film, however, is not their ordinariness or the social reality that helps shape them, but the mythic quality Penn endows them with. It is a quality conveyed both by the glamor of stars like Beatty and Dunaway and by Penn's camera, which captures in long shot and close-up the outlaws' vitality, spontaneity, and style. Penn frames their actions with painterly, beautifully composed, and melancholy images of sweeping wheat fields and prairies and Walker Evans–like small towns. This treatment culminates in their slow-motion death, dressed in white (signifying innocence?), twitching like rag dolls in a montage of violence. Their death is both mythic—the tragic death of a heroic duo— and concrete, for the bullets are real and leave them truly dead.

The myth of Bonnie and Clyde works for Penn in aesthetic terms—the beauty of alienation and outlawry—and captures something of how integral violence and the unfettered assertion of self and will were both to American mythology and the sixties. It is when Penn wants his outlaws to be seen as romantic rebels against an unjust social order—Clyde returning money he stole from a bank to a poor farmer, or the gang being embraced as people's heroes at a migrant camp (straight out of The Grapes of Wrath)—that the film becomes most simplistic and even dangerous. It is clear that Penn wants Bonnie and Clyde to stand as symbols for the rebellious and high-spirited youth of the 1960s while the banks, Deputy Sheriff Homer, and Pa Moss represent a callous, rigid, and hypocritical adult world. There are also suggestions, in the exaggerated, murderous use of police firepower (for example, a bloody shoot-out where the police use an armored car), of the American military's penchant for overkill in Vietnam.

However, no matter that Clyde talks about protecting poor folk, the pair's social consciousness is no more than a contrivance of Penn's. The only community Bonnie and Clyde are members of is the criminal one, and though the film might not have had any more pernicious influence than getting somebody to buy a snap-brim hat, it did give symbolic sanction to certain nihilistic values and strains permanent in both the counterculture and the New Left. The film fed the contempt many of the young had for the adult world and its work ethic. More significantly, by affirming crime as a viable means of social, political, and cultural protest, it fed the growing contempt that many of the young felt for more orthodox forms of political organization and action, and ominously romanticized sociopathic violence by confusing it with acts of social rebellion.[34]

These objections aside, *Bonnie and Clyde* was still the landmark film of the sixties. Along with revitalizing the formal dimensions of the Hollywood film, its focusing of attention on the young and the alienated gave some Hollywood luster to the 1960s revisionist impulse that saw American history and society from the bottom up. Once this road was embarked on, the facile shibboleths about American society that had been Hollywood's stock-in-trade since World War II became harder and harder to sustain. Much of this new perspective was transformed into films expressing a kind of bankable and facile pessimism accompanied by the same superstar actors as before. Nevertheless, the films projected a vision of a fragmented America no longer as secure of itself and its values as it had once been.

Nowhere is the crumbling of these values more clearly illustrated than in Mike Nichols's homage to the young, *The Graduate* (1967), a commercially and critically successful film whose most compelling moment is the postnuptial abduction of the beautiful Elaine Robinson (Katherine Ross) by the romantically obsessed Benjamin Braddock (Dustin Hoffman in his first film). Not only did this scene break with a whole genre past that upheld the sanctities of the marriage vow above everything else, it was the ultimate and shrewdest—it gave Hollywood a breakthrough into the 18–25 market—assault in a whole series of attacks on the values of the affluent, upper-middle-class American.

The embodiment of this challenge in *The Graduate* is somber, bright, and inexperienced Benjamin Braddock, who returns to the emptiness and sterility of his parents' vulgar Southern California world of swimming pools and material comfort. Out of a sheer sense of ennui and alienation, Ben begins a sexually satisfying but emotionally starved and mechanical affair with the bored, cynical wife of his father's law partner, Mrs. Robinson (Anne Bancroft). The first stages of this affair allow Hoffman to display his talent for giving richly textured performances. Before his transformation into a romantic hero, Hoffman's Braddock is filled with anxiety and self-doubt—speaking in half-finished phrases, wheezily expelling breath, and never quite sure of what his hands are doing while fending off Mrs. Robinson's seductive wiles. The affair is simultaneously comic and pathetic, and probably the most poignant section of the film.

The deadness of his affair with Mrs. Robinson is contrasted with the spontaneity and openness he finds with her daughter Elaine. It's a relationship the predatory Mrs. Robinson violently objects to. And Nichols skillfully evokes empathy from the youth audience for both Elaine's freshness and vulnerability and Benjamin's truth-seeking and rejection of a plastic, unfeeling adult universe.

Combining the New Wave techniques of jump and flash cuts, extreme close-ups, and subjective view and telephoto lens shots (throughout one senses Nichols's eclectic, stylistic borrowings from Antonioni, Fellini, and Godard) with the music of youth-culture heroes Simon and Garfunkel, Nichols successfully creates a world of honest young people surrounded by stereotyped adults who are either predators or fools. The gilded surfaces of the adults predictably cover empty lives and dead marriages all echoing, in the words of Simon and Garfunkel, the "sounds of silence."

In such an emotional and moral void the mere act of honestly being in love is perceived as liberating and capable of shattering old taboos, even the supposed eternal links of "I do." Consequently, Mrs. Robinson's shriek at the runaway Elaine, that it's "too late," can be met with the reply, "not for me." This hardly guarantees a "they live happily ever after" fade-out; and the film ends with the couple's blank and ambiguous stares as they leave the scene of the wedding in the back of a municipal bus.[35]

Regardless of this final seed of doubt about the future, The Graduate still remains a hymn to the young. Like Bonnie and Clyde, it grants all energy, integrity, and life to the young. However, in contrast to the origins of Bonnie and Clyde's revolt, which was loosely tied to the poverty of the Depression, the reasons for Ben's alienation supposedly can be found in the sterility of upper-middle-class affluence. Taken together, both films affirmed the discontent of the young. The Graduate underlined that dissatisfaction by locating it precisely at the moment when the American dream seemed to have reached its peak of material fulfillment—creating a paradigm for the type of sixties' film that attempted to subvert the values that had dominated American films since the 1940s. Not only were the language and sexual detail franker in The Graduate, but the insistence on a moral perspective that unambiguously repudiated social convention and mores was relatively new to Hollywood. With its oblique references to 1960s radicalism when its locale is shifted from Southern California to Berkeley (where a harried Benjamin follows Elaine) and a comic landlord who dislikes outside agitators makes a brief appearance, The Graduate hinted that there might be even more to Benjamin's anguish than alienation from the values of the upper middle class and existential angst. However, The Graduate was based on a 1950s novel by Charles Webb and the film's few 1960s allusions did little to update the novel or illuminate the sources of student rebellion and alienation in the 1960s.

Still, something about the intensity of Bonnie and Clyde's violence and the extremity of Benjamin's alienation suggested that political events had some effect on the nature of the two films. The event that most profoundly affected the politics of the young and American politics in general was the war in Vietnam. Aware of the divided nature of American public opinion about the war, producers hesitated to tackle the subject directly. However, for a right-wing superstar and patriot like John Wayne, a film about the Vietnam War, *The Green Berets* (1968), with himself as star, was a means of winning the hearts and minds of the American people.

Since the 1940s and films such as *Wake Island* (1942), *They Were Expendable* (1945), and *Sands of Iwo Jima* (1949), John Wayne had become the symbol par excellence of the tough, efficient, patriotic American fighting man. The Wayne image was indelibly imprinted on every American schoolboy's imagination and every raw recruit's dreams. Nor was there anything ironic or calculating in Wayne's own devotion to the image, as exemplified by his red-baiting leadership in the McCarthyite Motion Picture Alliance for the Preservation of American Ideals, and his support of bellicose right-wing politicians like Barry Goldwater and Ronald Reagan.

Choosing as the subject of his Vietnam film the elite military unit, the Green Berets, Wayne was returning to the world of John Ford, his mentor. Ford's cavalry units, perched at the edge of the frontier, were bastions of communal honor, tradition, camaraderie, and pride, fighting an often little-appreciated and less-understood battle for civilization and decency against the barbarians. Wayne's notion of the Green Berets was similar: He saw them as a fortress for muscular and professional anticommunist values whose most serious challenge came, ironically enough, not from the communists, but from a liberal, skeptical reporter, George Beckwith (David Jannsen). For Wayne, those soft liberals who undermined our patriotic will were far more dangerous than regiments of savage Vietcong. However, Beckwith's piddling doubts are suppressed as soon as he is exposed to the murderous brutality of a Vietcong raid on a desolate Vietnamese village.

If the first half of the film is mediocre John Ford—the Vietcong even scale the Green Berets' fort, which is aptly named Dodge City, with ladders—the film's second half is pure Richard Nixon. In this section, Wayne uses all manner of advanced technologies and dirty tricks, including a Hollywood-style Mata Hari female decoy, and kidnaps an enemy Vietcong general. The general's aristocratic and decadent values make even the revolutionary politics of the Vietcong suspect. Through all of this Wayne's hero (Col. Mike Kirby) hovers about like a good paterfamilias, granting absolution to the liberal columnist for his political sins and providing fatherly comfort to a cute Vietnamese orphan who in Wayne's fadeout comment is "what this is all about."[36]

Although *The Green Berets* turned out to be financially profitable, rather than setting Americans' minds at ease about the righteousness of their cause it produced new evidence of the national split on the war. Indicative of that polarization was some of the critical reaction to the film. In previous years Wayne films had rarely raised anything more than a critical ho-hum. However, *The Green Berets* provoked *New York Times* critic Renata Adler's withering comment that "*The Green Berets* is a film so unspeakable, so stupid, so rotten and false that it passes through being funny, through being camp, through everything and becomes an invitation to grieve not so much for our soldiers or Vietnam (the film could not be more false or do greater disservice to them) but for what has happened to the fantasy-making apparatus of this country."[37]

Adler's comment recognized that Hollywood's myth-making abilities had lost power and resonance, and that consequently the old Hollywood formula could no longer capture the nation's imagination and spur it to a greater commitment to the war. No longer could Wayne's war-loving, patriarchal figure, spouting the old patriotic and macho certainties and clichés about decent, freedom-loving Americans and brutal, totalitarian Vietcong, capture and dominate the moral center of the American imagination as it once had. Instead, Wayne's values existed in uneasy proximity to Hollywood's new revisionism, which featured genre films that not only undermined Wayne's most cherished certitudes but covertly and slyly evoked a Vietnam War that had horror rather than honor as its dominant motif.

One such film was Sam Peckinpah's (a descendant of pioneers) brilliantly cut and richly composed western *The Wild Bunch* (1969). Paradoxically *The Wild Bunch* drew much of its power from working against the Ford–Hawks tradition that had done so much for Wayne's reputation. For instance, *The Wild Bunch* took place when the frontier was physically closed and the ethos of the Old West was disappearing fast in the wake of new technologies such as the motor car and machine gun. Also fading with it were the elite band of mythic professional good-bad Robin Hoods that often populated the moral landscapes of Hawks and Ford. In *The Wild Bunch* we have the interminable wranglings and whorings of Pike Bishop's (William Holden) gang of bank robbers and payroll snatchers, who are in turn pursued by a group of craven, rednecked, lumpen bounty hunters led by Pike's old confederate, the melancholy, trapped Deke Thornton (Robert Ryan). In addition, the traditional Hollywood western town, which often contained some people who could express communal pride, concern, and virtue, has been replaced by a passive, foolish citizenry, too cowed and confused to make even more than a token protest when the streets of their town erupt with bloody, chaotic violence. The only seemingly active members of the town are its children, who mimic the shoot-out and are demonically amused by burning to death the scorpions and ants they have been playing with.

With society corrupt and rapacious and the mythic West gone, the film follows the Bishop bunch's involvement in the Mexican Revolution (whose political character Peckinpah cares nothing about), in the process trying to establish some kind of rough principles. The one most valued is group loyalty, the kind embodied in Bishop's comment that "When you side with a man, you side with him all the way—otherwise you're an animal." Ultimately, this sense of loyalty grows among the outlaws and even includes the primal, savage Gorch Brothers (Ben Johnson and Warren Oates) and the Mexican bandit Angel (Jaime Sanchez). Almost as significant is the value placed on genuine authority in a world of corrupt betrayers where traditional institutional power is dominated by debauchees like the gross, murderous Mexican general Mapache (Emilio Fernandez) and the ruthless railroad executive Harrigan (Albert Dekker). Society's corruption makes it imperative, according to Pike's lieutenant Dutch (Ernest Borgnine), to heavily weigh the fact of not only giving your word (the old code), but also considering "who you give it to."

However, whatever scrupulousness the outlaws exhibit toward their code is not matched by any restraint on Peckinpah's part in his depiction of violence in the film. For a supposed moralist, Peckinpah's use of graphic, elongated, and sensational violence throughout the film—a horse stomping on a woman and dragging a man along the ground and countless bodies falling in slow motion with blood gushing from them—again raised questions about the origins and effects of screen violence. The answer this time was not only the usual talk about the psychology of the director and Hollywood's tendency to indulge in and exploit blood and gore, but also a crediting of responsibility to the audience's increasing receptivity to violence, some of it caused by the nightly scenes of Vietnam bloodletting they saw on the television screen.

The climax of The Wild Bunch, with its stylized, orgiastic massacre, raised questions not only about the often incoherent blend of moralism and nihilism pervading Peckinpah's work, but also about the hopelessness reflected in many of the films of the late 1960s. Although The Wild Bunch ends on a supposedly revolutionary note, with the last survivors both of the outlaws and of the bounty hunters, wise Old Sykes (Edmond

O'Brien) and Deke Thornton, joining with the revolutionaries, the gesture seems a hollow afterthought following the more emotionally and
aesthetically intense and compelling slaughter scenes. In fact, Peckinpah's deepest and most sentimental loyalties clearly have nothing to do
with social commitment. It is men like Pike, seen in low-angle shots
walking tall to a drum beat and resolving to die heroically, who elicit
Peckinpah's deepest feeling. Pike and the men of the wild bunch may be
brutal killers who belong to the past, but Peckinpah grants them a final,
heroic eulogy reminiscent of Ford's *Fort Apache* (1948). He superimposes
over the film's final images – in their one moment of transcendence – the
bunch riding out of a Mexican village to the applause and serenades of
its inhabitants.[38]

The *Wild Bunch's* mixture of intellectual incoherence and imaginative
and powerful imagery was symptomatic (though in exaggerated form) of
the problems that many of these late sixties' films exhibited. The filmmakers reveled in the freedom they had to pursue previously forbidden
subject matter and imagery, but were often incapable of doing more
than evoking a portrait of a world gone awry. They were clearly more at
home with images and feelings of human corruption, alienation, confusion, and rebellion than with incisive and complex social and political
critiques. And they were more attuned to feelings of anger and resentment towards established institutions and the desire for freedom from
conventional mores than to any overviews of the social malaise and political and cultural movements of the sixties.

A number of films touched on aspects of the counterculture. Films like
Richard Lester's psychologically suggestive and self-consciously stylish –
excessive flash cuts, a splintered narrative – *Petulia* (1968) were primarily
interested in satirizing the callousness, crassness, and obliviousness of
American society of the sixties. The film does provide brief, unpleasant
glimpses of the counterculture; Lester depicts its adherents as being just
as uncaring and mean-spirited as conventional middle-class society, and
providing little hope as a social alternative. And Paul Mazursky's box
office success *Bob and Carol and Ted and Alice* (1969) gently satirizes the
Southern California, upper-middle-class version of the counterculture.
Mazursky's well-heeled professionals go to Esalen (for primal scream,
twenty-four-hour marathons, and other pop therapies), smoke pot, and
struggle to achieve emotional and sexual liberation. The film has charm
and wit, and Mazursky conveys an insider's knowledge of his characters'
foibles. He never, however, probes beyond the externals of their behavior or asks larger social questions about why they behave as they do,
preferring to play it safe and mute his satiric jabs.

Arthur Penn's elegiac and loosely episodic *Alice's Restaurant* (1969) goes a bit further. Its primary purpose was to provide a critical but loving evocation of the counterculture. Using a ballad-like structure and centering the film around a solemn, honest, pure Arlo Guthrie (playing himself with consummate impassivity), the film touches on Arlo's relationship with the old left (via visits to his dying father, the legendary folk singer Woody Guthrie); his conflicts with the establishment—college, police, army; and his involvement with the counterculture.

Arlo has long hair, plays a guitar, smokes dope, and takes refuge in a counterculture commune presided over by his more animated and complex surrogate parents, sensual earth mother Alice (Pat Quinn) and her insecure, hostile, dreamer husband Ray Brock (played with manic intensity by James Broderick). Penn's sympathies are clearly with the counterculture as he wittily portrays Arlo's victories over the police (he beats a conviction for littering) and the draft. These scenes wryly and satirically (the film recreates the twenty-minute talking-blues hit "Alice's Restaurant Massacre") capture the estrangement between the generations in America. Nonetheless, though Penn likes the young's openness and spontaneity, he sees the counterculture as having its own painful limitations. For though Arlo can serenely triumph over traditional institutions, another member of the commune dies of an overdose of heroin. And the image of the commune as a beatific refuge (they even reconsecrate an abandoned church) coexists with a profound sense of the whole venture's futility and failure. The film concludes with a despairing Ray desolately fantasizing about creating one more commune, and with Penn's camera tenderly panning around Alice, who stands vulnerable and alone with both the commune and her marriage heading for disaster.

Alice's Restaurant is filled with luminous, poetic, and painterly images, and exhibits a real empathy for the counterculture. Penn can grace us with scenes that catch both the absurdity—the dim, clichéd talk about getting one's head together—and the sense of human possibility and community of the counterculture. However, at times it seems that there are too many tones inhabiting the work—comic, pathetic, and ironic—ultimately dissipating some of the film's emotional and intellectual impact. *Alice's Restaurant* also never gets sufficiently close to the Brocks or especially to the other members of the commune—who are merely colorfully dressed hippie extras—to get to the heart of the film's personal and communal breakdowns.[39]

If *Alice's Restaurant* is not a fully realized and coherent portrait of the counterculture, a film like the left-leaning, strikingly cinematic *Medium*

Cool (1969) tends to sacrifice its narrative and characters to the evocative documentary footage that its director had amassed. *Medium Cool's* hard-boiled, apolitical hero is a TV cameraman, John (Robert Forster), who views contemporary events with professional detachment; he treats the nature and substance of the event as much less significant than the process of getting the story—until he discovers that the FBI is being allowed to use his footage to identify radicals. He suddenly realizes that the act of pointing a camera is itself a political gesture.

John's job as a TV cameraman allows *Medium Cool's* director Haskell Wexler to mix cinéma vérité—documentary and neo-documentary footage (a reconstruction of the assassination of Bobby Kennedy)—with a loose fictional narrative in order to create a telling portrait of sixties' social reality. And though there are scenes that go in for easy ironies (e.g., "Happy Days Are Here Again" can be heard on the sound track as protestors are beaten by Chicago police) and take facile potshots at targets like insensitive, white, middle-class liberals, the film is filled with incisive sequences depicting angry, knotted-up black militants subtly playing with white fears and guilt, Illinois National Guardsmen receiving riot training, and the chaos and repression of the Chicago 1968 Democratic Party Convention and police riot. However, the purely fictional scenes lack conviction and are often left aimlessly suspended as the more powerful vérité scenes are inserted between them.

Even in the vérité scenes *Medium Cool* sometimes indulges in awkward Pirandello-like effects—the actors wandering past the Chicago police and protestors, and the audience viewing Wexler and his crew self-consciously shooting the final fatal accident scene and turning the lens toward the audience. That final scene, where John and a woman friend, Eileen (Verna Bloom), die in a car crash, ends the film on a dark note, which both conveys a sense of the fatality and destruction of the sixties,[40] and suggests that "we are implicated both as voyeuristic viewers and as potential victims of the camera's imaging of violence and death."[41]

Wexler is unambiguously on the side of the sixties' protesters, but he knows full well that the exposure of repression on film, including his own, may merely titillate its audience—that "the whole world may be watching" on television the brutality of Mayor Daley's police, but their actions will probably arouse little concern in the audience. For a committed filmmaker like Wexler, the feeling that politically engaged films might ultimately make no more social difference than the most detached, commercial works was not a hopeful sign for the success of the sixties' movements.

Easy Rider (1969), which was the most culturally significant and com-

mercially successful of cinematic attempts at capturing the rebellious and
alternate life styles of the 1960s, was no more sanguine about the future.
Initially conceived of as a kind of American International Pictures ex-
ploitation quickie about the hippie scene, like the *Wild Angels* (1966) and
The Trip (1967), it had to be finished with independent financing by its
star, Peter Fonda. Its subsequent box office success compared to its small
initial investment made it a model for what became known as the New
American Cinema. Its characteristic products were independently financed, low-budget films, made by non-studio-trained directors, who
combined highly personal or politically radical stories that broke with
conventional Hollywood narrative techniques while borrowing heavily
from the respective styles of New Wave, cinéma vérité, and avant-garde
films. Offshoots of this tendency were *Wild 90* (1968), Brian De Palma's
Greetings (1968) and *Hi Mom* (1970), *Putney Swope* (1969), *Coming Apart*
(1969), *Ice* (1970), and other films of the late sixties and early seventies.

Crucial to *Easy Rider's* enormous commercial success and cultural significance was its ability to capture on a visceral level certain primary
themes and concepts of the counterculture and the sixties—mysticism,
personal freedom, "the land," drugs, and communes. It begins as a re-
verse road film in which a pair of hippie motorcyclists—the cool, detached, oracular Wyatt (Peter Fonda) and the tense, angry, comical Billy
(Dennis Hopper)—sell a kilo of dope to a Los Angeles hippie capitalist
and then head east to New Orleans for Mardi Gras in what ostensibly is
a search for freedom. Along the way *Easy Rider* becomes a laid-back
bildungsroman as the duo visit old-time ranchers and hippie communes,
spend time in jail and in brothels, and take acid trips. The journey is
enhanced by the film's exciting use of landscape, space, light, movement,
and sound (especially the contemporary rock music of Jimi Hendrix, the
Byrds, Steppenwolf, and others).

Unfortunately, the film is often painfully inarticulate, shallow, and
pretentious when it forgoes its tracking camera and tries to turn its vision into words. Most of it takes the form of particularly banal and pretentious pronouncements by the hippie saint Wyatt, who gives a
benediction to a rural commune that has faced hard times—"they're
gonna make it"—or pays pious reverence to the simple life-style of a
toothless old rancher with a beaming Mexican wife who is "doing his
own thing, in his own time."

However, in its depiction of Us against Them—the supposed free long-
hairs versus the vicious, redneck straights, who universally treat Wyatt
and Billy with murderous contempt—the film does strike a powerful social and emotional chord. In the process the film gave up its penchant

for indulging in ersatz and sentimental beatitudes and connected itself to the disillusionment felt by many, especially the young, about sixties' America. Its most poignant expression comes in the comments of an articulate, witty, alcoholic lawyer, George Hanson (Jack Nicholson), who joins the two on their quest. After they are attacked by local goons Hanson points out that "this used to be a helluva country," but that it seems to have lost its way. He adds that though the rednecks may ostensibly believe in the idea of freedom they are scared of free individuals.

Hanson's remarks set the tone of the second half of the film, which is as pervaded with a sense of doom, failure, and despair as the opening half was a paean to the exhilaration of traveling on the open road. Wyatt's and Billy's own violent fate is prefigured in George's murder by a group of rednecks. Although the two do make it to the Mardi Gras, and take an extravagantly filmed acid trip (fisheye lens, overexposed images, and overlapping dialogue) with some prostitutes in a cemetery, their pathetic destiny seems so sealed that we get hints of it in flash-forwards. It is a climax that not only acted as a judgment on their personal quest but seemed to extend to the American experience as a whole.

Such was the outrage of some critics at this judgment that an elite, cultural custodian like Diana Trilling (who had not raised more than an eyebrow at films since her tenure as a reviewer for the New Republic in the forties and fifties) was moved to call the film "devious." She particularly questioned the appropriateness of Wyatt and Billy as symbols of our social and cultural condition and complained that "Wyatt and Billy lack the energy to create anything, comment on anything, feel anything, except the mute, often pot-induced pleasure of each other's company."[42]

However, though one may clearly quarrel with the presumptuousness of using two dope-dealing drifters as symbols of freedom and making judgments on something as vast as the "American experience," there is little doubt that Easy Rider captured the sense of foreboding and doom that dominated many of the films of the sixties, and heralded those of the seventies. In fact, the deaths of Wyatt and Billy seemed a reflection of what had been the fate of Martin Luther King, Malcolm X, and Robert Kennedy, and—some felt—could be the lot of anyone whose dissent and protest truly threatened the power structure of America.

Of course, Billy and Wyatt were far from being political rebels or critics, but in their dim, self-destructive way they were searching for some alternative vision to the dominant culture. Easy Rider is a tongue-tied film that succeeds in evoking the mood of a decade. In its mixture of intellectual simple-mindedness, striking imagery and editing, and conscious and unconscious intuition into the decade's confusion and alienation, it was one of the most representative of late 1960s films. In fact, Wyatt's despairing comment grants unintentional pop-cultural symmetry to a decade that began with the sense of political possibility embodied in lyrics of songs like "Blowin' in the Wind" and ended with the pessimism of a line like "We blew it."

NOTES

1. William L. Langer, *Political and Social Upheaval, 1832–1852* (New York: Harper and Row, 1969).

2. Godfrey Hodgson, *America in Our Time: From World War II to Nixon, What Happened and Why* (New York: Vintage, 1978).

3. Hodgson, *America in Our Time*, pp. 491–99.

4. William L. O'Neill, *Coming Apart: An Informal History of America in the 1960s* (New York: Quadrangle, 1971), pp. 29–103.

5. *Ibid.*

6. Hodgson, *America in Our Time*, pp. 179–99.

7. *Ibid.*

8. *Ibid.*

9. Hodgson, *America in Our Time*, pp. 200–24.

10. *Ibid.*

11. Doris Kearns, *Lyndon B. Johnson and the American Dream* (New York: Signet, 1976), pp. 220–62.

12. Kearns, *Lyndon B. Johnson*, pp. 263–323.

13. Frances Fitzgerald, *Fire in the Lake* (New York: Vintage, 1973).

14. David Halberstam, *The Best and the Brightest* (New York: Fawcett, 1973).

15. Kirkpatrick Sale, *SDS* (New York: Vintage, 1974).

16. Morris Dickstein, *Gates of Eden: American Culture in the Sixties* (New York: Basic Books, 1977), pp. 51–88, 128–53.

17. Hodgson, *America in Our Time*, pp. 326–52.

18. O'Neill, *Coming Apart*, pp. 396–428.

19. *Ibid.*

20. James Monaco, *American Film Now: The People, the Power, the Money, the Movies* (New York: Oxford University Press, 1979), pp. 1–48.

21. *Ibid.*

22. *Ibid.*

23. Thomas Schatz, *The Genius of the System: Hollywood Filmmaking in the Studio Era* (New York: Pantheon, 1988), p. 489.

24. Pauline Kael, *Going Steady* (New York: Bantam, 1971), p. 115.

25. Gerald Pratley, *The Cinema of John Frankenheimer* (Cranbury, N.J.: A. S. Barnes, 1969).

26. Susan Sontag, *Against Interpretation* (New York: Dell, 1969), p. 215.

27. Norman Kagan, *The War Film* (New York: Pyramid Publications, 1974), p. 142.

28. Norman Kagan, *The Cinema of Stanley Kubrick* (New York: Grove Press, 1975), pp. 111–44.

29. Pauline Kael, *Kiss, Kiss, Bang, Bang* (New York: Bantam, 1969), p. 79.

30. Albert Auster and Leonard Quart, *How the War Was Remembered: Hollywood and Vietnam* (New York: Praeger, 1988), p. 25.

31. Lewis Mumford, quoted in Kagan, *The Cinema of Stanley Kubrick*, p. 132.

32. Donald Spoto, *Stanley Kramer: Filmmaker* (New York: G. P. Putnam's Sons, 1978), p. 2.

33. Norman Mailer, *Armies of the Night* (New York: Signet, 1968), p. 47.

34. Robin Wood, *Arthur Penn* (New York: Praeger, 1969), pp. 72–91.

35. Hollis Alpert and Andrew Sarris (eds.), *Film 68/69: An Anthology by the National Society of Film Critics* (New York: Simon and Schuster, 1969), pp. 235–41.

36. Alan G. Barbour, *John Wayne* (New York: Pyramid, 1974), pp. 121–22.

37. Renata Adler, *A Year in the Dark* (New York: Berkeley, 1969), pp. 199–200.

38. Joseph Morgenstern and Stefan Kanfer (eds.), *Film 69/70: An Anthology by the National Society of Film Critics* (New York: Simon and Schuster, 1970), pp. 148–56.

39. Wood, *Arthur Penn*, pp. 92–116.

40. Morgenstern and Kanfer, *Film 69/70*, pp. 165–72.

41. Robert Sklar, "When Looks Could Kill: American Cinema of the Sixties," *Cineaste*, xvi, 1–2 (1987–88), p. 51.

42. Diana Trilling, *We Must March, My Darlings* (New York: Harcourt Brace Jovanovich, 1977), pp. 175–86.

5

THE SEVENTIES

On March 18, 1969, newly elected President Richard Nixon ordered the secret bombing of neutral Cambodia. It was the first in a series of events whose consequences were to dominate American politics and society during the first half of the seventies. Given Nixon's past history—his hawkish foreign policy views and his gift for manipulating anticommunism to further his political career—there should have been little surprise that he ordered the bombing. But in 1968 Nixon had come to power primarily on the strength of the vague promise that he knew how to end the war in Vietnam, understanding that at this point in the Vietnam War neither Congress nor the public would approve its escalation.[1]

Despite his political promises, however, Nixon was clearly not ready to abruptly terminate American involvement. Nixon and his advisers had no use for the Johnson–Humphrey idea that the war was fought for democracy and "winning the hearts and minds" of the people, and displayed little interest in geopolitical rationales like the fear of toppling Southeast Asian dominoes. The Nixon–Kissinger justification for continuing U.S. involvement was summed up in the strategic concept of "credibility." They believed that the war was being fought to maintain America's reputation "as a guarantor"—to assure her allies, and more particularly her enemies, that the United States would be firm in confronting a crisis.[2]

Inextricably connected to the idea of "credibility" was the notion of "American will." The Nixon administration felt it had to assure the world that America would take the necessary painful steps, like the bombing of Cambodia, to back up words with action. After the American people finally became aware of the bombing, the president affirmed the notion of credibility by stating, "it is not our power but our will and character that is being tested tonight."[3]

To the Nixon administration that will seemed badly shaken after years of interminable bloodshed, the investment of billions of dollars, and the often violent political debate and struggles of a profoundly divided nation. Some people in the administration felt the national will had been permanently damaged not only by the war, but by social welfarism, government intervention in the economy, and the leadership of a decadent elite and establishment.

In order to renew America, Richard Nixon set about attacking the media, liberal-left intellectuals, and government bureaucrats — institutions he viewed as bastions of an enemy establishment. It was a campaign motivated almost as much by Nixon's own sense of personal powerlessness and private grievance as by his ideological and political commitments. In the process of initiating this attack Nixon dismantled much of the "Great Society" legislation of the Johnson presidency, stacked the Supreme Court with supposed judicial conservatives (though Justice Harry Blackmun surprisingly turned out to be a liberal on a number of issues), and attempted the political mobilization of a segment of the American population he dubbed the "silent majority." They were supposedly ordinary Americans who adhered to traditional verities like patriotism and were antagonistic to the values of both the establishment and the war protesters.

Given that Nixon's policies were dependent on smears, innuendo, confrontation, and polarization, they succeeded only in fragmenting any semblance of an American will. They pitted race against race, old against young, class against class, and region against region, leaving division rather than unity in their wake. This further disruption of the American will did not contradict the goals of the Nixon administration, for what he and his associates were really interested in creating was not a harmonious and cohesive American society and spirit, but an administration which embodied and defined the national will. This confidence (megalomania?) that his administration really was an expression of the American will provided Nixon with the rationale to indulge in whatever he felt politically necessary: to concentrate power in the White House; to use war methods against domestic enemies; and to use the power of the federal government to promote and maintain the image and reputation of the administration. In fact, for Nixon and his cohorts the image the administration projected was more significant than the substance, a notion that was far from new to American politics, but clearly gained much strength during the 1970s.[4]

In promoting its image the Nixon administration initiated a campaign of illegal activities. In 1971, after the release of the Pentagon Papers, the administration created a group of undercover operatives nicknamed "the plumbers." It was the covert activities of this group that led to the break-in at Democratic headquarters in June 1972 and the resulting Watergate scandal. The public revelation of the scandal and the administration's cover-up led to Nixon's resignation—though even in his final days of power Nixon was unable to confront and admit his own responsibility in the whole affair. Forcing Nixon and his hatchet men out of office (e.g., Vice President Agnew—for bribe-taking) undermined both the institution of the presidency and the whole American political ethos. The public began to distance itself from politics, expressing only cynicism about the rhetoric and programs that politicians proposed. By 1973 it was clear that the political passions and polarization of the sixties had died, replaced by a general sense of political alienation and apathy.[5]

Paralleling that shift in the public mood was the replacement of Nixon by his appointed vice president, Gerald Ford, the perfect figure to preside over a period of political stagnation. In 1976 Ford led a bicentennial celebration of American independence. The frenetic activity and the overblown rhetoric were a self-conscious attempt by Americans to demonstrate their confidence in the country despite almost fifteen years of wars, recessions, riots, and the assassinations and resignations of its leaders. The most poignant expression of this need for self-congratulation occurred in New York City. In 1975, perhaps symbolic of American society and especially of its older urban areas, New York had been brought to the brink of bankruptcy by a combination of such factors as middle-class flight, rising crime, a reduced tax base, increased demands for public services from a growing poverty population, economic demands of municipal unions, and the callousness and rapacity of the city's major banks. Only a last-minute loan guarantee by the federal government staved off financial catastrophe.

However, despite, or more likely because of, these economic and social conditions, New York staged "Operation Sail," one of the most impressive of the bicentennial ceremonies. During this celebration a fleet of white-sailed schooners and frigates from all over the world sailed up and down the Hudson River to the applause of immense crowds. New York's elaborate ceremony seemed to embody the nation's desire to affirm the power and resilience of the American will—no matter what the social realities were like.[6]

In fact, Jimmy Carter based his campaign for the Democratic presidential nomination in 1976 precisely on the nation's need to renew its belief in itself. Carter, a man of deep religious convictions (he was a "born-again" Christian) was aware of the country's need for spiritual talk rather than political rhetoric and programs. In his standard speech he talked about a government as good as its people, implicitly affirming a belief that the American will and spirit were still strong and vital. He also shrewdly sensed that after Nixon, the "character issue" was an important one for the American public and he promised in Sunday-school terms never to lie to the people.

In addition, Carter benefited from other American social and political strains. A "New South" had emerged since the 1960s, for with de jure elimination of racial segregation, Carter no longer had to deal with the southern politician's albatross of the Civil War, Reconstruction, and Jim Crow. Secondly, Carter was not a national politician or party chieftain; he was an outsider (one-term governor of Georgia) who could be projected as a fresh face untainted by Watergate. Finally, the all-pervasive power of the media had made it possible for a political figure to jump from obscurity to celebrity merely by making a number of successful television appearances.[7]

Carter's campaign avoided dealing with the issues or taking hard positions, and by invoking moral pieties and capitalizing on his outsider status he won a narrow victory over Ford in the 1976 election. However, though he was a skilled diagnostician of the public's yearnings, Carter's political talents did not seem to extend beyond the pursuit of power and the winning of elections. His first year in office was committed more to populist symbolism than to substance. Informal state dinners, telephone talks with ordinary citizens and nights spent at their homes, and wearing a cardigan sweater while announcing an energy plan that he conceived as the moral equivalent of war did not help him with Congress. Carter confronted an assertive Congress, which after Vietnam and Watergate was profoundly wary of the executive branch. Furthermore, Carter carried over from his campaign a blurriness over issues and an inability to make hard decisions. He equivocated in the Bert Lance scandal, tarnishing his image for integrity, and seemed to lack control over his cabinet and his low-comic brother Billy. More and more there existed a growing feeling that Jimmy Carter was too small a man to handle the presidency.[8]

In July 1979, after repeated attempts to untangle his administration, Carter tried to liberate himself from his ineffective and incompetent image by firing a number of cabinet members (Califano, Blumenthal, et al.) and making a speech updating his energy policy. It was more than just a speech about energy; it was in typical Carter style an expression of moral concern which attempted to rouse the American people from their malaise. It was a call to strengthen the American will by ridding it of its self-indulgence: "The erosion of our confidence in the future is threatening to destroy the social and political fabric of America . . . we have learned that piling up material goods cannot fill the emptiness of lives which have no confidence or purpose."[9]

Though this ministerial oratory was no substitute for a coherent energy policy, Carter's rhetoric did have cultural resonance and significance for the seventies. It paralleled the writing of culture critics such as Christopher Lasch and Tom Wolfe, who had called the 1970s a narcissistic era, the "me decade." They conceived the age as a period when people went about polishing, cultivating, and doting upon themselves and their relationships without regard to politics, society, or posterity. The mid-seventies had produced a culture built on a cult of personal relations which was often simply a result of a chaotic and destructive social world and devastated and empty private lives. This culture was characterized by a craving for intimacy without genuine human connection and sacrifice, material plenty without productivity, and success without real content or accomplishment. Hedonistic consumerism and the ethic of self-preservation—including an interest in the body ("working out," natural diets)—had become the order of the day.[10]

To some extent this collective narcissism was partially brought on by the failure and collapse of the New Left and counterculture in the early seventies. The "Movement" always differed from the old left by being concerned with problems of personal identity and authenticity. These problems, especially for those who were political or social activists, were rarely separated from a commitment to transforming American society. Of course, there were always activists who treated political action as merely a substitute for personal therapy. But by the seventies many of the survivors of the Movement had decided that one of the reasons for its failure (neglecting or dismissing historical and political explanations) was the nature of political commitment itself. What was now necessary to achieve some sense of peace and fulfillment was getting directly to the bottom of the self or losing oneself in various self-awareness movements (such as EST, Rolfing, and Arica), oriental gurus, and religious cults such as the Moonies and Jim Jones's suicidal People's Temple and bioenergetics.[11]

The premise underlying this intense preoccupation with the self was the assumption that unlimited personal growth would coincide with unlimited material prosperity. The belief was based on the post–World War II notion that continuous expansion was inherent in the very nature of the American economy; and, though blatant racial and economic inequities existed in America in the years from 1945 through the early seventies, America had the resources to create an economy successful enough to satisfy the material needs and yearnings of the majority of the people. Within that expansionist framework, American capitalism could vitiate resentment by keeping unemployment low, increasing social services, and mediating between the interests of capital and labor.

However, in the mid-1970s a change in public consciousness occurred. For the first time in American history public opinion polls reported that the American people were no longer optimistic about the nation's future. The country was beset with an economic crisis, which in fact was an underlying cause of Carter's 1976 victory. But Carter was ultimately unable to turn the economy around. By the end of his term rising oil prices, a debt-laden balance of payments, and the lack of competitiveness of the motor and steel industries had again thrown the American economy into severe recession.

In the 1980 election Carter was soundly defeated and the ex-actor and California governor Ronald Reagan was elected by a landslide to the presidency. There were many reasons for the repudiation of Carter and the Democrats—a recoil from big government and liberalism (though Carter was no liberal), personal rage and resentment towards Carter's supposed weakness and incompetence, and most importantly the hope that Reagan would resurrect the American will from its malaise. The public craved a candidate untouched by a sense of complexity and ambiguity, who could successfully package a simple belief in American might, power, and opportunity to right the ills of the nation. However, in 1980 the rebirth of the American will existed only in the realm of political rhetoric; the country was beset with perilous economic, social, and international difficulties which clearly would not be resolved by the intoning of patriotic and moralistic platitudes.[12]

During the seventies the film industry and its product reflected the confusion and malaise permeating the American will. At the beginning of the decade the industry was a chronic invalid, with studios losing a combined aggregate of 500 million dollars between 1969 and 1972, only to renew itself financially during the second half of the decade with grosses of almost 3 billion dollars. Early in the decade the old studios connected their fortunes to those of huge conglomerates like Kinney National Service. As a result, the men who produced the films had their eyes glued to the balance sheets rather than to the rushes. That meant fewer pictures, but those that were made had generous publicity budgets geared primarily to a youth audience between the ages of twelve and twenty-six.

Another element in this process was the changing relationship be-tween the movie industry and TV. It began with a period of all-out war in the fifties, moved to the casual embrace of the sixties, and by the seventies had become a passionate one. By preselling films both to pay and commercial television and cashing in on new video software (cas-settes, discs, and so on), Hollywood had minimized the possibility of losing immense sums of money on films. No longer did a studio have to worry about possible bankruptcy if one heavily financed film failed.[13]

There was at least one beneficial result from the financial difficulties of the seventies. In groping around for any means to make a comeback, the studios began to take chances and reach out to relatively untried film-makers such as Robert Altman, Martin Scorsese, Brian De Palma, Peter Bogdanovitch, Steven Spielberg, Michael Ritchie, and Francis Ford Coppola.[14]

What distinguished these directors was their awareness of film history, technical competence (sometimes gained from working on small-budget quickies or being trained in university film schools), and self-conscious, personal visions. A number of these directors made films that were self-reflexive in nature and veered from the formal stateliness and order and even, at moments, the sense of verisimilitude of the classical narrative. For instance, Robert Altman directed films that were highly personal, idiosyncratic versions of popular genres (e.g., film noir) like *The Long Goodbye* (1973), engaged in social comment and satire in *Nashville* (1975), and made dreamlike, European-style art films like *Three Women* (1977). Brian De Palma's varied output included the anarchic *Hi Mom!* (1969) and the Hitchcockian *Obsession* (1976). Francis Ford Cop-pola transformed the gangster film (*Godfather I* and *II*) into a tragic epic about the nature of Americanization.

In stark contrast to the old studio days when these directors and their cinematic styles and themes would have been subordinated to a whole battery of executive producers, they now retained a great deal more con-trol over scripts and actors. They often even had the power of the final cut. The studios had become primarily financiers and distributors, treat-ing film more as a business than an industry and consequently taking more interest in profit margins than in the substance of their product.

The transformation of the studios and the success of this more per-sonal form of filmmaking did not mean that Hollywood had opted for dispensing with the traditional genres. Genre films with their well-de-fined characters, actions, and iconography still resonated with Ameri-can audiences. In the sixties a number of films (e.g., *Easy Rider*) both cut across and modified the traditional genres focusing on buddies (rather than Hollywood's usual solitary hero), the counterculture, and blacks. However, despite *Easy Rider*'s becoming a landmark for the directors of the seventies, these new genres did not sustain their audience appeal. A number of the seventies' directors did make films that turned back to conventional genres like the gangster film and the thriller, but the effects of the counterculture and the New Left of the sixties and the sense of alienation and anomie were too great to make films that adhered to the structure and rules of classics like *The Big Sleep* (1946) and *Little Caesar* (1930). The genre conventions often existed now as a springboard for social commentary, psychological revelation, or parody and satire.[15]

The best examples of this use of genre were the protean Francis Ford Coppola's *The Godfather* (1972) and *The Godfather II* (1974). In their emphasis on the murders, violence, and Machiavellian manipulations of criminals, these films indirectly reflected American involvement in Vietnam and the political crimes of Watergate. The films also echoed Balzac's famous comment that behind every great fortune there rested a crime. But beyond these images of American corruption, the two films used a driving narrative rhythm, a luxurious use of light and shadow, and voluptuous camera movements to evoke the destruction of the American Dream.

Coppola based the films on Mario Puzo's commercially successful pulp novel and used it to invert the whole tradition of the gangster film. As Robert Warshow once wrote of the gangster film: "Since we do not see the rational and routine aspects of the gangster's behavior, the practice of brutality—unmixed criminality—becomes the totality of his career."[16] In the *Godfather* films Coppola begins with the very rituals and emotions that have been left out of the traditional gangster film—baptism and marriage, family solidarity and love—all of which serve as the foreground for the life of criminality, violence, and murder to which the characters remain committed.

The Godfather I centered on the idea of family and those rites of passage that celebrate and validate it. Dominating the film is gravelly-voiced Don Vito Corleone (Marlon Brando), an almost mythological figure—a murderer who is totally at ease with his authority and power. He is a man whose primary goal is to keep his family from dancing to another's strings, and who is committed to maintaining their security, dignity, and independence. Don Vito is a powerful force who can absolve people of their guilt and protect them from hurt. He is a monster, but in Coppola's view an almost sacred one. In *The Godfather*, for every dark, shuttered room where business and murder are plotted, there are still scenes where children play, marriages are held, and familial and communal warmth and light exist. The Don may live by violence, but Coppola allows him to die peacefully among the tomato plants in his garden.

Some of *The Godfather*'s audience appeal must have derived from the sense of order it evoked. In a time when many Americans felt the world had gone mad with assassinations, war, corrupt politics, and economic recession, there was a longing for a sane place where experience was relatively coherent and secure. In a nostalgic film like George Lucas's *American Graffiti* (1973) the time of innocence – of cruising and proms – is placed in the fifties, and in *The Godfather* that haven was the ethnic family. *The Godfather*, however, was a film drenched in blood, and neither the depiction of strong family roots nor the Don's rough, natural sense of justice could quite cancel out the image of a family whose business and success were totally involved in intimidation, violence, and murder.[17]

In *Godfather II*, Coppola decided to pursue the underside of the American success ethic in much greater depth. Using Don Vito's son and heir, Michael (Al Pacino), as the central character, the film captures the transformation of the American Dream into a nightmare of alienation and dissolution. In *Godfather II* the old tribal Mafia of Don Vito's New York–based Genco Olive Oil Company, with its numbers, juke boxes, and prostitutes, has begun to transform itself into a Lake Tahoe–based, acculturated, depersonalized, multinational corporation. With the abandonment of the old traditions, the quest for a veneer of corporate respectability and legitimacy has only tragic consequences.

Michael and "the family" have made it in America, and are powerful enough to command the support of a hypocritical and venal U.S. senator and to gather with the heads of other ("legitimate"?) multinational corporations to divide up the spoils in pre-Castro Havana. However, the family's mobility and new status have brought neither happiness nor repose, just pain and fragmentation. Michael is somber, remote, and unfeeling, all his life energies projected into the "business." His success results only in his sister Connie's (Talia Shire) hatred, in betrayal by his ineffectual, envious brother, Fredo (John Cazale), and in estrangement from his WASP wife Kay (Diane Keaton).

The decline of the family is filmed in dark, dimly-lit interiors and in sterile, luxurious rooms, where people can often be seen only in silhouette. It is a joyless world, and by intercutting and counterpointing luminous flashback sequences of the life of the young Don Vito (Robert De Niro), Coppola succeeds in vividly heightening the bleakness and desolation of Michael's universe. For though the immigrant world of Don

Vito's Little Italy may be impoverished and murderous, it is enveloped in golden-toned colors and light and shot in soft focus, nostalgically evoking a world of warmth and community. Don Vito himself is depicted in a heroic mold, a venerated, urban Robin Hood—courtly, self-possessed and courageous—a man who can help his fellow-immigrants by frightening an exploitative landlord out of his rapacity. Coppola does not hide the fact that Don Vito is a criminal, but he is one whose profound familial feelings and natural grace make his criminality almost socially acceptable.

However, in the move from the world of tenements, pushcarts, and religious processions to the armed fortress in Lake Tahoe, the personal and the familial have been lost. The haven of the family and the ethnic community (however claustrophobic and prescriptive) cannot be sustained under the fragmenting pressures of the capitalist success ethic. Coppola depicts Michael as attempting to hold onto aspects of the code—he believes in machismo and the sacredness of the family—but they exist for him primarily as abstract and formal ideals, and he is never able to convey the love for his children which the young and old Don Vito basks in. In fact, it is Fredo who acts as surrogate father for Michael's unhappy, melancholy son, Anthony. By the end of the film the unforgiving Michael has murdered and lost almost everything he has cared for and is seen in close-up sitting in tragic isolation, his face turned into a ghostly death mask.

The *Godfather* films did not pretend to provide a sophisticated left critique of capitalism and its ethos. However, while operating within the genre conventions, they were able to convey some of the perniciousness of the American success ethic. The films projected an epic of dissolution, conveying how Americanization and mobility turned the murderous passion and loyalty of the immigrant Mafia into an impersonal, rootless nightmare. Implicit in the films was the feeling that the nightmare extended far beyond the parochial confines of the Mafia into the heart of American history and society itself.[18]

Another film which, in a similar fashion, was consciously influenced by the political and cultural ferment of the sixties was Robert Altman's *Nashville* (1975). The film was Altman's epic and ironic attempt at capturing both middle-American consciousness, and the perniciousness and life energy of America's popular culture, which both helps shape and express it.

Indicative of the film's importance was that the *New York Times* assigned then-associate editor Tom Wicker to write a think piece about it. In it he called *Nashville* "a two and a half hour cascade of minutely detailed vulgarity, greed, deceit, cruelty, barely contained hysteria and the frantic lack of root and grace into which American life has been driven by its own heedless vitality."[19] In *Nashville* Altman interweaves twenty-four characters who are either participants in or dream of entering the world of country and western music. Using an open-ended, improvisatory style which centers around the actor, *Nashville* is built on privileged, seemingly disconnected moments, filled with dazzling aural effects and visual images, and demands close viewing from its audience (to pick up the elusive detail in frames packed with overlapping actions). In the film Altman evokes a callous, grasping, violent world in which everyone either gropes for stardom or lives off the fantasies and myths popular culture creates. The country and western stars are manipulative, absurd, hysterical—in the main, empty, vain people obsessed by crowd applause and their own status, while their public's behavior ranges from breathless adulation and emulation to petulance and rage.

Among Altman's "Grand Hotel" of stars is the doyen of country western music, Haven Hamilton (Henry Gibson), a self-important, narcissistic, and petulant tyrant stuffed into a tailored, sequined cowboy suit with a slightly askew toupee. Hamilton is a tough, ambitious little rooster whose songs "We Must Be Doing Something Right" and "For the Sake of the Children" exemplify the soporific and saccharine values of Nashville. The lead singing star, Barbara Jean (Ronee Blakley), a madonna dressed in white, is childlike, fragile, and neurasthenic. She is a symbol of how media success can help victimize and destroy a performer, painfully embodying the agony that lies between an unstable private self and a star's public role.

Altman's other characters run the range from a handsome, totally egoistical stud rock singer who plays tapes of his songs while he sleeps, to a pathetic off-key singing waitress, a dim, bizarre-looking, promiscuous groupie, and a ridiculous and pretentious BBC journalist. They inhabit a world where almost all relationships are subordinated to hustling for the main chance or to promiscuous scoring. It is a fragmented and alienated world where the characters, in the main, exist from moment to moment, and there is almost no person in the film capable of listening to or caring about what another person is saying. Altman's cool, idiosyncratic sensibility succeeds in turning Nashville's country music world into a metaphor for American life—a chaotic din where everybody is struggling for or has a gold record.

In *Nashville* everything is packaged, including politics. From the opening frame, when the sound truck of the Replacement party's presidential candidate, the pseudo-populist Hal Phillip Walker, patrols the predawn empty streets, to the final shot of his limousine leaving the climactic assassination scene, politics play a significant role in the film. It is a politics built on a canned voice and an invisible candidate; we never see Walker, just the detached, quietly contemptuous advance man, Triplette (Michael Murphy). And the party, with its slogan "new roots for the nation" and its platform calling for a new national anthem and the removal of lawyers from Congress, seeks national moral renewal by selling nostalgia and bumptious iconoclasm. The party is one more image without substance: boosters and a sound truck hawking the vagaries of the platform in the same way as the record albums are hyped over the opening credits.

Altman has created, through dynamic and seamless cutting and unrelenting movement within his densely packed frames, a frenzied world. It's a landscape he simultaneously loves and despises. One thinks of Whitman's catalogues of America now gone amuck; sound tracks overlap as cars crash, planes roar, marching bands perform, and TV newsmen drone on. This grasping, frenetic universe has its apotheosis in the assassination of Barbara Jean at a benefit concert for the Replacement party in Nashville's Parthenon. In this dazzling set piece of a finale, a seemingly innocuous boy with a guitar, acting out of some Oedipal rage or possibly out of the violence that permeates every pore of the society, shoots Barbara Jean. The act is an echo of the Oswalds, Sirhan Sirhans, and Arthur Bremers—the assassins and psychopaths that wander and menace the streets of contemporary America.

In the aftermath of the assassination the crowd, stunned and milling about, begins to participate in the ironic and chillingly repeated lyric, "You may say I ain't free, but it don't worry me." What sounds at first like a stirring song of solidarity and the courage to go on is one more turn of the screw, accentuated by the fact that a black choir leads the singing. The camera pans to close-ups of people in the crowd giving voice to the words, and then zooms away to a long shot of a stupefied, acquiescent mass. The song is a hymn to apathy and accommodation, a metaphor for an America which unthinkingly accepts its bondage to the media's plasticity, artifice, and banality.

Altman is a director who is in love with the ambiguity and complex texture of his images, behavioral tics, and social surfaces. His work is built on observation rather than exposition, intuition rather than analysis, and on a vision of a society based on chance rather than on one whose values can be systematically traced to a set of causes. Consequently, Altman is not interested in exploring popular music's historical and cultural content or dissecting the power groups that help shape the music industry. But he understands just how bountiful and destructive American popular culture is, and how the world of appearances and hype often beguiles and rules Americans. When his suggestive metaphors and images come alive, as they do in *Nashville*, they conjure up a monstrous and irrational America which is vivid, resonant, and true.

Nashville's vision of the role of the media—especially in the political arena—has grown more apt and pointed with each passing decade, though there was no denying the power of the media to shape American public opinion during the late sixties and seventies. In fact, other films were made during the decade like Michael Ritchie's *The Candidate* (1972) and Sidney Lumet's *Network* (1976) that criticized the power of the media.

The Candidate used a semi-documentary technique—natural sound, panning and tracking with a handheld camera, and a mixture of professional and nonprofessional actors—to evoke richly the mechanics of the political process and the power of the media to shape it. The film's protagonist is an idealistic, Kennedy-style, public service lawyer, Bill McKay (Robert Redford), who runs for the Senate in California against a glib, right-wing conservative. As the campaign evolves the frank-speaking, socially committed McKay acquiesces to being transformed into a handsome commodity who hedges on the issues and learns to speak in empty political slogans and vaporous rhetoric about "courage and compassion" so he can win the election.

The film does little with McKay's private self or marriage, but it has a political insider's knowledge of how to produce thirty second spots, write position papers, win endorsements, and engage in campaign debates, rallies, and speeches. The television cameras are ubiquitous in the campaign, and the candidates must learn to gear their persona and positions to the camera eye and sound bite. *The Candidate* is satirical about the nature of a media-governed politics, but it's too shrewd and knowing to offer quick fix alternatives to a political process with a genius for co-optation.

Network—winner of four Oscars—is utterly different intellectually and stylistically from *The Candidate*. Written by Paddy Chayefsky, it's a dark, shrill, sometimes expressionist comedy filled with television lampoons, rousing monologues, collective primal screams, and savage portraits of freaked-out anchormen and TV revolutionaries. Shot mainly in close-up and medium shot, *Network*'s images are totally subordinated to Chayefsky's speeches. In them he brings his wrath down on a corrupt and dehumanizing television world built on corporate jockeying and an obsession with Nielsen ratings. In Chayefsky's pessimistic vision the left is totally absurd, "the people" mesmerized sheep, and there is only one weary, honest, news department head—Max Schumacher (William Holden as an Edward R. Murrow clone)—to stand for what is honest and true.

Network is a moralistic, overstated film that strains for significance. But there are moments when it draws blood—it is especially good both in portraying the media's capacity for turning everything into a marketable commodity and in conveying the feeling that the television image has become reality for many Americans. Yet, in its desire to be outrageous, the film ironically often seems to be doing what television does— merchandising iconoclasm.

The two films may have savaged the role of television, but it's clear that without TV the antiwar and women's movements in the seventies would have had a lesser impact. Television covered feminist sit-ins at leading women's magazines and mass marches and demonstrations and held debates on men and women's changing roles and identities. Of course, television also vulgarized and merchandized feminism in various sitcoms and commercials such as the one for Virginia Slims cigarettes.[20] And its underlying attitude towards women and feminism was at best ambivalent and at worst destructive, but it succeeded in forcing the movement into the consciousness of the American public.

Hollywood in turn had no journalistic function, so it had even more difficulty in dealing with women's issues; especially since they went far beyond equal rights and equal pay and challenged sacred movie industry canons about the nature of sexuality and the family. For a time in the seventies Hollywood seemed to have banished most women from the screen and replaced them with buddy films such as *Scarecrow* (1973), *Little Fauss and Big Halsey* (1970), and *The Sting* (1973), works which concentrated on macho exploits and homoerotic bonds.

At the same time, however, Hollywood was being prodded to pay attention to changes in women's consciousness both by the women's movement and by powerful and popular actresses like Barbra Streisand and Jane Fonda. In addition, the rise of an independent women's cinema—which produced documentary films like *Joyce at 34* (1973), *Nana, Mom and Me* (1974), and *Union Maids* (1976) and features like Joan Micklin Silver's film about Jewish immigrants' adjustment to America, *Hester Street* (1975), and Claudia Weill's *Girlfriends* (1978)—dealt with women defining themselves through work and in other ways where their relation to men did not have primacy. These varied influences moved the mainstream film industry to make a stab at producing films where a women's exploration of identity was a central theme. One of the first of these, *Klute* (1971), was not only a box office success but an Academy Award–winner as well.[21]

Klute is John Klute (Donald Sutherland), a strong, silent, small-town policeman who comes to New York to pursue leads in the disappearance and possible murder of a close friend. The film is stylishly directed by Alan Pakula (*All the President's Men*, 1976), creating a paranoid, noirish New York of wiretaps, dark hallways, and lurking silhouetted figures. Pakula's compositions are nervous, with his characters placed on the extreme edge of the frame, and he often blacks out part of the screen to create feelings of isolation and tension. But the real focus of the film is not urban paranoia or the sadistic, murderous violence that lies behind respectable, corporate facades; it lies in the struggle for self-definition of a prime suspect in the case, a call girl, Bree Daniels (Jane Fonda).

Bree is a witty, seemingly confident, cynical, and self-destructive woman who wants to control her life but can only maintain some equilibrium when she operates as a call girl. It is a life she knows is going nowhere. Nevertheless, as she tells her therapist about her tricks: "I'm in control. When they come to me they're nervous; I'm not. I know what I'm doing. I know I'm good." In contrast to her power over the johns who share her bed, she has little control over the rest of her life. Although able to simulate sexual excitement and manipulate male fantasies as a call girl, she is merely an object or image, a commodity to be dismissed, when she pursues her acting and modeling careers.

What little control Bree has in her life is increasingly threatened by her love for Klute, an emotion she tries to fend off by continually manipulating and hurting him. Some of the film's best moments take place during Bree's sessions with her therapist, where she describes how she tries to destroy her feelings for Klute for fear they will engulf her and she will lose whatever autonomy she has. It is one of the few times in the history of American film that a therapeutic session seems natural and irreducible to psychological clichés and magical resolution.

Unfortunately, Klute's character does not quite transcend Hollywood stereotypes. He is portrayed as a man whose self-sufficiency is merely a muted affirmation of traditional Hollywood rites of machismo and whose passivity is a form of aggression. But the character of Bree gives the film a genuine sense of the problems of the seventies' "new woman." Breaking away from the old roles based on female dependency and commitment to domesticity and family means all sorts of new and anxiety-laden relationships and situations. At the end of the film Bree gives up her compulsive need to manipulate and control and leaves with Klute for his hometown. But she remains ambivalent about the relationship and informs her therapist in a voice-over: "I may be back in a couple of weeks."[22]

While Bree does not make the complete break with the traditional women's role in Hollywood—her possible happiness is predicated on her having a man to emotionally support her—the film does provide some feeling of a woman's struggle for a new identity. In a faltering manner, the film industry made a number of other gestures towards confronting the social and psychological issues raised by the women's movement. Films such as Paul Mazursky's satiric sex comedy *Blume in Love* (1973) and Martin Scorsese's film about a working-class widow who seeks to create a life of her own, *Alice Doesn't Live Here Anymore* (1974), reflected, in a compromised and commercialized fashion, the industry's struggle with constructing an image of the "new woman." There was also the lushly romantic—a great many soft focus close-ups and reaction shots— Streisand–Redford film *The Way We Were* (1973), about the doomed love affair of a passionate, Jewish leftist with a cool, handsome, uncommitted WASP. Streisand's aggressive heroine, being a committed activist, is willing to lose her love over a matter of moral principle, but the film subordinates its feminist and political strains to its romantic nostalgia.

Some of the women's films made during the second half of the decade tended to trivialize the problem by tying it to outworn genres like the "weepie" (*The Turning Point*, 1978) or a literate, female version of the buddy film (*Julia*, 1977). There were also films that dealt with supposedly liberated women, such as the comfortably feminist *An Unmarried Woman* (1978) and *Kramer vs. Kramer* (1979), which either provided talented, loving Prince Charmings to ease the pain of "liberation" or implicitly criticized the callousness of the newly emancipated women.

Kramer vs. Kramer was 1979's biggest commercial and critical hit, winning five Oscars (including ones for best film, director, and actor) and grossing over 60 million dollars domestically. It was the kind of work that *Time* could tout as a minefield of contemporary social issues. And though it did indeed deal with the breakdown of traditional concepts of marriage and family and with the male assuming the maternal role, much of its massive success rested with its remaining human and cozy in the old Hollywood style. It is a film that keeps under control the despair and chaos inherent in the abandonment by the liberated wife-mother Joanna (Meryl Streep) of her husband Ted (Dustin Hoffman) and her son, emphasizing instead the growing warmth and love between father and son. It also comforts rather than disturbs the audience, assuring them that in a time of fragmentation where egoism had become a prime virtue, humane qualities such as loyalty, decency, and self-sacrifice still exist.

Despite these limitations, *Kramer vs. Kramer* is an intelligent and accessible work which succeeds in conveying fresh and unsentimental truths about parents and children; the relationship between father and son is evoked in all its anguish, pleasure, and complication. The intensity of the father's love is most powerfully communicated in a scene where the boy receives a severe cut by falling off some playground monkey bars. The camera then focuses on Ted's despairing and guilt-ridden face as he races wildly with his son in his arms to the hospital. There are also perceptive scenes where Ted not only must try to be patient and compassionate with his son, but must feign affection and interest when he does not feel it or has his mind on other matters. And though Ted is clearly depicted as a caring, devoted father, he also can at times become prickly, tense, and easily irritated.

Nevertheless, *Kramer vs. Kramer* is a film that takes few formal or intellectual risks. Its emotions and images don't reverberate beyond what is presented within the frame. There is also a strain of antifeminism inherent in the film. It is Ted who garners the film's sympathy and applause by displaying the humanness and emotional strength (not without difficulty) that makes him capable of both pursuing a career and being a nurturing, committed parent. The wife's consciousness is never explored (except for the opening moments where in desperation and sorrow she prepares to tell her husband that she is leaving), and she is given relentlessly packaged feminist clichés (which in the context are unsympathetic): anguished-women-submerged-by-domesticity-careerist-husband-in-search-of-self.[23]

Despite these limitations there were clear advances for women in the films of the 1970s. Women's issues were consciously foregrounded and built into the narrative of the films, in ways the Joan Crawford and Bette Davis films about strong, well-defined women rarely did. For example, in *Norma Rae* (1979), a sentimental liberal film about a successful textile strike, the interest is focused more on the unformed heroine's (Sally Field) realizing her potential than on labor issues. Spunky Norma Rae has spent much of her life being used and abused by men, but the strike grants her the opportunity to discover that she is a courageous, intelligent, and independent woman. Still it's a man, an articulate, aggressive New York Jewish labor organizer, Reuben (played with broad, ethnic strokes by Ron Leibman), who acts as her intellectual and political mentor and guide. Though Norma Rae does not end the film in a classic romantic clinch with Reuben—submerging her identity in his— the majority of the other seventies' films still saw women usually back in place next to their man at the climax, despite the struggles for autonomy they engaged in through the body of the narrative.

In sharp contrast to the increasing number of films about women's quest for selfhood was the disappearance of the few serious films about black life (it was as if Hollywood decided to echo the Nixon–Moynihan notion of "benign neglect"). Black films had been commercially successful in the early seventies, with movies about heroic black studs and pimps like *Shaft* (1971) and *Superfly* (1972) ushering in a whole new genre called blaxploitation films (though they began to disappear by the mid-1970s).

There was also writer-director Melvin Van Peebles's more outrageous and controversial hit *Sweet Sweetback's Baadasssss Song* (1971), whose hero (played by Van Peebles) transforms himself from an apolitical black stud, who works in a whorehouse, into an indomitable avenging angel at war with and in flight from the police. The film is contemptuous of whites, who are seen as murderous brutes and buffoons, while it romanticizes the communal spirit of ghetto blacks. The anger and defiance at the heart of the film is more an expression of black rage towards whites than a coherent politics; the film is "dedicated to all those who have enough of the man." And among those who have had enough are a group of ghetto inhabitants—prostitutes, campy preachers, unwed mothers, and gamblers whose lives Van Peebles does not prettify, but still affirms and even exalts.

Sweetback is an overheated, overdirected film—inundated with flash cuts, tilts, freeze frames, voice-overs, double exposures, and the use of a split screen. However, it's a vivid and vital work, and though it is politically counterproductive to turn a sauntering pimp into a superhero and attempt to frighten and intimidate whites, the film's abrasiveness and rhetorical commitment to black power was successful in reaching a large black audience in 1971.

Films, in turn, that involved much less action and dealt with less sensational aspects of black life, such as *Claudine* (1974), *Conrack* (1974), and *The Bingo Long Traveling All-Stars* (1976), did not do well at the box office. With rare exceptions, black films needed a star personality such as Diana Ross (*Lady Sings the Blues*, 1972) or Richard Pryor (*Greased Lightning*, 1977), to get the crossover audience—whites who would not normally go to see a film about blacks. And although these stars could generally sell a film, they tended to be well-crafted escapist works rather than films that dealt with the psychological and social reality of black life. Hollywood clearly sensed that in the seventies both white guilt about the social status and problems of blacks had begun to disappear, and black civil rights organizations had lost much of their political potency and power. As a result, beyond the few black stars who had crossover appeal, black actors mainly played minor character roles. Hollywood's decision to avoid dealing with the complexity of black life and lives was clearly in tune with the dictates of the market and the political and social climate of the 1970s.

Of course, early seventies' Hollywood films did not speak in one voice. Not all films engaging in a critique of American society and culture were made from the perspective of women or blacks or by people adhering to left-liberal politics or the counterculture. There were a great many people in the sixties and early seventies who were appalled by what they perceived as a period dominated by permissiveness and social breakdown. Their answer to the political protests and alternative life styles was a return to traditional values of home, family, and law and order. Part of this yearning was turned by Hollywood into a nostalgia for a lone man with a gun bringing law and order to an untamed frontier, only this time that frontier included the city as well. *Death Wish* (1974) and *Walking Tall* (1974) were two prime examples of this film genre, but the best and most archetypal one was Don Siegel's brilliantly edited *Dirty Harry* (1971), starring Clint Eastwood.

Dirty Harry was a film about an avenging knight of a San Francisco police inspector, Harry Callahan, whose major targets besides criminals were the liberals and politicians whose laws and sentiments helped create a permissive social climate. In the film Harry pursues a psychopathic, hippie killer who has tortured and killed a number of people and culminated his series of atrocities by kidnapping a bus filled with children. Harry is a solitary, lean, indefatigable figure who will not be deterred by mere legalities, like civil liberties, or police rules until he has killed this personification of pure evil—there are no psychological or social explanations for the killer's behavior. Using heroic low-angle and full shots of the demigod Harry the film totally identifies with his perspective, making his superiors seem lame and weak, and Harry's skill at providing vigilante justice the only protection against a violent, demonic world. At the film's climax, in a scene reminiscent of *High Noon*, Harry throws his badge away into the water where the killer's corpse is floating. Obviously, it is only a beau geste, for in sequels like *Magnum Force* (1973) and *The Enforcer* (1976) Harry continues to relentlessly wage all-out war against radicals, homosexuals, and other groups he perceives as flotsam of a permissive society.[24]

Many of the films of the early and mid-seventies nicely illustrated how long it took for major cultural changes and trends to register in Hollywood. Whether or not their points of view were inspired by the political right or the left, many of these films were a spillover from the political

conflicts and social tensions of the sixties. For example, Alan Pakula's
Parallax View (1974) was a stunningly visual thriller (e.g., a wonderful
use of wide screen space and unique settings) about a politically nebulous right-wing conspiracy's assassination of a Kennedy-style politician,
which a government commission (i.e., the Warren commission) white-
washes by attributing the murder to a lone psychopath. The conspiracy
is all-encompassing, and the sullen, unflappable reporter Joe Frady's
(Warren Beatty) heroics are insufficient to defeat this omnipresent, evil
power. Another skillful, paranoid thriller and commercial success was
Sydney Pollack's *Three Days of the Condor* (1975), which evoked a desolate world of betrayers who work for the CIA. The film's last scene sees
its isolated hero played by Robert Redford going off to take his story
about a renegade organization that has gotten inside of the CIA to the
New York Times — a variation on Daniel Ellsberg and the Pentagon Papers. However, in this case, the film bleakly suggests that even the good,
respectable *Times* could be part of the conspiracy and may not publish
the story.

One film that acknowledged some of the major political and social
trends of the early seventies was Alan Pakula's big box office hit, *All the
President's Men* (1976). The film was based on the Woodward–Bernstein
book which painstakingly followed their investigation for the *Washington
Post* of the Watergate burglary and all its more ominous political ramifi-
cations. Shot in the characteristic Pakula mode — shadowy night streets
and apartment interiors, parts of the screen blackened out, the reporters
seen isolated on the frame in extreme long shot or dwarfed by Washington's buildings — the film combines the style of the thriller and the televi-
sion-style documentary drama which dramatizes actual events.

The two dogged, driven reporters — Woodward and Bernstein (Robert
Redford and Dustin Hoffman) — are treated here as icons, who use the
freedom of the press to preserve our constitutional rights and democracy. Their private lives and individual personalities — except for sketch-
ing the surface of Bernstein's tense, aggressive, chain-smoking
persona — are totally subsumed in the detailing of the investigation. The
film tries and sometimes succeeds in adding drama to the endless car
rides, phone calls, and meetings with the editors by creating an all-pervasive sense of danger. It sets a number of scenes in the murk of an
underground garage — complete with threatening footsteps and screech-
ing car tires — where Woodward meets his prime informant, Deep Throat
(Hal Holbrook). In this Pakula film the conspiracy is, of course, defeated,
and we are made to feel good about the press and the American system.
Still, the film eschews a full exploration of the political motivation and

institutional accommodation that was at the root of Watergate for the usual Hollywood emphasis on the courage of two individuals—Woodward and Bernstein.

Despite these conspiracy films, the industry sensed that the public sought some release from the years of Vietnam and Watergate. It turned, in the main, to mirroring political slogans like Ford's "time of healing" by relentlessly packaging escapist entertainment. Some of the films, such as the bicentennial blockbuster *Rocky* (1976), resurrected traditional American values like the Horatio Alger dream of "rags to riches." The fairytale dimensions of the film were projected both on and off the screen, since it was written by an unemployed and practically destitute actor, Sylvester Stallone, who became an overnight sensation and superstar and won an Academy Award.

Rocky was a film about a broken-down pug who also moonlights as an enforcer for a mob loan shark. However, in this fairy tale Rocky was depicted as combining the body of a circus strongman with the saintliness of St. Francis. He was kind to animals and small children and gave a break even to those who were behind in their payments to the loan shark. Rocky's big moment comes when the black heavyweight champion grants him a shot at the title. The scenes of his training and his Dionysian struggle with the champion Apollo Creed turn into a crudely stirring evocation and endorsement of the importance of honesty, perseverance, and hard work.

Rocky not only revived the Alger myth, it made ethnic, working-class Americans the prime actors and agents of the dream. In Rocky the film had created a character who existed as some prepsychoanalytic being, a man who could invoke nostalgia for a purer, simpler past. For the general film-going audience, working-class lives had, for the moment, become a preserve of spontaneity, warmth, and masculinity.

In fact, the success of *Rocky* made the white working class briefly fashionable in Hollywood again. The trend took off into solid, commercial hit like *Saturday Night Fever* (1978), and less successful films such as Paul Schrader's *Blue Collar* (1977), *F.I.S.T.* (1978), and *Bloodbrothers* (1978), all of which highlighted working-class characters and situations, though they were as interested in exploiting genre conventions as in exploring class realities.[25]

In *Saturday Night Fever* the hero, Tony Manero (John Travolta), conveys on the surface much of the same mixture of macho charisma, gentleness, and vulnerability as Rocky. But instead of the heroics taking place in the ring, his arena is the dance floor, where he is the local king of the disco. His undulating energy and dynamism on the dance floor, however, aren't sufficient to grant him a way out of his neighborhood wasteland. Tony's bound to a world composed of a stereotypical Italian-American mother and unemployed construction worker father, both of whom spend much of their time either putting him down or shouting at each other; a pill-popping, gang-banging, and fighting, oafish group of friends; and a job without a future as a clerk in a hardware store.

   Saturday Night Fever is a more complex and suggestive film than *Rocky*. Though *Rocky* cannot escape touching on certain social realities, such as decaying ethnic neighborhoods and racial conflict (Rocky as "the great white hope"), it still blurs, even obliterates, those tensions in a magical act of transcendence. However, *Saturday Night Fever* allowed much more of the anxieties of working-class life to intrude before submerging them in the romantic music of the Bee Gees and disco scenes shot through multicolored filters by a fluidly zooming and panning camera.

   Tony, however, though more sensitive, decent, and perceptive than his friends, is not another saintly Rocky. His character is built on a blend of crude street humor, macho posturing, and self-absorption. He can use and dismiss friends (male and female) without much sensitivity to their feelings. The film also touches on working-class sexism, frustration, rage, and the sense of social inadequacy working-class people feel when dealing with an upper-middle-class culture. *Saturday Night Fever* is still primarily a commercial, escapist work which does not delve too deeply into the full meaning of these problems and emotions. In fact, like *Rocky* (though in much more muted fashion) the film offers a second chance to Tony, a romance with an upwardly mobile secretary, Stephanie (Karen Lee Gorney), and the repudiation of his Brooklyn world for a supposedly more humane and exciting life in upper-middle-class Manhattan.[26]

   Along with *Rocky*'s affirmation of the American Dream came a revival of the traditional Hollywood theme of the uncommon common man. For example, in Steven Spielberg's *Jaws* (1976), the family man as hero is affirmed amidst blockbuster technical effects and a consummate building of tension and suspense. The most memorable elements in *Jaws* are the skillfully edited scenes of a killer shark's attack on a summer resort. However, though the ominous shark has a great deal of life, the film's central characters are thinly sketched. Among them is a middle-class family man, police chief Martin Brody (Roy Scheider), who battles against the cover-ups of the town's corrupt mayor and ultimately kills the shark. He only does that after the upper-class technologisms of ichthyologist Matt Hooper (Richard Dreyfuss) and the working-class machismo of the Ahab-like sailor Quint (Robert Shaw) have failed. By turning Brody into the film's hero, *Jaws* implicitly celebrated the virtues of fidelity and family instead of glorifying the heroic loner.[27]

But even *Jaws* was touched with the anxieties of the real world. In George Lucas's *Star Wars* (1977), the ultimate in escapism was achieved by creating a magical world, somewhat similar to the American West, where heroic action could find its proper setting. The audience no longer had to be bothered by images of real streets, problems, and people; it could lose itself in outer space. In *Star Wars* Lucas threw everything he knew into the picture—a catalogue of genre entertainments of the last thirty years—and capitalized on America's passion for technology. The film is populated with almost-human, cuddly robots, computers, and alien beings (looking like an ape version of the *Wizard of Oz*'s cowardly lion), and scenes of glorified combat with rocket fighters right out of the World War II films—all of it placed in a fantasy galaxy. Lucas's inventiveness is framed within a story of a "quest" for the "force" in a hierarchical world which does not only consist of robots, but contains knights, villains in black, princesses, and priests, all of which were staples of adventure fiction, comic books, and fairy tales. Even if Americans were no longer willing to follow the lone cowboy as he eternally cleaned up the frontier, they flocked in record numbers to see Luke Skywalker and his cohorts as they blasted through space and shot it out with Darth Vader.[28]

Shoring up this return to past values and genres were films evoking occult dread and divine power. Starting with *The Exorcist* (1973), a terrifying film directed by William Friedkin (*The French Connection*, 1971), these works began to denounce the sins of modernism and implied that only true faith could ensure peace and tranquility. *The Exorcist* was conceived by its scriptwriter, the Jesuit-trained William Peter Blatty, as part of his "apostolic work."[29] The film describes how two gentle, heroic priests invoking Christ's name cured or exorcised of demonic possession (at the expense of their own lives) the young daughter of a free-thinking, divorced actress after all else, including impotent doctors and psychiatrists had failed. Besides preaching the true faith, *The Exorcist* and other similar works—for example, *The Omen* (1976) and *Exorcist II* (1977)—also undermined the idea of individual or moral responsibility for one's behavior. *The Exorcist*, though primarily a work of well-crafted horror—using sound and elaborate makeup to evoke anxiety and fear in its audience—still projected in a cold and impersonal manner that the acts of human beings are determined by powerful demonic forces.

Though little intellectual credibility could be given to a belief in demonic forces, *The Exorcist* was symptomatic of a number of Hollywood films of the second half of the decade. In contrast to films of the first half of the decade, which either attacked American capitalism and culture for its corruption, murderousness, and creation of ersatz values, or saw criminality aided by liberalism overwhelming traditional institutions, many of the second-half films affirmed traditional American values such as a belief in mobility, family, technology, and religion.

That is not to say that there weren't a number of major films that didn't quite fit into either category. One of the best American directors of the 1970s and 1980s was Martin Scorsese, whose work was built on emotional extremity, pulsating energy, and formal boldness. Two of his most original and imaginative works were critical successes and starred Robert De Niro. *Mean Streets* (1973) is an edgy, violent film which fuses realist and expressionist imagery to unsentimentally evoke the codes and rituals of "the boys" in New York's Little Italy.

Taxi Driver (1976) was a more murderous, alienated, and hallucinatory film than *Mean Streets*. It centered on a paranoid, solipsistic, and strangely innocent New York City cab driver Travis Bickle (De Niro), who, isolated behind his glass partition, drives all night around nightmarishly beautiful Manhattan streets filled with junkies, pimps, and twelve-year-old hookers. Bickle is a man who carries "bad ideas in his head," and with an arsenal of weapons wants to clean the city—"an open sewer"—of its scum. *Taxi Driver* is not *Dirty Harry*—Scorsese is not advocating vigilante justice—neither is the film a social reformer's portrait of urban squalor and disintegration nor is it a critique of the condition of 1970s America.

Scorsese's obsessions are primarily psychological and aesthetic rather than social and political. *Taxi Driver*, with its cinematic references, voice-over, restlessly moving camera, high overhead shots, semi-abstract sequences, extremely tight close-ups of Bickle's mad eyes, use of slow motion, and its sweltering night city of shadows, neon lights, shimmering shapes, and manhole covers emitting steam is not interested in providing a documentary or social realist view of the city. The emphasis here is on one alienated man's personal hell—most of the film shot from Bickle's point of view—which is shaped by the dark ambience of film noir and Scorsese's own personal demons and fantasies and fragmented view of the world. Scorsese has made a riveting, virtuosic work, where, breaking from classical Hollywood conventions, he creates no truly redeemable characters and concludes the film on an ambiguous, open-ended note.

Another major director of the seventies whose work could not easily be placed in either category was Woody Allen, America's prime comic auteur. By the late 1970s Allen's films were no longer nightclub-based, cartoon-style works filled with one-liners and pratfalls (e.g., *Bananas*, 1971), but comedies with serious moral intentions and characters capable of genuine suffering. The best of them was *Manhattan* (1979), a tragi-comedy with a coherent narrative and a distinctive visual style. The film opens with a glorious, loving montage of Manhattan icons and avenues—Lincoln Center, Park Avenue—the final image being a spectacular fireworks display over Central Park. Allen's New York is not Scorsese's; it's chic, comfortable, safe, and romantic, and it sways to a Gershwin tune. His upper-middle-class, urban New Yorkers, however, though they may live in a cultivated city whose beauty can "knock you out," are neurotics—irresponsible and egoistic individuals unable to sustain commitments to work or to other people.

Allen, of course, still remembers how to be funny. He wittily satirizes the cultural games New York intellectuals and demi-intellectuals engage in: Mary's (Diane Keaton) seamless flow of pretentious art crit jargon, and talk of the wrong kind of orgasm at a MOMA fund raiser. But in *Manhattan* he never allows a sight gag or a one-liner to disrupt the film's moving, comic-pathetic portrait of intelligent people who live self-deluded, unrealized lives.

Allen's film, like Scorsese's, could be read, on one level, as a critique of contemporary American urban life, but his perspective was neither shaped by nor derived from the movements of the sixties. As an antidote to contemporary moral decay, Allen constructs a personal pantheon which includes Willie Mays, Ingmar Bergman, Groucho Marx, and Louis Armstrong. His heroes aren't hip or politically radical; they have a sense of purpose, discipline, and genius—virtues that Allen clearly sees as having been lost by the often emotionally flabby and intellectually compromised characters that inhabit his cinematic universe.

Allen and Scorsese's films were anomalies: *Rocky* came much closer to what the Hollywood mainstream was all about in the second half of the decade. The ultimate test of this renewed commitment to patriotism and the American Dream was to see how Hollywood would handle the Vietnam war. All through the war it had shied away from any films that dealt directly with the conflict. Despite some films (*Bonnie and Clyde, The Wild Bunch*) which could be seen as oblique metaphors for the war, there was doubt whether Hollywood would ever directly confront the issue. In an industry whose basic operating premise is that an appeal to the lowest common denominator is one of the keys to making a profit, dealing with a war that was so divisive and controversial was seen as a recipe for financial disaster.

However, as a number of successful novels and memoirs on the war were published, and people's passions about Vietnam cooled, films dealing with the war began to seem less risky. Moreover, books such as Tim

O'Brien's National Book Award–winning novel *Going After Cacciato*, and Michael Herr's dazzling, feverish *Dispatches*, projected the feeling that only a film could convey the nightmarish and absurdist imagery of the war–making the ultimate statement about Vietnam and integrating it into the national consciousness. Consequently, after the release of a number of smaller films about Vietnam, (*Boys in Company C*, 1978; *Tracks*, 1978; and *Go Tell The Spartans*, 1978), the war and its impact were treated in three big-budget films: *Coming Home* (1978), *The Deerhunter* (1978), and *Apocalypse Now* (1979).

Coming Home, directed by Hal Ashby, was a film structured around a traditional love triangle which mixed a touch of feminism and some painful Vietnam realities to give the film political and cultural significance. The primary focus is on a romantic affair between a Marine Corps captain's wife and former cheerleader, Sally Hyde (Jane Fonda), and a paraplegic Vietnam veteran, Luke Martin (Jon Voight). Sally is transformed by her love for Luke from a repressed, conventional wife into a sexually liberated and somewhat independent woman, while Luke changes from an embittered, totally dependent cripple into an empathetic, politically and sexually active handicapped person. The third person in the triangle, eager, ambitious Marine Captain Bob Hyde (Bruce Dern), goes off to Vietnam without any hesitation and returns submerged in suicidal despair, evoking the alienation and moral disintegration that often accompanied front-line service in Vietnam.

The romantic triangle and the radical transformations of character in the main seem simplistic and unconvincing. Sally's changes lack internality and are built on her achieving orgasm with Luke (aided by the Beatles' "Strawberry Fields" on the soundtrack), and they are expressed primarily through stylistic changes in dress and hairdo. Luke's emergence as a caring, almost saintly figure is too sudden to be credible and makes the film seem smug about America's capacity to turn the resentful vets into symbols of postwar hope.

Despite the facile Hollywood touches, there are moving moments where the film captures a great deal of the texture of the war's terrifying legacy. The scenes in the veterans' hospital of the crippled GIs oppressed by nightmares, talking unselfconsciously, and often with black humor, about the war and the pain they experience, seeing them being sponged, fed, and getting high, carries a great deal of emotional resonance and authenticity. The hospital's physical condition and medical care are no horror show, but the vets feel walled in–they see themselves as carrying too much of the war's reality for ordinary people to deal with except by treating them as objects of pity.[30]

Coming Home is a film openly critical of the war, which never quite goes to the heart of the Vietnam experience. The nightmare of combat is left to our imagination and whatever can be gleaned from Bob Hyde's memories. More importantly, the film shies away from the war's political and historical context – emphasizing its link to American machismo – and tries to mute the specific terrors of the war by providing overly-neat moral and psychological transformations and an upbeat final image of Luke and Sally spending a joyous, sunny day on the beach.

The terror of Vietnam was clearly not purged from Michael Cimino's *The Deer Hunter*. Cimino's controversial epic was alternately condemned as being racist or a total distortion of the truth or praised for being cinematically brilliant and emotionally devastating by critics and Vietnam war correspondents. The film even brought on hostile demonstrations by anti-war activists when it won the Academy Award in 1978.

The three central figures in *The Deer Hunter* are three apolitical, young, Russian-American steelworkers, Michael – the film's central figure – (Robert De Niro), Nicky (Christopher Walken), and Steven (John Savage), from a milltown in western Pennsylvania who go off, without qualms, to fight in Vietnam. These are men who are linked to each other and their ethnic community not by words, but by a number of visible and invisible strands of ritual and memory. Cimino is in love with their rituals and turns every experience (e.g., lip synching rock songs, drinking, and hunting) into an elaborate ceremony. And he is more concerned with constructing images of a warm, working-class community than with illuminating the social structure and culture of that world. The apotheosis of Cimino's homage to traditional, working-class life is the ethnic wedding sequence. It is lovingly detailed with the camera dollying around the wedding participants, which include young children, stocky Slavic housewives, grizzled older workers, and all the film's major characters, evoking the joy, energy, cacophony, and brawling stupidity of the celebration.

Despite Cimino's use of long takes, natural sound, and nonprofessional actors to capture the formlessness of authentic experience, he gives a sentimental gloss to his working-class milieu. It's a more intact and satisfied community than ever graced *Rocky*, *Saturday Night Fever*, or factory towns in the late 1960s. *The Deer Hunter*'s steel mill is no "dark satanic mill" filled with alienated and resentful workers, but an elegant monolith where sooty, sweating workers labor with gusto and even pleasure amid intense noise and blast furnace flames. The three steelworkers are untouched by dreams of mobility and feel that all they have ever desired in life "is right here."

This almost Edenic image of the working-class community serves to make what follows in the second half of the film in Vietnam even more horrific. The second half begins with the use of a handheld camera to make the audience viscerally feel the terror of Vietnam combat. There are no limits in this war—everyone, including civilians and soldiers, women and children, can be either shot or burned alive. However, Cimino's focus is not on combat, but on the emotional effects of the war on the three steelworkers, whose point of view the film embraces.

Vietnam's abattoir disrupts them all to different degrees, and their connection to each other and their community is almost totally torn apart. The only one of the trio who comes out of Vietnam able to function (though disoriented) is Michael, the deer hunter of the title. Cimino conceives Michael as a working-class superman in the romantic tradition of James Fenimore Cooper's *The Deerslayer*, a frontiersman who stood on the periphery of his society and struggled with nature to define his manhood. Michael, in turn, is still one of the boys who wrestles, jokes, guzzles beer, and has a deep link to his friends. But like Cooper's Bumppo he is silent, stoical, and sexually chaste, given to inarticulate poetic yearnings beyond the emotional understanding of his friends. He is also a man of almost superhuman will—an indomitable, fearless figure who is able to calmly confront and triumph over death. It's his will that saves the trio through the slaughter of their National Liberation Front captors when they are tortured in an emotionally draining, politically manipulative, and stunningly edited Russian roulette session (purely a fictional conceit of Cimino's).

If the film lacks a conscious, coherent political ideology, its total identification with Michael's rectitude and heroism has the politically invidious effect of inverting history, making the Americans innocent victims and the Vietnamese the aggressors in the war. In close-up the Vietnamese (including the South Vietnamese) are seen as "the other," demonic or decadent variations of "the yellow peril." The film suffers from a case of political and moral amnesia, forgetting that it was the Americans who were the aggressors and extended the basically civil and colonial conflict, who carpet-bombed and napalmed the Vietnamese and adulterated and destroyed the social fabric of South Vietnam. *The Deer Hunter* ultimately personalizes history, constructing a war where good Americans struggle to survive against bad Vietnamese, rather than one where political ideology, Cold War politics, and nationalism play a determining role.

The film's final scene provides a perfect illustration of Cimino's gift for moving us emotionally with action that is politically and intellectually

callow. After Nick's funeral, Michael and his friends sit in numbed silence and then suddenly begin to sing "God Bless America" in tremulous
voices. Their singing uneasily affirms a tattered American will and community. One wants to believe that Cimino is providing, on one level, an
ironic commentary on their continued patriotism, but there is no sign of
irony in the sequence. Given the terror and extremity of the Vietnam
charnel house the film depicts, it is impossible simply to empathize with
this ritual of reconciliation. Obviously, Cimino's artistic strength lies in
using mise-en-scène and editing to create striking, indelible images and
to arouse us emotionally. What the film lacks is the kind of historical
and social imagination that would allow it to go beyond its working-class
superman conceit and evoke the political heart of Vietnam.[31]

Despite its intellectual limitations and distortions, The Deer Hunter did
convey a sense of the spiritual desolation and destruction that Vietnam
caused for many Americans. However, the film not only raised a great
deal of controversy, but was often taken by audiences as a homage to the
American cause in Vietnam. As a result, it made the final release of
Francis Ford Coppola's Apocalypse Now (1979) that much more eagerly
awaited. There was a feeling that this film would provide for the public
an emotional catharsis and be the final word about the war. Coppola
reinforced these expectations when he equated the making of the film
with the war itself. He said that he had made Apocalypse Now just the
way America made war in Vietnam. That there were too many people,
too much money spent and equipment used there, and little by little the
cast and crew went insane.

Apocalypse Now was loosely based on Joseph Conrad's Heart of Darkness, particularly its evocation of the emotional and moral rot of imperialism. It opens with an image of apocalyptic flames superimposed over a
sweating, drunken Willard – the novella's Marlow (Martin Sheen). Willard has the mad eyes and ravaged looks of a man who has lived and
seen too much. In the film he is a burnt-out government hit man with
six kills to his credit, whose mission is to terminate the life of Colonel
Kurtz (played with little sign of real involvement by a bulging, mumbling Marlon Brando), a rogue Green Beret colonel who had set himself
up as a tribal God, engaging in a private war against the North Vietnamese and Vietcong in the Cambodian jungle.

Using Willard's pilgrimage as a framework Coppola constructs a hallucinatory, surreal Vietnam – the war as absurdist epic. The film is filled
with spectacular scenes touched with a sense of the absurd: an exhilarating Gotterdammerung helicopter attack led by Colonel Kilgore (Robert
Duvall as an exaggerated version of General Patton), to whom napalm is

the perfume of victory and the purpose of destroying a Vietcong village is to discover the perfect wave for surfing; the revolt of sex-starved soldiers as they rush the stage after being tantalized and provoked by a garish USO bump and grind show of undulating Playboy bunnies; and an officerless and forgotten platoon of anxious black GIs despairingly shooting into the darkness (accompanied by atonal music, disembodied voices on the soundtrack, and flares lighting up the sky) in the "asshole of the world"—the last American outpost on the border between Vietnam and Cambodia. These set pieces and a number of Coppola's other terrifyingly luminous images grant the film great visual power and a genuine feeling for the chaos and lunacy of the war. Still there is something excessive about much of it—not enough repose and moral balance to give some perspective on the almost unrelieved madness and abundance of special effects that fills the film's frames.

What hurts the film most is that the ultimate confrontation between Kurtz and an empty and exhausted Willard is anticlimactic. Willard is too saturated in death and a sense of nothingness to be morally transformed (as Marlow is in Conrad's version) by meeting Kurtz. In fact, there is little interaction between them, as an imprisoned Willard sits passively listening to Kurtz's gnomic and pretentious monologue, which is permeated with literary allusions ranging from Eliot's *The Hollow Men* to the *Golden Bough*.

In Kurtz, Coppola has created a metaphysical abstraction—the superman incarnate—a man who speaks of himself as transcending conventional opinion and morality. He advocates, in almost Nietzschean terms, that judgment defeats us and "we must make friends with moral terror." And Coppola's superman engages in the ultimate assertion of will: he wills his own and his followers' death.

Nevertheless, all Kurtz's philosophic musings and imperial posturing turn him into such a self-conscious symbol that the particular historical and social reality of the Vietnam war and America's role there is replaced by an abstract and nebulous notion of civilization's madness. The terror is universalized—it's seen as a part of the human condition, not as a product of concrete political forces. In constructing his version of Kurtz, Coppola strains for significance, trying to sum up the highly charged and sometimes overly-spectacular imagery of the film's first two-thirds with a symbol that has little emotional or political resonance.

In addition, Coppola demonstrates little critical distance from his conception of Kurtz. One senses that though Coppola may, on the one hand, morally recoil from the war's murderousness and madness, on the other, he identifies, even embraces, Kurtz's megalomania and extremity.

So when Dennis Hopper's manic photojournalist speaks of Kurtz as a "great man," as an archetypal figure who has his own "dialectic logic"—he is not parodied for his portentous babbling but is seemingly expressing one strain in Coppola's vision. In *Apocalypse Now* that vision itself was often blurred, Coppola sacrificing clarity for stylistic effects.

There is a German proverb that states that a war creates three armies: an army of cripples, an army of beggars, and an army of the unemployed. The Vietnam war had created a fourth army: one of filmmakers. But in the seventies these were directors who substituted a gift for inventive metaphors and symbols and startling images for an ability to penetrate the heart of darkness that was Vietnam.[32]

Of course, Hollywood has rarely tried to penetrate that heart—in either Vietnam or at home in New York or other American cities. It has usually used well-honed conventions and ceremonies to mute those profound anxieties and avoid looking too closely at what is. The Academy Award ceremonies of 1978 were just the sort of an occasion where Hollywood utilized its genius for shaping public rituals and neutralizing what was politically or emotionally threatening. John Wayne (in his last public appearance before his death) was called to present the Oscar for best film to Michael Cimino for *The Deerhunter.* In the sixties and seventies Wayne had become synonymous with the traditional American verities and with a virulent, jingoistic right-wing politics. Though *The Deerhunter* was clearly no left-wing film, its alienated and maimed soldiers (though there was still a stoical, courageous hero) caught in a futile war were a far cry from the tough, confident, uncomplicated fighting men portrayed by Wayne in *They Were Expendable* (1945) and *The Sands of Iwo Jima* (1946). The ceremony brought together the two Hollywoods: Wayne, who had gone through the ranks from bit player to icon, and Cimino, who without the long apprenticeship common to the old studio system (he had made only one previous film, *Thunderbolt and Lightfoot,* 1974) found himself with a multimillion-dollar picture in his hands. As it had done so often in the past, Hollywood had found the appropriate ceremony to absorb, exploit, or mute what could be seen in some ways as deviant and new.

Even without the death of John Wayne giving the decade a symbolic capstone, the seventies were an end to an era in American films. Gone forever were even the remnants of the old Hollywood production system, and in its place the studio had become a financial clearinghouse, dependent on independent producers rather than a rationalized assembly line. The old Hollywood which could produce family pictures cheerily affirming individual mobility and success, family, and patriotism had almost disappeared. Its values were now open to question or even repudiation, and the films conveyed a greater sense of uncertainty about what was true and right than in the past. None of these changes, however, meant that much of the old Hollywood had not survived. It was still an industry where big-budget films were dominant, where stars called the shots as much or more than they ever did, and where television staples like situation comedies provided a large portion of the creative models for filmmakers. And in a faltering and confused way, Hollywood still had the commercial magic and potency to create worlds which could simultaneously hint at what American social reality was like and skillfully obscure it.

NOTES

1. Jonathan Schell, *The Time of Illusion* (New York: Alfred A. Knopf, 1976).

2. Godfrey Hodgson, *America in Our Time: From World War II to Nixon, What Happened and Why* (New York: Vintage, 1978), pp. 239-40.

3. Hodgson, *America in Our Time*, p. 398.

4. Schell, *The Time of Illusion*, pp. 77-134.

5. Theodore H. White, *Breach of Faith* (New York: Dell, 1975).

6. Gerald R. Ford, *A Time to Heal* (New York: Berkeley, 1980), pp. 378-80.

7. James Wooten, *Dasher* (New York: Signet, 1978).

8. Wooten, *Dasher*, p. 298.

9. Wooten, *Dasher*, p. 301.

10. Christopher Lasch, *The Culture of Narcissism* (New York: Warner Books, 1979).

11. *Ibid.*

12. Lou Cannon, *Ronald Reagan* (New York: G. P. Putnam's Sons, 1982).

13. James Monaco, *American Film Now: The People, the Power, the Money, the Movies* (New York: Oxford University Press, 1979).

14. Diane Jacobs, *Hollywood Renaissance: The New Generation of Filmmakers and Their Works* (New York: Delta, 1980).

15. Monaco, *American Film Now*, pp. 54-68.

16. Robert Warshow, *The Immediate Experience* (Garden City, N.Y.: Anchor, 1964), pp. 38-39.

17. Jacobs, *Hollywood Renaissance*, pp. 115-18.

18. Leonard Quart and Albert Auster, "The Godfather, Part II," *Cineaste* VI, 4 (Winter 1976), pp. 38-39.

19. Tom Wicker, quoted in Judith M. Kass, *Robert Altman: American Innovator* (New York: Popular Library, 1978), p. 193.

20. Leonard Quart, "Altman's Films," *Marxist Perspectives* I (Spring 1978), pp. 21-33.

21. Molly Haskell, *From Reverence to Rape: The Treatment of Women in the Movies* (Baltimore, Md.: Penguin, 1974), p. 366.

22. Haskell, *From Reverence to Rape*, p. 369.

23. Leonard Quart and Barbara Quart, "Kramer vs. Kramer," *Cineaste* X, 2 (Spring 1980), pp. 37–39.

24. Stuart M. Kaminsky, *Don Siegel, Director* (New York: Curtis Books, 1974), pp. 268–83.

25. Leonard Quart and Albert Auster, "The Working Class Goes to Hollywood," in Philip Davies and Brian Neve (eds.), *Cinema, Politics and Society in America* (Manchester, U.K.: Manchester University Press, 1981), pp. 163–75.

26. Albert Auster and Leonard Quart, "Saturday Night Fever," *Cineaste* VIII, 4 (Winter 1978), pp. 36–37.

27. Peter Biskind, "Jaws between the Teeth," *Jump Cut* 9 (Fall 1975), pp. 3–4.

28. Dan Rubey, "Star Wars," *Jump Cut* 18 (Summer 1976), pp. 9–14.

29. Josh Rofkin, "The Exorcist," *Screen Talk* (September 1975), p. 54.

30. Albert Auster and Leonard Quart, *How the War Was Remembered: Hollywood and Vietnam* (New York: Praeger, 1988), pp. 50–52.

31. Auster and Quart, *How the War Was Remembered*, pp. 58–65.

32. Auster and Quart, *How the War Was Remembered*, pp. 65–71.

6

THE EIGHTIES

The politics of the 1980s were dominated by Ronald Reagan's serene, amiable personal style and right-wing politics. Reagan's political "philosophy" was built around aggressive anticommunism and an antagonism to big government and the welfare state. These commitments, ironically, made this enemy of state intervention into the best friend in government that the American military-corporate power structure ever had. The 25 percent tax cut enacted in his first year in office delighted business, as the almost ten percent increase over inflation in military spending pleased the Pentagon. And his cuts in domestic spending—health care, low-cost housing, and income maintenance programs—elated conservatives, who saw them as the beginning of their long-hoped-for counteroffensive against five decades of the welfare state.

At first, however, Reagan economic policy—critics named it "voodoo economics" as a contemptuous substitute for its original "supply side" title—resulted in the worst bout of unemployment (one factor in the creation of a subculture of homeless people who continue to wander and often sleep on the streets of American cities), bankruptcies, and corporate deficits since the Great Depression. Nevertheless, despite the growing income gap between the rich and poor and the failure of what were essentially his "trickle down" economic tenets, Reagan rigidly held onto his beliefs, shoring them up with anecdotes about welfare "cheats" and a philosophy of voluntarism that seemed to owe as much to Frank Capra (a Capra without a social conscience) as to Herbert Hoover.

Nor was this film-based political vision confined to economic affairs.

In foreign policy, during his "Darth Vader" speech, Reagan referred to the Soviet Union as an "evil empire," and extended the Star Wars metaphor even further by justifying his massive military buildup with allusions to as yet unbuilt space weapons that would presumably deter Soviet aggression. It seemed as if America had finally acquired a president who was deeply committed to all the crackbrained fantasies and mindless, empty rhetoric peddled by Hollywood ever since it became the center of America's popular culture.

Obviously, Reagan's saber rattling (which included the arming of a rebel force, the contras, against the leftist Sandinista regime in Nicaragua and the overthrow of an ultra-left revolutionary government on the island of Grenada in 1983) had a disquieting effect on America and its allies. If nothing else it helped relaunch antinuclear and disarmament campaigns that had lain dormant for a number of years. In small towns and large cities people all over the world began again to protest against the Strangelovian nuclear policies of the last forty-five years. In a similar fashion, by unleashing free market forces, particularly on the air, land, and workplaces of America (dismantling the Environmental Protection Administration (EPA) and placing people in charge who unblinkingly served the special interests), Reagan incurred the ire of the nation's environmentalists.

Nonetheless, despite these problems, midterm election losses, and an unemployment rate of over ten percent, Reagan continued to gain the approval of the majority of Americans. Much of it had to do with his undoubted charm, his quickness with a quip and his calming nice guy demeanor, media assets that, when coupled with his actor's talent for assuming the presidential role and playing the "Great Communicator," led him to an easy election victory over a serious, uncharismatic Walter Mondale in 1984. Reagan's triumph clearly demonstrated that the American public's obsession with imagery and personality went so deep that this politically unreflective and callow figure—this shallow man who seemed all persona—could do no wrong in their eyes.[1]

Of course, by 1984 the economy had revived, though there was an immense budget deficit, economic weak spots in the old industrial areas of the Northeast and Midwest, and blacks and the poor were clearly economically worse off. In fact, in the 1980s the living standard for the bottom fifth of the population dropped by 8 percent while the top fifth's standard of living rose by about 16 percent.[2] Wealth became increasingly more concentrated as a result of Republican policies. The public, however, cared little about the difficulties of the poor—the poor living at a great remove from most people's daily experience. The public also felt that times were prosperous and success was open in America to anybody who worked hard at achieving it. And even a precipitous decline of the price of farm commodities in 1985, and a trade shortfall of 170 billion dollars in 1986–with protectionist Japan flooding America with better-quality VCRs and autos (though it aroused the anger of unions and business groups)–did little to undermine the public's sanguine mood about the American economy. Union opposition had little effect on Reagan's policies, as they had in the main allied themselves with the Mondale campaign and were in a weakened state, their membership declining by 1985 to nineteen percent of the work force.

Reagan's base of support also included members of Protestant fundamentalist groups (e.g., the Moral Majority) whose prime political aims were not in the economic sphere but in the active promotion of a social agenda including prayer in the schools, prohibition of abortion, traditional family values, and law and order. Reagan paid constant lip service to this constituency in innumerable presidential pronouncements but did little concrete to put their program into effect beyond taking their interests into account in his Supreme Court nominations (e.g., Scalia and Bork).

The last years of his administration saw a scandal–"Irangate"–finally stick to Reagan (the "Teflon President") personally. This was a secret arms-for-hostages deal with Iran where profits from weapons sales were covertly shifted to the contras–a deal that broke the law and overrode the Constitution. Reagan attempted to deny his own responsibility for the affair by claiming total ignorance of the activities of subordinates like Chief of the National Security Council, Vice Admiral John Poindexter and superpatriot Colonel Oliver North. Of course, denying knowledge of the affair made Reagan look publicly like a bumbling, ineffectual figure incapable of controlling his underlings. Some of his diminished popularity was regained at the Gorbachev–Reagan summit conference in Iceland in 1986 when for the first time the superpowers agreed to eliminate a whole weapons system (all medium range missiles in Europe).

Nevertheless, by 1987 the Reagan administration seemed moribund: the President vague and detached; some former aides indicted for influence peddling; and the president and Congress at a stalemate over Star Wars, the budget, and other issues. But the Democrats were incapable of transforming the troubles of the Reagan administration into a victory in the presidential election of 1988. The Democrats, led by an intelligent but inexpressive and rigid technocrat who emphasized "competence" rather than social vision–Michael Dukakis–ran an inept, defensive campaign, which helped turn lightweight George Bush into a formidable candidate and Republican winner. Bush was also aided in his victory by skillful debate preparation and well-crafted and vicious and racist negative campaign ads. In its first year the popularity of the Bush administration benefited greatly from being in power as the Cold War wound down, and revolutionary political changes in Eastern Europe, the Soviet Union, and Nicaragua took place (though the political and economic future of almost all these countries remains uncertain and even precarious). Bush demonstrated little talent or imagination for using the historical moment to project an inspiring vision of democracy, but his affable, cautious style also meant that he did not say or do anything that could undermine these momentous developments. On the domestic front, Bush's tepid, consensual, right-of-center politics muted much of the ideological abrasiveness of Reagan conservatism without breaking the faith on issues like abortion or tax policy. He also indulged in rhetorical gestures of concern for the poor and homeless and made a legislative commitment to educational and environmental reform—without any of it being sufficiently far-reaching to make even a dent in social problems (e.g., drugs, crime, housing, teenage pregnancy) that grew more profound and explosive with each passing year.

More significant than any specific Republican legislation during the eighties was Reagan's ushering in a culture of unbridled greed and materialism—where lining your own pocket was the primary goal. The public realm was devalued and treated negligently and contemptuously. There was, of course, the close to 2 trillion dollar debt that the federal government built up over the decade. More than that there was the corruption and influence peddling that permeated the Department of Housing and Urban Development, the tax money necessary to clean up waste from badly managed nuclear plants like Hanford in Washington, and the exorbitant cost (estimates run as high as 500 billion dollars) to the public of the savings and loan spree that was supported by both the Reagan administration and Congress casting a blind eye to ongoing abuses. Conversely, the marketplace and the private realm and pleasure were deified. In a sense it was a second Gilded Age where conspicuous consumption was the norm—a great many stretch limousines and a great deal of nouvelle cuisine—an age whose commitment to profit, hedonism, and modern technology basically subverted its conservative political rhetoric. Its heroes—and Reagan's speeches promoted individual heroism—were vulgar, aggressive entrepreneurs like Donald Trump and sharp Wall Street pirates like Ivan Boesky whose operations skirted and went over the line into illegality. In fact, the people who did best financially during the decade were paper entrepreneurs (e.g., investment bankers) who made their money through deal making and asset rearranging—hostile takeovers, leveraged buyouts, junk bonds—rather than creating anything of value. The tone for the decade was set by Reagan's first inaugural which cost 8 million dollars, opening with an 800,000 dollar fireworks display at the Lincoln Memorial, followed by two nights of show business performances, and topped off by nine inaugural balls serving 14,400 bottles of champagne. The inaugural exemplified both Reagan's aesthetic and his moral perspective, which was based on the notion that the "beautiful was the expensive, the good was the costly."[3]

This distorted moral vision gave sanction to a decade of narcissism whose most representative figure was the yuppie. Yuppies may have been subjects of jokes and social satire, but in their emphasis on financial success, consumption, and self-development they embodied the period. The archetypal yuppie jogged, ate health food, was obsessed with brand names and what was fashionable, and was a workaholic. Work was a means to a greater status and a more affluent life-style, and happiness could be realized only by relentlessly pursuing one's own needs. And little sense of larger social, moral, and communal concerns was allowed to intrude on this hunger for personal mobility. Of course, not every yuppie neatly fit this repellent archetype, or should I say stereotype, but enough conformed to type to help define the social character of the decade.

It was not clear, however, that his old industry, Hollywood, reaped any immediate benefits from the Reagan era. Not that times were bad—overall income and profits being up for most of the major studios. Yet, as always in an insecure industry, anxieties were heightened by Reagan's economic policies, especially since they swelled interest rates. Since the life blood of Hollywood is borrowed capital, the number of films produced each year suffered a severe cutback. At the same time, Hollywood looked for economic shelters, usually in the arms of huge conglomerates that had enough internal excess capital to avoid high interest rates. So the conglomeratization of Hollywood that started in the sixties and seventies continued apace, with the gobbling up of previously unattached studios like Columbia by Coca Cola in 1982 (the studio has recently been bought by Akio Morita's Sony) and the mergers of old giants like MGM and United Artists. In the process tycoons like Kirk Kerkorian, Ted Turner, and Rupert Murdoch (he picked up Twentieth Century Fox in 1985) all got into the movie business.

The conglomerates positioned themselves to take control over some of the theaters they had lost long before—acquiring since 1985 more than

3,500 of the country's 22,000 screens.[4] They also took advantage of the explosion in new telecommunications technology – cable, cassettes, video discs – and their need for product by selling their old film libraries to them at a great profit. Despite the mergers, independent production companies (e.g., Island, Vestron) grew in the 1980s until the stock market crash of 1987.[5] By 1988 many of these independent companies were on the verge of collapse, unable to produce the box office hits that would keep them solvent. However, though by the end of the decade Hollywood was under the tight domination of the entertainment combines, who, in the main, eschewed innovative and risky filmmaking for conventional blockbusters with established stars, there were still independent production and distribution companies like Miramax and New Line functioning and making films that were too idiosyncratic and personal for the mass market.

At the beginning of the decade, industry insecurity was heightened by the failure of Michael Cimino's intellectually vacuous and inchoate western epic, *Heaven's Gate* (1980), a total economic and critical disaster. Suddenly studios were calling into question the whole policy of allowing big-budget laissez faire to directors with only one or two hits to their credit. A search was initiated for highly marketable properties based on pre-sold reputations – sequels like *Superman II* and *Rocky III* (a film which exploits racial fears and stereotypes by creating a villain who is a brutal, black boxer with an intimidating, baleful look).[6]

It was perhaps this insecurity and the quest for bankable commodities that made it easier for Robert Redford to direct a film. Redford had been the producer of well-received and even financially successful films like *Downhill Racer* (1969), *The Candidate* (1972), and *All the President's Men* (1976), and this time around decided himself to direct a film based on Judith Guest's novel, *Ordinary People* (1980).

To some extent the material of *Ordinary People* was made to order for Redford with his Hollywood image of the WASP golden boy in films like *The Candidate* (1972) and *The Way We Were* (1973). The film evoked the dark side of an upper-middle-class, suburban WASP family – the Jarrets. The family's placid, comfortable life is disrupted by the accidental death of their eldest son Buck, and the subsequent suicide attempt and hospitalization in a mental hospital of his guilt-ridden, bright, and sensitive younger brother, Conrad (Timothy Hutton).

The villain of the film is not the middle-class materialism or the conformist wasteland of the suburbs of a film like *The Graduate*, but WASP repression and control as epitomized by Conrad's handsome, compulsively neat mother, Beth (Mary Tyler Moore). She is conceived as a woman so obsessed with appearances and so fearful of allowing her emotions to get out of control that she deals with the family tragedy by remarking that "We'd have been alright if there hadn't been any mess." The Jarret family "mess," and, in particular, the terror in self-lacerating Conrad's eyes, only begins to be worked out when Dr. Berger (Judd Hirsch), a warm, commonsensical, and iconoclastic Jewish psychiatrist, starts getting through to him. Berger not only helps Conrad but as a bonus shakes his passive, somewhat unconscious, but loving father Calvin (Donald Sutherland) out of his bondage to his wife's rigidity.

Ordinary People is a small, intelligent film, which has an assured feel for the cocktail chatter and the green lawns and back yards of the insulated, all-white suburb of Chicago (Lake Forest) where the film was made. However, the film is primarily a work of two shots and interiors, a domestic work much more interested in the tensions of family life than the world and values of the upper middle class (there is no evidence in the film that Calvin's values are much different from Beth's). Despite subtle touches such as Dr. Berger's office becoming darker as Conrad gains more insight into his problems, the film is marred by Redford's habit of sometimes reducing the complexities of familial conflict to conventional formulas.

From Conrad getting just the right, jargon-free psychiatrist, to his meeting up with the most understanding and loveliest of high school coed girlfriends (Elizabeth McGovern), the film has a tendency to be too pat. What helps *Ordinary People* transcend some of its clichés and melodramatic contrivances (the boating accident itself) is Redford's gift for having his actors use their faces and body movements to convey a wide range of emotions. In an especially inspired bit of casting, Redford garnered Mary Tyler Moore (America's sitcom sweetheart) to play against type, giving a performance which avoids turning her frigid, golf-playing, napkin-folding mother into a mere stereotype. She successfully communicates the profound desperation and insecurity that lies underneath her need to cleave to the surfaces of life and coerce the people around her to do the same.[7]

However, though her ability to project feelings of anxiety adds nuance and dimension to the role, the mother is still the film's villain, bearing primary responsibility for Conrad's problems. It is Beth who is unwilling to contemplate changing herself by going to therapy and incapable of giving any love to Conrad. And it is the mother's cold-bloodedness and egoism that links the implicit point of view of *Ordinary People* with sophisticated, often unconscious feminist backlash strains inherent in films like *Kramer vs. Kramer* and even *Tootsie* (1982). Like the wife in

Kramer, Beth flees home and familial responsibility and leaves her husband to assume the nurturing, maternal role—the family becoming a male preserve. In both films the central female characters are portrayed as being either irresponsible or uncaring, with Beth carrying the added burden of being insidious as well.

Tootsie, of course, is a very different sort of work from the other films we have linked it with. It was one of the big box office hits of 1982, a genuinely clever and funny film with beautifully timed gags, witty one-liners, and a virtuoso performance by Dustin Hoffman. It is built around the classic comic gambit of the man who dresses up as a woman and then cannot have his identity revealed (for example, *Some Like It Hot*, 1959). However, Hoffman and the film's director, Sydney Pollack, were not satisfied with merely making a film which left audiences howling, and they began to make serious claims for the film as an exploration of gender and sexual roles.

Tootsie is the sort of film that baldly states that each of us carries both maleness and femaleness, and that a man can acquire greater sensitivity and humanness by getting in touch with his femaleness. It also touches on other feminist issues and insights by dramatizing the insults and patronizing behavior constantly bestowed upon women at work by their bosses and, of course, asserts that women must stand up for their dignity. However, despite the film's self-conscious feminism, the reality of *Tootsie* is much more conventional than its ambitions. As Dorothy Michaels, soap opera star, Hoffman continuously affirms his maleness beneath the female impersonation; there is little sense of Hoffman having truly experienced his female side. And Dorothy Michael's feminism is troubling since it ends up that the strongest and, in fact, the only feminist in the film is a man, the other female characters being either neurotically insecure or vulnerable and dependent on a man to provide direction. *Tootsie* is a skillful, entertaining film which breaks little new ground, for it ultimately demonstrates how a man can become a feminist and leave the traditional sexual patterns in place. Just as in *Kramer vs. Kramer* and *Ordinary People*, the new hero-heroine of *Tootsie*'s brand of feminism turns out to be a man.[8]

Though small personal works like *Ordinary People* and a farce with pretensions to social significance like *Tootsie* were popular in the early eighties, probably more symptomatic of the period were the works of Steven Spielberg. In the seventies Spielberg directed blockbuster hits like *Jaws*, and his *Close Encounters of the Third Kind* (1977) almost single-handedly resurrected the fortunes of Columbia Pictures. But after the failure of his comedy *1941* (1980), his career seemed on the wane, until aided by his friend and University of Southern California schoolmate, George Lucas (the film's executive producer), he directed *Raiders of the Lost Ark* (1981).

As in his previous films—the hunt for the malevolent shark in *Jaws*, the extraterrestrials in *Close Encounters*, and the Japanese submarine in *1941*—*Raiders* is essentially a story about a quest. The search focuses on the competition between an intrepid and invulnerable American archaeologist, Indiana Jones (Harrison Ford), and the Nazis to find the lost ark of the covenant, which will give its possessor unlimited power.

Although the film does go in for an awesome, though nonsensical, religious display at its finale, and there is talk of the gleaming gold ark having infinite power, the film's appeal and even its subtext aren't built around religious belief. *Raiders* is a reflection of the old Hollywood and its skilled manipulation of an audience's need to feel anxiety, lose itself in harmless fantasy, and become nostalgic.

In fact, from the film's opening credit where the Paramount fades into a snow-covered Andean peak, to a fade-out where it recreates the final scene in *Citizen Kane*, we are treated to a whole host of images and themes borrowed from old Hollywood—particularly the cliffhanging serials of the thirties. Following the genre conventions, the whip-snapping, unreflective Indiana and his hard-drinking, tough but dependent girlfriend, Marion (Karen Allen), face down poison darts, snakes, rotting corpses, assorted gun-toting villains, and finally outsmart and outfight the inhuman Nazi hordes. The upshot of it all is not so much to reassure us about good triumphing over evil—Indiana's only real commitment is to adventure and acquiring the ark (even Marion is an afterthought)—but to enclose us in a claustrophobic world of action for its own sake. The result is that *Raiders* comes as close as a film can to being a children's comic book.[9]

It is that very same child that exists in all of us that Spielberg appealed to so imaginatively and skillfully in *E.T.* (1982). Written by Melissa Mathison, who wrote the scenario for the lyrical children's film *The Black Stallion*, *E.T.* managed to hit on a mine of primal fantasy. It is basically the story of a benign extraterrestrial (who looks very much like one of the aliens in *Close Encounters*), who is left behind when his spaceship takes off without him, and a young boy, Elliot (Henry Thomas), who befriends, protects, and helps him return to his home. The story is as simple and familiar as any about a boy and his pet dog. However, there is more to the film than a bare sketch of the plot would suggest. *E.T.* contains numerous references and images invoking children's films (i.e., *Bambi*, 1943; *Peter Pan*, 1953; and *Mary Poppins*, 1964). The film also carries a feeling of religiosity that alternately transforms the cute, doll-like extra-terrestrial into a loving father substitute and, possibly pushing its significance a bit too far, a Christ figure (E.T. dies and is resurrected in the midst of a family where the mother's name happens to be Mary).

Of course the qualities that made *E.T.* a great commercial success — within less than a year of its release it was assured of becoming one of the top grossing films of all time — went far beyond its *Bambi*-like forest imagery or its possible religious resonances. Among the most significant of these was the emphasis it gave to the need that all of us have for unwavering affection, which is conveyed in the spiritual union between E.T. and Elliot. Pervading the whole film was Spielberg's commitment to child-like innocence, reinforced by his ability to visualize the world the way a child does.

As a result of the film's emphasis on a child's perspective adults and adult authority are either treated warily or distrusted altogether. Even Keys (Peter Coyote), the benevolent and sympathetic head of the government scientists sent out to find E.T., wants to subject him to scientific scrutiny, and that alone places him in the adult realm. None of the adult males in the film, including Keys, are ever shown beyond their midriffs; they are a faceless, ominous, almost malevolent group — the real aliens. Elliot's mother is portrayed as ineffectual — she has difficulty coping with being a single parent — and his father as irresponsible — he causes Elliot distress by running off to Mexico with another woman. In *E.T.* the children ultimately triumph over the adults, helping E.T. to elude their grasp and reach his home — the victory of feeling over rational and scientific thought.

E.T. was essentially a fairy tale, sometimes a bit too cute and sentimental for its own good — a film whose meaning is much less significant than the feelings it elicits. Still its general mood paralleled a number of cultural tendencies in early eighties' America. In its affirmation of innocence, its simple optimism, and its distrust of authority, particularly the state, it consciously mirrored some of the certainties and pieties offered to the American public by Ronald Reagan. Indeed both E.T. and Ronald Reagan were eminently lovable, and just as Spielberg's Elliot found solace from his problems in a fantastic creature, Reagan mouthed platitudes about traditional values and fled the complexities inherent in bringing about social change or reshaping the economy.[10]

The fact that the audience also shared this nostalgia for old verities need not rest solely on the election returns but can be confirmed from the grosses and awards to a film like *On Golden Pond* (1981). In fact, if nothing else, *On Golden Pond*, with its saccharine shots of rippling water and loon-filled lakes, evoked the sterile aura of a Norman Rockwell painting. Despite the banal imagery, the film did have an important theme and moments of truth about a rite of passage — aging and the confrontation with the imminence of death. Nevertheless, by casting Henry Fonda and Katharine Hepburn in the leading roles as the eighty-year-old, ailing Norman Thayer and his radiant, vital wife Ethel, the film paid less attention to gerontology than to Hollywood iconography.

It is not that Fonda's portrayal of the dying Norman was not a fitting culmination to a brilliant career. In fact his characterization of the surly curmudgeon, with a soft streak, who delivers lines like, "I think I'll read a new book — see if I can finish it before I'm finished. Maybe a novelette," is letter perfect. Likewise is his confusion and anxiety when a well-known path suddenly becomes unknown to him, due to his failing memory.

It was not the characters or the neatly turned, sentimental narrative that drew audiences. What did was the teaming of Fonda and Hepburn, and the cinematic memories it evoked of her costarring roles with icons like Grant, Tracy, and Wayne, and their combined five decades of starring roles from Mary, Queen of Scots to Tom Joad and Mr. Roberts. In addition, in casting herself as his estranged daughter Chelsea, Jane Fonda stirred resonances of her real-life, often embattled relationship with her father. Finally, it also gave Hollywood the chance to make amends to an actor who had given so much to the industry and audience over the years by granting him an Academy Award for best actor.

The long overdue award to Fonda (Hepburn also won for best actress) was yet another symptom of Hollywood doting on its past. The problem was that this tendency was more than mere nostalgia, for it indicated not just a sentimental longing for the past, but an active use of its ideas and images in lieu of any new subjects, themes, or forms. Hollywood's yearning after its past almost seemed symptomatic of a more general longing for an America of a vigorous work ethic and powerful, growing industries, whose policy of speaking softly and carrying a big stick was enough to keep any foreign government, at least the Latin American ones, in line. It was a simpler, more buoyant and heroic past which stood in sharp contrast to a contemporary America where smokestack industries decayed and closed leaving its workforce standing on unemployment lines, and a seemingly growing number of Central American Fidelistas thumbed their noses at American power.[11]

To some extent it was this yearning after a heroic past that contributed to a decidedly peripheral trend in the early eighties — the impulse to make epic films dealing with grand themes. This thread ran through

Heaven's Gate (1980), a muddled, inarticulate attempt to deal with class warfare in the American West, and Milos Forman's respectful, intelligent, but stolid effort in *Ragtime* (1981). *Ragtime* was based on E. L. Doctorow's jaunty, ironic, cinematic novel of the same name and attempted to deal with the American success myth and American racism—a trend that finally regained some critical if not economic respectability with Warren Beatty's *Reds* (1981).

In many ways *Reds* was as much a personal film for Warren Beatty as *Ordinary People* was for Robert Redford. Like Redford, Beatty's previous successes as the producer-star of *Bonnie and Clyde* (1967), *Shampoo* (1975), and *Heaven Can Wait* (1978) insured him the industry clout necessary to make a film about, of all things, an American radical and communist. Also in line with Redford's work, Beatty's film was inspired by personal experience. In the late sixties Beatty had taken a trip to the Soviet Union where, whenever he met older communists, they told him how much he physically resembled John Reed. When he returned home, Beatty delved into researching Reed, which set off an almost-two-decades-long campaign to do the film about him.[12]

Ultimately, it was a combination of this personal obsession coupled with his awareness of what made for success and failure in the film business that deeply influenced *Reds*. First of all, Beatty (who won an Oscar for direction) decided to limit the focus of the film to the last four years of Reed's life: concentrating on his love affair and marriage to Louise Bryant (Diane Keaton); their experience and reporting of the Russian Revolution; and Reed's subsequent commitment to building an American Communist party. Of course this left out important aspects of Reed's life: his equally intense involvement with wealthy Mabel Dodge Luhan, who ran a literary salon in the Village; and his participation in the Mexican Revolution and the struggles of the International Workers of the World (an anarcho-syndicalist labor organization operative during the first two decades of this century), of which we receive only brief glimpses. Also, Beatty's decision to portray Louise as a poor little woman who clings to her man offended many feminists who saw her as much more forceful, defined, and talented than the Keaton role conveyed.

Significant as these omissions were, even more glaring was how basically safe the film truly was—especially on a formal level. Of course Beatty faced an insurmountable problem in making a commercially viable film with a 35 million dollar budget which at the same time treated two American communists sympathetically. In making *Reds*, except for his inspired use of the "witnesses," Beatty never strayed beyond the conventional romantic epic. In fact, despite its links to Stieglitz photos and

Eisenstein's *Ten Days that Shook the World*, it owed its greatest debt to David Lean. In one episode Beatty had Louise, in her attempt to unite with an imprisoned Reed, doing a pointless reprise of Dr. Zhivago's trek across the frozen tundra to Lara. The film also had a tendency to transform the chaos of the revolution and the squalor and poverty of war communism into Hollywood operatics and glamor. In *Reds* historical credibility is sacrificed so that the revolution can become a carefully choreographed magical tableau.[13]

Unfortunately, in this quest for commercially viable elements Beatty often skirted perilously close to romantic comedy, complete with cute puppy dogs and running gags like Reed bumping into a chandelier. The most problematic element, however, was the film's depiction of two main characters and their relationship. Keaton is able to bring some complexity into the role of Bryant when she communicates both her insecurity and her resentment at being treated as a mere adjunct to Reed during their early Village days—especially when Emma Goldman curtly dismisses her as she painfully struggles to find the right words. Still there is nothing in her performance of the passion and sensuality of the woman whose touch, according to Eugene O'Neill, could set you afire. Indeed, the only time she conveys a bit of that intensity is in her scenes with O'Neill, played with great brio and force by Jack Nicholson. In addition, the scene where Bryant begins to offer trenchant political criticism of the relationship between the American Communist party and the working class feels utterly incongruous, as if a ventriloquist's dummy were doing the talking.[14]

Beatty in turn struggles to capture a life of the scale that Reed lived— his romantic individualism, his contentiousness, and the passion and intensity of his political commitment. Though he makes him an attractive figure, nowhere does one get the sense of a man whom Walter Lippmann described as "Many men at once . . . there is no line between the play of his fancy and the responsibility to fact: he is for the time the person he imagines himself to be."[15] Beatty with his boyish charm, winsome smiles, and sheepish looks is not so much protean as eager to please. And the complicated, painful, and contradictory relationship between Reed and Bryant, which is made the focus of much of the film, is superficial and seen primarily from the outside, through meetings, partings, and passionate reconciliations, rather than through illuminating its intricate internal life and motivation.

Despite these limitations *Reds* remains both stirring and provocative. It was one of the rare times a Hollywood film had both at its center an appealing hero who was fully committed to left politics and made the history of the American left accessible and engaging. And though the film may concentrate too much on the Bryant–Reed relationship, *Reds* successfully captures the feeling of two people living on the rim of a new world that will usher in a cultural and sexual revolution as well as a political one. Of course, it may be absurd to hear the "Internationale" played with such exaltation while Reed and Bryant make love and at the same time the Bolsheviks take over the government. But it is also striking to see an image of politics, more American sixties than Communist party, that merges the personal and the political—as much a revolt against bourgeois culture as against capitalism itself.

Coinciding with this image of a utopian—thoroughly romantic, impulsive, and exhilarating—political commitment is the most incisive and lucid political dialogue to appear in an American film. Undoubtedly the contribution of Beatty's screenwriting collaborator, British leftist playwright Trevor Griffiths (*Comedians*), there are moments, particularly in the film's second half, chronicling Reed's political battles within the American left and with the Comintern, that carry a dialectical electricity. For instance, in one especially insightful moment a weary and disillusioned Emma Goldman (Maureen Stapleton) and Reed debate the effects of the Russian Revolution. Goldman attacks the decline of the revolution into tyranny, stating that "The dream we had is dying, Jack. The centralized state has all the power. They're putting anarchists like me in jail, exterminating all dissenters. I want no part of it." To which, justifying himself, Reed replies, "What did you think anyway? It was all going to work right away? It's war, Emma. And we have to fight it with discipline, terror, firing squads—or give up." Then pausing, and expressing his own internal conflicts and misgivings, Reed ruefully says something with as much relevance to himself as to her: "Otherwise what has your life meant?"[16]

Unfortunately, when this sort of exchange is fused with brief portraits of Reed's political struggles with Comintern ideologues and political Czars Zinoviev (played by chic, Polish-born novelist Jerzy Kosinski) and Radek there was not so much the image of a man analyzing and brooding over the nature of the revolutionary process, or of a man conflicted between the bohemian writer and the disciplined revolutionary in himself, but the simpler, less introspective question whether or not Reed was ultimately disenchanted with the revolution. It was not that Beatty did not bravely begin to pose the other questions, but the film never truly pursues them. Of course, even the question of Reed's disenchantment is never really answered and is made to seem less significant by the only genuine unconventional formal technique in the film (a chorus and self-reflexive device): the use of real "witnesses" who were contemporaries of Reed and Bryant.

Like "petals on a wet black bough,"[17] as one critic, quoting Ezra Pound, referred to them, the poignant, intelligent, aged faces and voices of Adela Rogers St. John, Rebecca West, Dora Russell, Henry Miller, and other famous and once-famous figures comment on Reed and Bryant ("I'd forgotten all about them. Were they socialists?") and their times ("There was as much fucking then as there is today"). And the one inescapable conclusion drawn from these meandering and fragmented comments is the elusiveness and selectivity of human memory. Whether Reed would have turned against the revolution (as many of his friends like Max Eastman did) is probably less important than the larger truth that a person's historical place and role is difficult to discover and define. If nothing else, *Reds* at least rescued the figures of Reed and Bryant from historical obscurity and assured them a place in popular mythology.

There were other films during the Reaganite 1980s that dealt with the nature of the American left. Writer-director John Sayles made his first feature film, *The Return of the Secaucus Seven* (1980)—a low-budget ($40,000), independent work about a group of sixties activists who get together for a reunion in the late seventies. The group were never hard line, movement ideologues, nor had they been hippies. In Sayles's words, "they were the people who went to the marches, not those who planned them"[18]—strongly committed, issue oriented activists who liked to smoke dope. By the time of the reunion most of them are no longer activists—they are teachers, doctors, folk singers, speechwriters for liberal politicians. But the political values and culture of the sixties still have a powerful effect on their lives, without their ever losing a sense of perspective and some ironic feelings about the period.

Sayles's film had little camera movement, contained a number of scenes that needed editing, and was generally very raw and awkward on a technical level. However, it was a fresh, authentic and open-ended work, made by a man who understood the sixties from the inside, capturing the period's consciousness, language, and humor, and never dismissing or parodying the significance of the experience. Sayles's wondrously attuned ear and eye for the way different people speak and behave extended also to a "straight" liberal visitor and two working-class townies. Almost all his characters carried the kind of behavioral nuance that defied stereotyping.

It was, however, Lawrence Kasden's popular hit *The Big Chill* (1983), rather than *The Return of the Secaucus Seven*, that conjured up memories of the sixties for the general public. Using a plot device somewhat similar to that of *Secaucus*, Kasden structures the film around the reunion of a group of sixties friends for the funeral of their friend and guru, Alex — the only one who kept the 1960s faith — who has committed suicide.

Starring rising Hollywood stars like William Hurt, Kevin Kline, Glenn Close, Tom Berenger, and Jeff Goldblum, Kasden's film is slicker, better acted, and more dynamic — a great deal of neat and rhythmic cross-cutting between characters, witty one-liners, and a rousing 1960s soundtrack (e.g., "I Heard It through the Grapevine" and "You Can't Always Get What You Want") — than Sayles's work. Almost all the characters have achieved some semblance of upper-middle-class success — pop journalist, shoestore chain owner, real estate lawyer, and television actor. None of them work in social activist professions, and though they express some feeling about betraying their past ideals and a few pangs of conscience about their mainstream careers, there is little sign that these characters ever had any real politics to betray, except smoking dope, wearing long hair, and attending the odd antiwar rally. In fact, the malaise most of them feel has more to do with their own psychic make up than with conflicting values and ideals.

In fact, the film basically affirms yuppie values and rejects the notion of clinging to the ideals of the past. It's their generous weekend host, Harold (Kevin Kline), the owner of a chain of shoe stores, who is the most sympathetic and dominant character. Harold is lean, athletic, a loving father, and the only one of the group who is happily married. He is at home in the eighties — an investor and money maker, an integral part of his small town, and utterly realistic about what it takes to survive in the present. His antithesis is Nick (William Hurt), a bitter insomniac, a graduate school dropout, and, for good measure, a Vietnam vet who was wounded and as a result became impotent during the war. Nick sells drugs out of his run-down sports car, feels totally adrift, and hates his life. He inherits Alex's cabin and girl, but clearly there is nothing in his fragmented life that offers an alternative vision to Harold's complacent sense of well-being.

The Big Chill is an intellectually thin, well-crafted film which gives little sense of what the sixties were all about. The politics and culture of the period are reduced to fashionable tag lines, and the only sixties' legacy they have kept seems to be a capacity for greater emotional and sexual spontaneity and ease. That easy, bantering style separates them from the stiff, dull, workaholic ad man who is unhappily married to one of the group. It provides them with a feeling of superiority based on their hipness, but these feelings are based more on matters of personal style and sensibility than on some ultimate difference of values.

The Reaganite eighties were really the wrong historic moment for Hollywood to revive the politics of the sixties. But *The Big Chill*'s embrace of yuppie realism had strong links with aspects of the 1960s counterculture which emphasized "doing your own thing" and giving all one's energies to developing the self, with little consciousness that a society needed some idea of social interdependence to be at all cohesive and whole. In fact, *The Big Chill* was a perfect expression of the "temporary truce be-tween bourgeois and bohemian individualism as they joined together in a celebration of private life"[19] during the 1980s.

If it was difficult to make films that projected the political critique and culture of the 1960s in the period, films critical of American politics still were produced. *Missing* (1982), a box office hit, was the first American film made by French director Costa-Gavras (e.g., *The Confession*, 1970; *State of Siege*, 1972). The political thriller plot centers around the disap-pearance of young American writer Charlie Horman (John Shea) and the arrival of his naive, apolitical, conservative businessman father, Ed (Jack Lemmon). The purpose of the narrative is to indict the United States for the CIA's collusion in the right-wing military coup of 1973 which overthrew the elected Marxist government of Salvador Allende in Chile. And that end is achieved here by personalizing the experience for an American audience by having them identify with the pain of an American everyman, Ed Horman. He undergoes a political transforma-tion and becomes enraged with American policies after discovering that the government was involved in his son's execution.

The film's power does not lie in its political critique, which illuminates neither what the Allende regime stood for nor what the particular politi-cal dynamics of the coup were. Nor is Costa-Gavras particularly gifted at creating complex characters—the reasons for innocent Charles Horman and his wife Beth's presence in Chile (though Sissy Spacek gives an ex-tremely natural performance) are never made clear. What is most strik-ing is Costa-Gavras's gift for creating the terrifying atmosphere of a night city under martial law. It's a city where the sound of sirens and volleys of gunfire pierce the eerie silence, where pedestrians beg strangers for sanctuary, and a stadium's bleachers are filled with people rounded up because of suspected leftist connections.

Costa-Gavras embeds his unambiguous political critique within the conventions of the thriller, but a film like Mike Nichols's *Silkwood* (1983) eschews melodrama for a muted, ambiguous account of the dangers of nuclear power. Based on a true story about a woman who had become a political heroine, Karen Silkwood, the film uses very different aesthetic strategies from both *Missing* and the earlier nail-biting, Oscar-winning entertainment about a demonic nuclear power industry, *The China Syn-drome* (1979).

Silkwood avoids turning the problem of nuclear power into a schematic conflict between people of good will and a profit hungry industry. Its heroine, Karen Silkwood (Meryl Streep in a natural, unselfconscious performance), is a tranquilizer-swallowing, chain-smoking, sexually promiscuous blue-collar worker whose three children are being raised by her husband. This tense, crass, unsophisticated protagonist can alternately be both abrasive and deeply feeling. And the film spends more time, using long takes and medium two shots, to capture atmospheric detail – the clutter of her collapsing house – and realistically limn her difficult relationships (there are tedious moments as well as evocative ones) with her lover Drew (Kurt Russell) and her lesbian roommate Dolly (Cher) than in conveying the machinations of the nuclear power industry.

Silkwood's focus is on the feelings of ordinary people rather than on issues, and most of the workers are either too unaware or too frightened about the possible loss of their well-paying jobs to speak out about the plant's disregard for their safety. The workers are no heroic mass out of Eisenstein, the local union is ineffective, and the workers don't suddenly turn into angry, articulate critics of nuclear power. It's Karen who courageously and heedlessly takes the main role in agitating against the company and trying to bring to the *New York Times* evidence of falsified safety records – activity which is not simply aimed at changing company policy, but also motivated by an unstated desire to realize a greater sense of self. The corporation itself isn't conceived as a group of avaricious, stock villains, but as an impersonal, opaque, and ultimately more insidious organization. *Silkwood* is a restrained work, which leaves the cause of Karen's death in an auto wreck an open-ended question – it's either an accident or a cold-blooded murder by the company. And the fact that the company is ultimately shut down is only seen in a postscript without any inflated theatrics about the triumph of individual courage and virtue over the evil corporation.

Besides nuclear power other 1980s political and economic problems were touched on by Hollywood. During the early 1980s there was a run of farm bankruptcies, resulting in some suicides and even in the murder of a few mortgage-holding bankers by angry, frustrated farmers. A cycle of films like Robert Benton's *Places in the Heart*, Mark Rydell's *The River*, and Richard Pearce's *Country* (all in 1984) reacted to these events by focusing on small farmers – all of them strong women – struggling against the elements and the banks.

Places in the Heart was the most popular of the three films and won Academy Awards for star Sally Field and scriptwriter Robert Benton.

Set in rural Texas during the Depression – the world of Benton's youth – the film has a wonderful feel for the Texas landscape, climate, and the church services and dances which are at the heart of small town life. The film's narrative, however, is a thoroughly soft and sentimental fable, Sally Field playing a gutsy widow with two children who must make a profit on her cotton crop to save her farm. She is magically aided by two outsiders – a bitter, blind veteran, Will (John Malkovich), and a kind, black drifter, Mose (Danny Glover). It's soft-spoken, heroic Mose whose knowledge of the land helps save the farm, though the local Ku Klux Klan drives him off the land right before the film's conclusion. Benton's childhood memories are essentially sweet ones, and though racism pervades town life, and the local banker is unctuous and manipulative, the communal ethic remains strong, and even a defensive Will becomes less bristly and more emotionally open. The film concludes on a moving, phantasmagoric grace note with a church service where all the film's characters – living and dead, black and white – gather to affirm Christian and communal love.

Places in the Heart was basically an affirmation of the human spirit's capacity to triumph over adversity, but the other two farm films did make a stab at a political statement. The more interesting of the two was *Country* – a muted, unsentimental film about a farm family whose husband (Sam Shepard) collapses when their government loan is called in. The determined wife (Jessica Lange) maintains the family and organizes a group of small farmers to resist the government, resulting in her winning a temporary stay of foreclosure. The film's strength is its fidelity to the reality of farm life, and it uses few close-ups or dramatic scenes to distort the daily texture of that experience. However, though it attacked Reagan farm policy, the film blurred the nature of the political enemy by portraying it nebulously as "monolithic bureaucracy" and apathetic government.[20]

Besides making films like *Silkwood* and *Country* whose liberal values were at odds with Reagan policies, Hollywood also began to make films that projected right-wing political views. It was a trend that only gained momentum after Reagan's landslide victory over Mondale in 1984. The first of these films was John Milius's *Red Dawn* (1984), a paranoid action movie about the invasion of the United States by a combined Soviet-Cuban force, and the defense of the country left in the hands of a group of young patriots. It revived the specter of the Soviet threat and demonstrated that anti-communism fused with exciting, reconstructed tank battles could sell.

Following *Red Dawn*'s lead, Hollywood indulged in some Vietnam war revisionism with a series of films that exploited the remaining cause célè-bre, the 2,500 purported MIAs left behind in Vietnam. In the process Hollywood did nothing less than rewrite history and gave America a second opportunity to win the war, at least on the screen.

Of the reported 2,500 MIAs, many were presumed dead, but others were considered to be alive and held captive by the North Vietnamese. Anguished relatives and supporters initiated a campaign to obtain their release. And one former Green Beret colonel, James B. Gritz, was not satisfied with lobbying and led an abortive raid into Laos whose most notable accomplishment was that Hollywood could turn it into a film, *Uncommon Valor* (1983).

In its us-against-them portrait of a powerfully linked group of Vietnam vets against a craven government, *Uncommon Valor* reflected a pessimistic right-wing populism sharply critical of an uncaring society and government. In addition, the film provided a retrospective affirmation of Vietnam as a noble cause, whose only seeming limitation was that we didn't win the war. The narrative structure of *Uncommon Valor* also provided a model for other revisionist Vietnam works.

Uncommon Valor leaned heavily on one of America's most enduring archetypical forms, the captivity myth, which originally evolved from the Puritan fear that the American wilderness would corrupt them spiritually. The myth was built around a tale of pure white men and women taken prisoner by barbaric Indians who tempted them into sins of the flesh and spirit. The Indians don't succeed in subverting their piety, and, in fact, the prisoners rediscover God's will.

As these tales were modified in the nineteenth century, there emerged a fearless, stoic hunter-hero—Davy Crockett, Hawkeye—whose intimacy with Indian and wilderness lore gave him the skill to wrest the land away from the Indians, and projected into the future the vision of a white man's agrarian Arcadia as the nation's destiny. That destiny helped justify our expropriation of the wilderness through methods that historian Richard Slotkin called a "regeneration through violence."

In films like *Uncommon Valor* the Indians became the Vietnamese and the MIAs the prisoners of the captivity myth, but the central figure in the film, Marine Colonel Jason Rhodes (Gene Hackman), was too much the dignified, stoic professional soldier to become a hunter-hero. Hollywood, however, had other aspirants for the role, the first being half-Indian, karate champ Chuck Norris, who had already established a screen persona of a mild-mannered, taciturn loner who puts to rout hosts of sleazy villains (e.g., *Force of One*, 1978).

In films constructed in the captivity narrative tradition like *Missing in Action* (1984) and *Missing in Action 2: The Beginning* (1985), Norris (Colonel Braddock) plays an inexpressive, solitary hunter-hero who liberates MIAs at the expense of literally hundreds of Vietnamese soldiers. The hunter-hero here is indomitable in the superman mode of a Michael Vronsky and is able to use the enemy's own guerrilla combat tactics, such as wearing a camouflage suit, to triumph over them. The films were extremely successful with the public, because they guaranteed a great deal of bloody action, little extraneous dialogue, and, for the politically unconscious, even the illusion of final victory of Vietnam.

The *Missing in Action* films served as a warm-up for the apotheosis of this developing cycle, *Rambo: First Blood Part II* (1985) — a sequel to *First Blood* (1982), an extremely popular film about the bloody visit of John Rambo (Sylvester Stallone), an alienated Vietnam vet and Congressional Medal of Honor winner to a small town in the Pacific Northwest. *Rambo II* was not only a box office success — 57 million dollars in the first two weeks — but became a political byword after President Reagan referred to it in a number of his speeches. For Reagan, Rambo was a symbol of American machismo and patriotism, and the film's crude Russophobia and narcissistic camera worship of its star Sylvester Stallone's glistening, nautilus-crafted body provided perfect fodder for Reagan's Hollywood brand of populism.

The film opens with Rambo's being freed from a prison stockade, where he was incarcerated after his *First Blood* rampage, so he can be sent on a secret mission into Vietnam to prove the existence of MIAs by photographing them. From that moment on the film becomes a rant against the U.S. government, embodied by an opportunistic bureaucrat, Murdock (Charles Napier), who both inspires the MIA mission and wants it to fail so he can bury the embarrassing political issue for good. Murdock is seen by the film as Rambo's prime enemy and a cartoon symbol of a soulless and impotent American government that ostensibly betrayed its own troops because it lacked the will to win. And Rambo's uncontrolled Luddite-style outburst at the film's conclusion — using a machine gun to destroy Murdock's computers — supposedly spoke for all the ordinary GIs who suffered the callous manipulations and rationalizations of these government experts in Vietnam.

Coupled with this populist, superpatriotic backlash was a revival of the Soviet menace. The real enemy in the film are the Soviets, not the North Vietnamese — the Soviets acting like an update of the Nazi SS, even to the point of being racists who view the Vietnamese as "yellow scum." And Rambo here is both a working-class echo of Colonel Kurtz, mumbling such aphorisms like "to survive a war you must become a war," and a hunter-hero, who moves through the jungle, stripped to the waist, looking like an Indian brave or a scowling noble savage.

There is an undercurrent in the film suggesting that the Rambos of the world will never receive justice from the American government, and that the only possible alternative is destructive rage. The film's dominant strain, however, is one of an America truly regenerated through violence—a resurrected nation bursting with pride, power, and unabashed aggression that can humble any enemy.

Nevertheless, by providing a touch of primitivism to the archetypes of the superman and hunter-hero, Stallone linked the character so close to his inarticulate persona that there was little possibility left for other films to work out new variations on the character. As a result, though Stallone succeeded in adding another mythic hero, along with Rocky, to his personal pantheon of America Redux, he helped bring the MIA cycle to a standstill. Of course, desiring better economic and diplomatic relations, the North Vietnamese themselves began to permit U.S. inspection teams to search for the remains of the missing—the kind of pragmatic behavior that made it difficult even for Hollywood to go on constructing aggressively patriotic fantasies.[21]

Still there were other films that fueled America's military build-up and Reagan's patriotic rhetoric. In 1986 Tony Scott's revved-up *Top Gun*—a film exulting in the military and in macho heroics—became one of the top box office hits. Its arrogant, adolescent hero Maverick (a grinning Tom Cruise) is obsessed with becoming "top gun," the best of the best pilots, at the U.S. Navy Fighters Weapons School. The film's strength is its virtuosic and lengthy flying scenes and simulated dog fights shot from a variety of camera angles, but the rest is laughable dialogue, a contrived plot, and an unbelievable passionate romance between the narcissistic Maverick and his aeronautics instructor (Kelly McGillis). Still the film would only be as disturbing as a glossy and banal navy recruiting ad, if, at the film's climax, Maverick did not become a hero by engaging an unnamed enemy in a real war situation over the Indian Ocean. That narrative twist turns *Top Gun* into a film that is dangerously unable to distinguish war games from real war—reducing life and death situations into a plaything for male egos.

Films like *Top Gun* and Clint Eastwood's *Heartbreak Ridge* (1986), where a career gunnery sergeant (played by Eastwood) follows the tradition of old World War II movies turning raw rookies into men—readying them for a triumphant invasion of Grenada—may still have been produced in 1986. But that year also would see the first Hollywood film to really confront the concrete realities of the Vietnam war, Oliver Stone's Oscar-winning *Platoon*. Stone was a Vietnam war veteran, whose film of remembrance and mourning had a cathartic effect for many Vietnam vets and nonvets alike. *Platoon* is most powerful and successful when it uses minimal dialogue and telling close-ups and medium shots to convey with great immediacy the war's everydayness: the stifling discomfort of the ants, heat, and mud of jungle and brush; the fatigue of patrols; the murderous cacophony and chaos of night firefights; and the boredom and sense of release of base camp. Stone also understood just how fear, fatigue, and rage could undermine some GIs sense of moral restraint and balance and turn them into savages who massacre civilians and torch villages.

Stone's Vietnam is a bleak, horrific world where the GIs face an almost-invisible, ubiquitous enemy. It's all seen through the eyes and voice-over narration (a number of self-consciously literary letters back home) of Chris Taylor (Charlie Sheen), an upper-middle-class Yale dropout and patriot, who like Stephen Crane's hero in *The Red Badge of Courage* is initiated into manhood and transformed by the war. Taylor discovers not only Vietnam's terrors, but a gallery of working-class and underclass GIs who are given a bit more nuance than the norm for Hollywood war films. There is baby-faced, beer-can-crunching Bunny (Kevin Dillon), who loves war and killing; gum-chewing Sergeant O'Neill (John MacGinley), whose obsequious attempts to find safety only lead him to greater danger; and a group of blacks of whom the earthy, wise King (Keith David) is balanced by the perpetually whining and malingering Junior (Reggie Johnson). The blacks are never merely turned into an anonymous mass, though the film's prime focus, as in most Vietnam films, is on the experience of white soldiers.

If the strength of *Platoon* is its ability to portray Vietnam as a world free of self-sacrificial heroics, where mainly angry, disengaged, and divided GIs try to survive the madness in one piece and just get on the plane back home, its main weakness is its penchant for overblown literary conceits. For besides his ordinary GIs inhabiting a realist film, Stone created two mythic lifers, the headband-wearing doper saint Sergeant Elias (Willem Dafoe) and the war-loving, demonic Sergeant Barnes (Tom Berenger), whose Manichean, melodramatic struggle tends to subvert the film's verisimilitude.

Both of them are constructed in larger-than-life terms: Elias is depicted as a gentle, Christ figure, critical of the war he has become weary of and given far too many self-consciously significant close-ups by Stone; while Barnes, his face crisscrossed with scars, is portrayed as a closet superman who asserts "I am reality" and is shot too often from a low angle to underline his forbidding character. These two portentous figures on one level serve as symbolic fathers warring for the soul of Taylor (a somewhat bland character who doesn't have too vivid a soul) and on another supposedly reflect the political divisions within American society.

Platoon, however, lacked a genuine political perspective. It was neither a film that dealt with the mixture of nationalism and Marxist-Leninism that underlay the North Vietnamese military effort nor did it explore the political culture and specific policies involved in American intervention. When Stone ventures to make a political point, as he does in the film's final moments, it's as vaporous as the physical world he conjures up is grittily alive. He has Taylor indulge in a sermonizing voice-over, which projects the facile, ethnocentric notion that the "enemy was in us" (as if America had fought the war to purge its own destructive impulses) and adds the harmless, banal sentiment that we must try "to find a goodness and meaning to this life."

Although *Platoon* was clearly not the final word on the war, it was an antidote to mindless political cartoons like *Rambo* and metaphysically confused works like *Apocalypse Now*. If Stone had little gift for capturing the political and social meanings of the war, he had at least echoed the dominant public feeling about Vietnam, that it was a self-destructive march into some kind of purgatory. Stone's authentic depiction of the mad and murderous world of combat was also so powerful an achievement that one could say that he had taken the first real cinematic step in Hollywood's coming to terms with Vietnam.

Platoon marked after years of avoidance, wavering, and regression Hollywood's total acceptance of Vietnam as a serious subject for film. In 1987 three films dealing with different aspects of the war were produced—*Hanoi Hilton*, Coppola's *Gardens of Stone*, and the only film worthy of a critical stir, Stanley Kubrick's *Full Metal Jacket*. Kubrick's work had grander aspirations than *Platoon*, dealing less with the concrete reality of Vietnam than with the military as an institution that breeds killers, and projecting a vision of an innately brutal and corrupt human condition.

That vision of human beings as potential destroyers and lovers of death, coupled with an Olympian, detached style, pervades almost all of Kubrick's work, notably *A Clockwork Orange* (1968), where a futuristic, delinquent gang engages in orgies of destruction. In *Full Metal Jacket* Kubrick brilliantly uses his unique style—overbearing close-ups, drained colors, harsh white and cold blue lighting, minimal dialogue, and an unnaturally severe barracks set—to choreograph the transformation of unformed recruits into trained marine killers.

Directing this dehumanization process is an obscenity-spouting, bullying drill instructor, Sergeant Hartman (Lee Ermey), whose relentless, sardonic barrage is so oppressively effective that it strips the men of their past identities and provides them all with new ones, naming one of them

Private Joker (Matthew Modine) and still another Cowboy. Hartman's harangues often attain the imagistic richness of a poet of the profane, and they are permeated with a sense of menace. Kubrick has never been clearer about the links between sex, aggression, and death—in this case, cocks and rifles.

Unfortunately, the compressed power of the forty-five minute prologue makes the film's second half—the Vietnam section—pale in comparison. Kubrick still dreams up inspired visual images and aural effects—a desolate, lunar-landscaped Hue (a city where some of the bloodiest battles of the 1968 Tet offensive were fought) constructed out of an abandoned gasworks outside of London, and after killing a female sniper, the chilling image of the marines marching into a blazing sunset singing "The Mickey Mouse Club Song"—sardonically fusing the carnage of war with the synthetic innocence of the popular culture that shaped the young marines. However, much of *Full Metal Jacket*'s second half is either conventional—a sniper sequence where one marine after another dies in blood-cascading slow motion is merely a more idiosyncratic variation on World War II films' battle action—or given over to heavy-handed ironies. The central, chorus-like figure, Private Joker, is a wry, ironic character, less defined than Sergeant Hartman. Joker's detachment is a projection of Kubrick's, but his exercise of irony too often feels like an overly literal cataloguing of the war's absurdities—the army newspaper *Stars and Stripes*'s attempt to provide happy news by calling search-and-destroy missions "sweep and clear" expeditions—rather than the kind of Brechtian mordancy that could get to the heart of the war's madness.

The ultimate and most striking irony implicit in Kubrick's version of Vietnam is that the film's most vital figures are its most lethal and brutal. Though Kubrick may not endorse the world of a Sergeant Hartman, he clearly has sympathy for characters who are at home in a nihilistic world. For Kubrick it's the misanthropic who dominate and often triumph amid the war's barbarism.

The most problematic element in *Full Metal Jacket* is Kubrick's Hobbesian view of human nature. Blaming it all on the savage nature of human beings may aptly describe some of the behavior on all sides in the war, but it is an evasion of its historical context. There was too much anguish present in the Vietnam abattoir to conceive it totally in terms of pitiless irony and black humor. It was a war whose intense torment demanded more than Kubrick's cool genius.[22]

At the end of the decade Oliver Stone returned to the subject of Vietnam and made a film which centered more on the cultural roots of the war effort than on the horrors of battle combat. *Born on the Fourth of July* (1989) was based on the autobiography of Ron Kovic, a paraplegic veteran whom the war transformed from a macho, working-class patriot into an articulate antiwar activist.

The film's opening scenes sketch in bold, underlined strokes how Kovic's (Tom Cruise) values were formed in the Long Island suburbs by a mixture of repressive Catholicism, John Wayne films, patriotic parades, and the American obsession with competition and victory. In depicting Kovic's coming of age Stone eschews subtlety for images which are almost operatic, even vulgar, in their intensity, and a swelling musical score to accompany them. Nevertheless, despite its sledgehammer style, the film captures with great poignancy and power Kovic's horrific experiences in a slum of a Bronx veterans hospital, his uneasy, angry return to his forbidding mother-dominated, conservative, pro-war home, and his descent into alcoholism and self-degradation, which reaches its apotheosis in a wild fight with another vet, Charlie (Willem Dafoe), while sitting in their wheelchairs in the middle of the Mexican desert. Stone is also much more adept at orchestrating emotional fireworks than in delineating the psychic and intellectual changes that Kovic goes through before he appears as a full-blown radical spokesman at the 1976 Democratic Convention. The transformation is too abrupt, but *Born on the Fourth of July* marks the public's acceptance of the fact that it was more than just a mindless, suicidal war. At least in Vietnam, America's intervention was a consequence of our need to assert our national will and demonstrate to the world our imperial power.[23]

Vietnam was clearly not the sole subject of 1980s film. Hollywood also spawned a flood of teen comedies like Amy Heckerling's successful and sometimes funny and fresh *Fast Times at Ridgemont High* (1982), about a group of high school students who spend their time surfing, hanging around the local mall, and obsessing about sex, which is never treated as a real problem. Another was Paul Brickman's *Risky Business* (1983), starring Tom Cruise (Joel Goodson) as a straight, careful suburban high school senior who lives in a comfortable, white Chicago suburb with the usual foolish and unseeing parents who populate teen films. Most of his time seems spent indulging in elaborate masturbatory fantasies and worrying about what college he'll attend. Joel's parents leave on vacation, and he decides to take a risk for the first time in his life—to say, "what the fuck." He gets involved with a pretty, shrewd hooker who provides sex and solace and then to make money hosts a party which provides hookers for all his friends and even for a Princeton recruiter who is there to interview him. Insecure, guilt-ridden Joel has overnight become a daredevil-driving, smooth-talking, middle-class pimp with shades, and the film cynically affirms this sleazy persona and his newfound talent for making the quick buck.

Risky Business is a perfect film for budding Reaganites. There is no danger here of Joel's risk-taking to lead him to question or break from his upper-middle-class world. It actually helps him get into Princeton – where he'll major in business – and gives him a good start at learning what it takes to become a "future enterpriser." The hooker girl friend is a sharp, tough businesswoman who will clearly be of help to Joel in acquiring a Porsche of his own and, after graduation, organizing hostile take-overs on Wall Street. *Risky Business* evokes a morally bankrupt world[24] where any action is justified if it will help you get ahead. It romanticizes both prostitution and cynical opportunism, and endorses the success ethos – without a hint of irony.

The master of the teen picture, John Hughes, produced and directed a whole slew of films during the eighties (e.g., *Sixteen Candles*, 1984; *The Breakfast Club*, 1985; *Weird Science*, 1985; and *Ferris Bueller's Day Off*, 1986), which conveyed some feeling for the social tensions and frustrations created by high school clique and life-style divisions – nerds, jocks, preppies, druggies, valley girls. Sometimes even class barriers are alluded to – someone coming from "the wrong side of the tracks" – but in 1980s America, despite the continuing reality of class, that idea had little emotional or social resonance for adolescent moviegoers.

Hughes's films were cute, wholesome, and relatively innocent – none of them as hedonistic or cynical as *Risky Business*. The only culture that exists in his films is a white, suburban adolescent one – the films treat with contempt an absurd adult and parental world – and Hughes seems to be able to enter totally and unselfconsciously into a world of teenage mating rites, dress codes, and argot (e.g., "asswipe," "geek"). Rebellion in a Hughes film is rarely anything more than a brash and spoiled kid hero like Ferris Bueller (Matthew Broderick) ingeniously and successfully flaunting school and other institutional rules but without ever deviating from a world that keeps him living a comfortable, possession-filled existence. All Hughes's films end neatly and happily, and in Elayne Rapping's words, Hughes's "kids are sui generis members of a self-sufficient, mysterious universe which operates not by the laws of capital but by magic, good Magic."[25]

One of the most popular teen films of the mid-eighties was Robert Zemeckis's *Back to the Future* (1985) (there have been two sequels so far), which combined teen comedy with science fiction. Starring television sitcom star Michael J. Fox (Marty McFly), the film combines time travel, a wild-eyed scientist (Christopher Lloyd) and his Rube Goldberg inventions, and nostalgia for the relatively innocent small town of the fifties. Diminutive and clever Marty travels back thirty years to the time when his parents met in high school, and inadvertently alters his own and his parents' future. The film is inventive and has some charm—playing with the emotional-Oedipal problems involved in time travel. Marty's mother is at first attracted to him rather than to his spastic, timid father. But Marty succeeds in averting the danger of this incestuous connection and pairs them off. In doing so he leaves a legacy for the future which transforms his seedy home and comic-pathetic 1980s parents—an overweight mother who is puritanical and drinks and a father with a lunatic laugh who allows himself to be mercilessly bullied—into a smooth, tennis-playing pair. The parents are now confident and successful and have moved up a couple of steps in class—the appropriate social background for a conventional teenage hero like clean-cut Marty. And though the film clearly endorses this Reaganite success story—Marty's time-traveling intervention aside—his father's ability to painfully assert his own will is the main reason he is able to create a new persona for himself; the parents are much more interesting as ineffectual, shambling failures than as stereotypical success stories.

During the Reagan years many of the black economic and social gains of the 1960s and 1970s, ranging from the rate of college attendance to the proportion of two parent families to relative income levels, began to decline while poverty and crime rates escalated. Hollywood, of course, was not interested in depicting these harsh, ominous realities but in finding black performers—who assert their black identity—like Richard Pryor (*Stir Crazy*, 1980) and Eddie Murphy who still would have crossover appeal.

In the 1980s it was Murphy who was the big box office draw in films like Martin Brest's *Beverly Hills Cop* (1984). The film actually opens with a graphic montage of Detroit which evokes a predominantly black ghetto world of windowless bars, abandoned buildings, polluting smoke stacks, and empty lots. The film, however, is not about the social reality of Detroit, but about a rule-breaking, undercover cop, Axel Foley (Murphy), who sets out from its impoverished, violent urbanscape to find the murderers of a boyhood friend amid the glitter and wealth of Beverly Hills.

The nonsensical plot, filled with soporific car crashes and shoot-outs, is merely a vehicle to provide the fast-talking, profane, homophobic Murphy a chance to do a number of routines and try out a number of voices. In his sweat shirt and sneakers he plays the irrepressible bad boy who tweaks authority and convention but is, at the same time, utterly apolitical and safe. Murphy's Foley may coolly manipulate and dominate his fellow white cops, but the edge of his behavior is muted by the film's projecting a vision of interracial camaraderie and ease between them. And when it comes to white women, Foley is utterly chaste. Murphy is an aggressive, hip, and funny comic, and *Beverly Hills Cop* is the perfect medium for him to reach a white audience—making them feel good so that they can root for a quick-witted black at the expense of dim whites (it also helps him hold a black audience) while preserving the racial status quo.

One of the rare films made during the early 1980s dealing with race was Norman Jewison's adaptation of Charles Fuller's prize-winning play, *A Soldier's Story* (1984). The film stars a predominantly black cast and perceptively explores the question of racial identity—what it means to be a black in a world dominated by whites—but it is set back in time in the Deep South of 1944. Another, more popular and commercial work, directed again by a white, was Steven Spielberg's adaptation of Alice Walker's Pulitzer Prize–winning novel, *The Color Purple* (1985)—a film about growing up a female victim in the Deep South.

Like the novel, the film is more about the oppression of black women by black men than about white racism. Celie (Whoopie Goldberg) is passive, subservient, and not very pretty. She is sexually and emotionally abused by almost all the men in her life—brutal, callous males who express their own rage against being demeaned by viciously scapegoating women. But Celie ultimately gains self-respect, becomes independent, and achieves happiness by forming a communal house dominated by women. And the women are the powerful, luminous figures here, loving, supportive, nurturing, and indomitable, while almost all the men are depicted as cruelly unseeing and uncaring.

The repressive, degrading nature of southern white racism is evoked, but the whites are peripheral to this feminist fable of female triumph. Spielberg's style tends to prettify, turning rural black poverty into a picturesque landscape filled with purple flowers, clear blue skies, green fields, and buzzing insects. There is also too much flashy editing, too many dramatic close-ups, and a couple of inflated musical sequences that look like they come from the MGM vault. Spielberg also plays it safe politically, merely skimming over Celie's passionate lesbian love for a sensual, free-living blues singer, Shug (Margaret Avery). *The Color Purple* may be a sentimental, overdirected film, but the portrayal of Celie's assertion of self and liberation from male domination leaves one emotionally stirred.

A more typical Hollywood treatment of racial issues was Alan Parker's *Mississippi Burning* (1988), dealing with the 1964 disappearance of three civil rights activists during Mississippi's "Freedom Summer." Parker, a sincere, socially conscious director, decided that the only way he could make a viable commercial film about the black civil rights struggle was to invert reality and feature whites and the FBI as heroes (the FBI's role in the South was essentially antagonistic to the movement, often spying on rather than protecting activists) and turn blacks into mute victims—obliterating the basic fact that the movement was built on black collective action and courage.

Parker's film was "simply the latest in a long line of historical films which subordinate complex political and social processes to individual heroics and spectacular set pieces."[26] In this case, the civil rights movement is denuded of all political and social nuance and replaced by excitingly edited action sequences and close-up confrontations between good FBI men—Anderson (Gene Hackman), a tough local boy who is willing to bend the rules, and Ward (Willem Dafoe), a by-the-book Yankee—and the ignorant rednecks who are Klan members and unadulterated scum. That makes for a film which is strong on small town atmosphere and the recycling of buddy film conventions and devoid of any feeling for historical fact or reality.

It was only during the last half of the decade that the films of a group of young black directors—Robert Townsend, Keenan Ivory Wayans, the Hudlin brothers, and the most original, Spike Lee—began to appear. Their works were rooted in black concerns and language and possibly signaled "the emergence of a new esthetic sensibility within Black America."[27] And, despite the fact that they were centered in the specificity of black reality, they were able to have some appeal to white, mainstream audiences.

Spike Lee's films, the low-budget *She's Gotta Have It* (1986), *School Daze* (1988), and *Do the Right Thing* (1989), were personal works about aspects of black life that the larger public almost never saw before on the screen. The most politically controversial and formally imaginative of his films up to now is *Do the Right Thing*, which received a great deal of critical praise even as it was virulently attacked by some black and white critics. There were white critics who saw the film as stirring up race riots and as a black racist work, while a number of black critics saw it as being insufficiently militant or given to stereotyping black life. Lee's film elicited the kind of charged, extremely varied responses that clearly went beyond its mise-en-scène and touched a raw nerve in black-white relations.

Do the Right Thing was flawed: a bit too many film school tics (e.g., gratuitous oblique angles and tight close-ups); a penchant for sanitizing some of the more destructive aspects of black inner-city life by eliminating both drugs and crime from the street; a sexist strain in its depiction of its central female character, Tina (Rosie Perez)—Mookie's (Spike Lee as an underachieving pizza deliveryman) undulating, nagging, foulmouthed wife; and most importantly, a political overview of the black relationship with white society which seems more dangerously facile (e.g., Public Enemy's rap song "Fight the Power") and muddled than dialectical or ambiguous. Lee may be genuinely groping for social answers—looking at Malcolm X and Martin Luther King as political role models—but the film seems less an expression of an artist exploring political alternatives than one mired in intellectual confusion.

However, despite these flaws *Do the Right Thing* was a rarity among American films; it was a serious, dynamic work about something substantial—successfully fusing realism and stylization to evoke a kaleidoscope of black community life and problems on one Brooklyn street during a summer heat wave. And Lee truly loves and knows how to grant cinematic life to the physical texture and language of the street. Using an episodic narrative and a great deal of rapid cutting and panning, point-of-view shots, talking heads, characters who skirt the edge of being cartoons, and other distancing devices like the disc jockey Love Daddy who provides commentary and narration during the film, Lee touches on a number of prime social issues that face the black community. They range from police brutality and white racism to gentrification, black hostility towards white and Asian storeowners, and the way black pride and protest should be manifested. Lee's Brooklyn street, enveloped in artificial light, has clearly been sweetened and romanticized, but he doesn't totally avert the camera eye from some of the painful realities of black inner-city life. For example, Mookie continually evades his responsibility as a father, and many of the black characters lack a work ethic, spending a great deal of time merely jiving, hanging around, and indulging in the kind of race rhetoric and idle fantasy that become substitutes for any sort of coherent, decisive action—be it political or personal.

Given Lee's profound identification with the black community and culture, it was a sign of his skill that the character granted the most dimension in *Do the Right Thing* is Sal (Danny Aiello), the Italo-American owner of the neighborhood pizzeria. Sal is depicted as an earthy, decent man whose life is his store. He has an amicable relationship with his black customers, whom he treats, despite an undercurrent of paternalism, as individuals. But Sal is also a product of a subculture where the use of racist epithets like "nigger" are not unusual. Enraged, Sal spews out racist invective, but Lee never dismisses or calcifies him as just a bigot. He treats him sympathetically (even a bit sentimentally)—an honest, feelingful man, in a frightening situation, whose dimensions he doesn't quite fully understand, responding the only way he knows how.

Lee's film may have heralded a breakthrough for black directors into the mainstream, but 1989 also saw a racially sensitive film like *Glory* evolve from more traditional and white Hollywood sources. Directed by Edward Zwick (creator of television's *thirtysomething*), the film dealt with the Civil War's 54th Massachusetts Infantry, an Afro-American volunteer unit led by a white abolitionist, Robert Gould Shaw (Matthew Broderick), who shed their lives in the cause of freedom. *Glory* would have likely been more profitable if it had centered the action on the idealistic white officer. This time around, however, Hollywood gave more than equal time to the courageous members of the black regiment (e.g., Rawlins [Morgan Freeman], Trip [Denzel Washington]), who, if not richly nuanced characters, are never reduced to stereotypes—either racial or military genre film ones.

There was one other extremely popular mainstream 1989 film to touch on racial issues. Bruce Beresford's luminously acted, Oscar-winning *Driving Miss Daisy* (Jessica Tandy won an Oscar for best actress) deals with the warm relationship of a crochety, elderly Jewish lady and her gracious, wise, black chauffeur Hoke (Morgan Freeman again). Set in the South of a couple of decades back, the film is a too neatly calibrated and predictable work which intelligently choreographs the nuances of their relationship without disturbing an audience either politically or psychologically. The relationship is an inequitable, mistress-servant one, but Daisy's power is muted by age and her dependency on Hoke. The friendship permits a white audience to feel emotionally and socially at ease because Hoke is a courtly and restrained man whom they like, one who almost never directly challenges the social status quo. The audience's sympathetic identification with this nostalgic, safe relationship makes them feel virtuous and liberal, without their ever having to confront the pain and tortuous complexity of present-day black-white relations.

Though the late 1980s saw the production of relatively sophisticated films about black life and black-white relationships, this heightened cinematic consciousness did not find a parallel in the society at large. General Colin Powell may have become the first black to head the Joint Chiefs of Staff under President Bush, Bill Cosby's sitcom one of the top-rated television shows of the period, and Spike Lee a popular director and pitchman for athletic shoes, but, in the main, white acceptance extended only to talented, elite blacks, not to the vast majority of the black population. In fact, during the 1980s the Reagan presidency signaled, by word and deed, that racism was acceptable; "decent," upper-class George Bush used coded racist appeals as part of his presidential campaign; and there was a marked increase in general racial tension, and even a proliferation of racial incidents on college campuses. What films like *Glory* possibly signified for a white audience was an affirmation of those democratic ideals that represented their best selves on questions of race. It was much less painful for the public to connect with this moral vision on film than to try to actualize these ideals by wrestling with all the complex and charged social variables surrounding everyday racial issues.

The 1980s not only saw several black directors finally get the chance to make films, but there was a minor renaissance of women directors as well. From its inception, male owned and controlled Hollywood had closed off the opportunity for women to play a significant role behind the camera. There were only a handful that were allowed to direct films—Alice Guy-Blache, Dorothy Arzner, Ida Lupino, and Elaine May—none of their work explicitly feminist. The feminist movement, however, changed the situation for younger women directors, and in the mid- and late 1970s overtly feminist films like Joan Micklin Silver's *Hester Street* (1975) and Claudia Weill's *Girlfriends* (1978) were made.[28]

After these films appeared, women directors could move away from expressly feminist content while rooting their work in the assumption that female characters no longer perceive themselves solely in terms of their relationships with men; and as a corollary that they would live more independent lives based on their own individual choices. Some of the most interesting 1980s films made by women directors were commercial, mainstream works like Barbra Streisand's *Yentl* (1983) and Susan Seidelman's offbeat second feature, *Desperately Seeking Susan* (1985), about two very different women switching identities (Madonna and Rosanna Arquette), while others were low budget films like Joyce Chopra's *Smooth Talk* (1986), an adaptation of Joyce Carol Oates' story about an adolescent girl's frightening sexual initiation, and Donna Deitch's film about a passionate lesbian love affair set in the middle America of 1959 Reno, Nevada, *Desert Hearts* (1986).

Yentl, the most mainstream, was the result of Streisand's fifteen-year dream to adapt an I. B. Singer story for the screen. Streisand, in the megalomaniacal mode of an Orson Welles, produced, directed, starred in (she sings every song) and even co-wrote this big-budget, overly or-

chestrated, and sometimes bathetic work about a rebellious, intellectually avid Jewish shtetl girl, Yentl, who dresses up as a boy in order to
study the Talmud. (Women were excluded from the world of learning in
the orthodox Jewish religious tradition of the shtetl.) Streisand loves to
underline, using split mirrors to connote Yentl's divided self and a bird
as a symbol of her flight from a traditional identity, panning to a chicken
as a metaphor for gossiping women, and bathing every sacred object
(e.g., a talis) in a golden light.

Nevertheless, despite its heavy-handed and bloated images, *Yentl* is an
ambitious, sometimes suggestive work which raises questions about the
role of women and about female bonding. Yentl, in her male disguise,
establishes a link with a beautiful, deferential, traditional woman, Hadass (Amy Irving), which is more intimate and tender than any male-
female relationship in the film. The relationship is open to a variety of
interpretations: as a homoerotic passion; as a nonsexual affirmation of
female bonding; as an appreciation of the role domestic, supportive
women play, which would appeal to Streisand's more conventional fans;
and as revealing the underside of her appreciation of Hadass—an independent woman's revulsion with Hadass's passivity and capacity for
shape-changing.[29] The film also concludes on a feminist note: Yentl sacrifices the man she loves—the kindly, manly, Talmudist Avigdor (Mandy
Patinkin), who wants her to stay at home and be a traditional wife,
maintaining that a wise woman knows everything without opening a
book—and heads for America to try out her wings and find room to
grow.

Besides Streisand there were other women who had an impact on Hollywood as producers. Jane Fonda formed a production company and
made *China Syndrome* and *Nine to Five* (1981), Jessica Lange produced
Country, Sally Field, *Places in the Heart*, and Goldie Hawn together with
Anthea Sylbert produced shallow, pop feminist films like *Private Benjamin* (1980) and *Protocol* (1984). Nevertheless, there is no guarantee that
the fact that some women achieved power in Hollywood would mean
that a more profound feminist perspective would inform its product,
since profits are Hollywood's governing reality, and risk-taking is usually
left to filmmakers outside the system.

Not only did the 1980s see a minor breakthrough for women directors
and producers and for films projecting a feminist perspective, but also
for films dealing with gay and lesbian sexuality as well. Until the 1960s
most Hollywood films submerged, displaced, or hid any mention of homosexuality. Then, with the relaxation of the Production Code, films
like *The Boys in the Band* (1970) and *The Killing of Sister George* (1968)
were made which dealt with openly gay and lesbian characters but

tended to perpetuate the most blatant, negative stereotypes—hysterically effeminate men and muscular and sadistic male hustlers, and angry
butch or sleek predatory lesbians. In these films gay or lesbian characters
were also rarely given the chance to have a happy, full life. However, in
1980s films like Bill Sherwood's *Parting Glances* (1985) and the aforementioned *Desert Hearts*, a gay and lesbian cinema that defined itself in its
own terms and voice made its appearance. It was best exemplified by the
openly lesbian Cay's (Patricia Charbonneau) remark in *Desert Hearts*, "I
don't act that way to change the world, I act that way so that the world
doesn't change me." The films were a hopeful augur of future works
which would authentically portray gay and lesbian life and consciousness, and neither romanticize nor denigrate it.[30]

Despite the clear shift in Hollywood's attitude towards women, and
greater openness to unstereotyped images of gay life, the last years of the
decade saw films that evoked strains of an anti-feminist backlash. In very
different ways films like *Baby Boom* (1987), *Fatal Attraction* (1987), *Broadcast News* (1987), and *Working Girl* (1988) affirmed marriage and often
projected negative images of independent career women. *Baby Boom* re-
verses the pattern of feminist films; it centers on an ad executive, played
by Diane Keaton, who leaves her high-powered job in Manhattan for a
fulfilling life as mother and apron-clad housewife in small town Ver-
mont. Adrian Lyne's slick, overheated, manipulative *Fatal Attraction*
skillfully creates frissons of suspense and fear, while constructing an implicitly regressive, anti-feminist vision. In *Fatal Attraction*, Dan (Michael
Douglas), a New York attorney with a loving home and happy marriage
to a beautiful, thoroughly domestic wife, has an intensely sexual, weekend affair with a seductive, single book editor, Alex (Glenn Close). Af-
terwards he tries to brush her off, but the career woman, who lives in an
inferno-like apartment, becomes vindictive and turns out to be a wild,
murderous figure. Though basically a well-made, predictable thriller, the
image it conveys of the unmarried, professional woman as pathetic and
mad reaffirms the value of marriage and home as havens of warmth and
stability and acts as a warning to women of the unnaturalness of living
independent, solitary lives.

The backlash elements in writer-director James L. Brooks's (creator of
the *Mary Tyler Moore Show*) *Broadcast News* are more subtle. This
briskly-paced film is filled with witty one-liners and has an insider's
knowledge of how television deals with the news and newscasters. However, *Broadcast News* is much less a critique of the content, role, and
value of television news than an updated portrait of a love triangle,
whose emotional life is no deeper than the wisecracks and the well-
honed set pieces that permeate the film. The romance is salvaged a bit

by three extremely strong performances by the film's leads: Albert Brooks as Aaron—a knowledgeable, committed reporter, who was born with a more aggressive version of Woody Allen's whine, insecurity, and self-deflective humor; William Hurt as Tom—a handsome, decent, intellectually limited anchorman whose pleasing and natural television persona make him the darling of the media executives; and Holly Hunter as Jane (an Oscar-winning performance), an extremely effective, bright, bossy news producer who has an unhappy private life. Implicit in the film is the notion that any woman like Jane, who is a driven, successful, morally serious professional, would, by necessity, live a tearful and solitary existence; that for a professional woman to have a happy personal life she would have to submerge some part of herself into a conventional female persona.

Even Mike Nichols's glossy, populist fable, *Working Girl*, projected an anti-feminist strain. Nichols's slight fairy tale about a sweet, working-class secretary from Staten Island, Tess (Melanie Griffith), whose financial wizardry both wins the heart of a Wall Street broker and turns Tess into an executive with a secretary and office of her own, is, on one level, a scenario for Reaganism—creating a world where overnight success and the big money (especially of the Wall Street variety) are available for anyone who has confidence and drive, and can appropriate the style and accent of the upper middle class. On another level, the film is a put-down of the type of cold, manipulative superwoman—Tess's boss Katherine (Sigourney Weaver), whose lack of softness and femininity help lead to her fall.[31] *Working Girl* is clearly not interested in engaging in a serious critique of the corporate world or of feminist claims, but in Tess it found a heroine who combines ambition, shrewdness, and female vulnerability—a perfect alternative to all those hard, threatening women whose supposed female virtues and characteristics disappeared with success in the public world.

Films containing strains of anti-feminism were just one of a number of cinematic currents during the last years of the decade. A popular, Capraesque fable like *Field of Dreams* (1989) sees the film's hero, Ray Kinsella (Kevin Costner)—a sixties activist turned Iowa corn farmer— resurrect what the film sees as the purity of the past, by following the instructions of a heavenly voice and transforming a cornfield into a baseball diamond filled with old ballplayers like Shoeless Joe Jackson. Kinsella does this not only to recover an idyllic America, but to ease the pain of a disenchanted writer so he can rediscover his muse, and to bring about his own reconciliation with the father he once rejected— baseball becoming both a social and psychological panacea.

Field of Dreams provides a great many simplistic soliloquies about both the need to dream and to recreate the innocence of childhood—a mixture of 1960s counterculture spirituality combined with the myth of the American rural past. It also attacks the utilitarian money culture and small-town censorship (an easy target), but its alternative vision is apolitical and nebulous, consisting of little more than a set of greeting card platitudes.

The soft-minded, nostalgic *Field of Dreams* was just one of the popular successes of 1989 which included a disparate group of films. Among them were the previously discussed *Do the Right Thing, Driving Miss Daisy,* and *Born on the Fourth of July,* a relentlessly middlebrow and pop homage to poetry and freedom like the *Dead Poets Society,* and big-budget summer films like the imaginatively designed (influenced by Fritz Lang's expressionist *Metropolis* and Reginald Marsh's painting) and totally impersonal, comic book epic *Batman,* and Spielberg's *Indiana Jones and the Last Crusade*—the third and most human (which is not saying much) of the playful boy's adventure trilogy. Clearly no single political and social trend could be gleaned from such radically different works, but the variety itself was a sign that Hollywood had become a touch less dependent on a teenage and action-oriented audience and could make a few films that would appeal to literate adults, albeit most of these films took few formal or intellectual risks.

In the final analysis, though Hollywood no longer plays the dominant cultural role it once did in the forties, it still has the capacity to create resonant, almost instantaneous cultural myths. It is for this power alone, if for nothing else, that the Hollywood film bears watching as an important barometer of America's dreams and desires, and of changes in its cultural and social values. There is also the possibility that the new technologies of video cassettes and cable television, which both compete with and act as a market for the industry, may force Hollywood to create a more variegated, imaginative, and adventurous product; that in the future more room may exist for films made by black and women directors; and that the work of such independent directors as Jim Jarmusch (*Stranger Than Paradise*, 1984), Tim Hunter (*The River's Edge,* 1986), and Steven Soderbergh (*sex, lies, and videotape,* 1989) will continue to develop and help renew mainstream Hollywood with films that both contain a personal voice and deal with human concerns rather than comic book heroes, special effects, or nonstop mayhem.

Though Hollywood's bottom line has always been profit, and art is usually seen as an afterthought or given no thought at all, who can be so complacent that he or she can predict the way the future of the world of film will evolve?

NOTES

1. Lou Cannon, *Ronald Reagan* (New York: G. P. Putnam's Sons, 1982), pp. 329–413.

2. Nicolaus Mills, "Culture in an Age of Money," *Dissent* (Winter 1990), pp. 11–17.

3. Mills, "Culture in an Age of Money," p. 13.

4. Gregg Kilday, "The Eighties," *Film Comment* (November–December 1989), p. 65.

5. Kilday, "The Eighties," p. 66.

6. Budd Schulberg, "What Makes Hollywood Run Now?" *New York Times Magazine* (April 27, 1980), pp. 52–88. See also Leslie Wayne, "Hollywood Sequels Are Just the Ticket," *New York Times* (July 18, 1982), pp. 1–17.

7. Veronica Geng, "Pearls Before Swine: Review of Ordinary People," *Soho Weekly News* (September 17, 1980), pp. 58–59.

8. Barbara Quart, "Tootsie," *Cineaste* XII, 4 (Summer 1983), pp. 40–42.

9. Richard Schickel, "Slam! Bang! A Movie Movie," *Time* (June 15, 1981), pp. 74–76.

10. Michiko Kakutani, "The Two Faces of Spielberg—Horrors vs. Hope," *New York Times* (May 30, 1982), pp. 1, 30. See also Pauline Kael, "The Pure and the Impure," *The New Yorker* (June 14, 1982), pp. 119–22.

11. Richard Schickel, "At Last, Kate and Hank!" *Time* (November 18, 1981), pp. 112–13.

12. Aaron Latham, "Warren Beatty, Seriously," *Rolling Stone* (April 1, 1982), p. 19.

13. Belle Gale Chevigny, Kate Ellis, Ann Kaplan, and Leonard Quart, "Talking 'Reds,'" *Socialist Review* 12, 2 (March–April, 1982), pp. 109–24.

14. *Ibid.*

15. Robert A. Rosenstone, *Romantic Revolutionary: A Biography of John Reed* (New York: Alfred A. Knopf, 1975), p. 4.

16. Richard Grenier, "Bolshevism for the 80's," *Commentary* (March 1982), pp. 56–63.

17. Joy Gould Boyum, "'Reds': Love and Revolution," *Wall Street Journal* (December 4, 1981), p. 35.

18. Al Auster and Leonard Quart, "Counterculture Revisited: An Interview with John Sayles," *Cineaste* XI, 1 (Winter 1980–81), pp. 16–19.

19. Fred Siegel, "Blissed Out and Loving It," *Commonweal* (February 9, 1990), p. 76.

20. Terry Christensen, *Reel Politics: American Movies from Birth of a Nation to Platoon* (New York: Basil Blackwell, 1987), pp. 165–66.

21. Albert Auster and Leonard Quart, *How the War Was Remembered: Hollywood and Vietnam* (New York: Praeger, 1988), pp. 99–112.

22. Auster and Quart, *How the War Was Remembered*, pp. 131–45.

23. Christopher Sharrett, "Born on the Fourth of July," *Cineaste* XVII, 4 (Spring, 1990), pp. 48–50.

24. Elayne Rapping, "Hollywood's Youth Cult Films," *Cineaste* XVI, 1–2 (Winter, 1987–88), pp. 14–19.

25. Rapping, "Hollywood's Youth Cult Films," p. 18.

26. Editorial, *Cineaste* XVII, 2 (Fall, 1989), p. 2.

27. Eric Perkins, "Renewing the African-American Cinema: The Films of Spike Lee," *Cineaste* XVII, 4 (Spring, 1990), p. 8.

28. Barbara Koenig Quart, *Women Directors: The Emergence of a New Cinema* (New York: Praeger, 1988), pp. 37–38.

29. Quart, *Women Directors*, pp. 83–85.

30. Andrea Weiss, "From the Margins: New Image of Gays in the Cinema," *Cineaste* XV, 1 (Fall, 1986), pp. 4–8.

31. Caryn James, "Are Feminist Heroines an Endangered Species?" *New York Times: Sunday Arts and Leisure* (July 16, 1989), p. 15.

SELECTED BIBLIOGRAPHY

Dean Acheson, *Present at the Creation* (New York: W. W. Norton, 1969).

Renata G. Adler, *A Year in the Dark* (New York: Berkeley, 1969).

James Agee, *Agee on Film: Reviews and Comments* (Boston: Beacon Press, 1966).

Hollis Alpert and Andrew Sarris (eds.), *Film 68/69: An Anthology by the National Society of Film Critics* (New York: Simon and Schuster, 1969).

Rick Altman (ed.), *Genre: The Musical* (London: Routledge & Kegan Paul, 1981).

Stephen Ambrose, *Rise to Globalism: American Foreign Policy 1938–1970* (Baltimore, Md.: Penguin, 1971).

Albert Auster and Leonard Quart, *How the War Was Remembered: Hollywood and Vietnam* (New York: Praeger, 1988).

Alan G. Barbour, *John Wayne* (New York: Pyramid, 1974).

Eric Barnouw, *Tube of Plenty: The Evolution of American Television* (New York: Oxford University Press, 1977).

Donald Bogle, *Toms, Coons, Mulattoes, Mammies and Bucks* (New York: Bantam, 1973).

Tim Bywater and Thomas Sobchack, *Film Criticism: Major Critical Approaches to Narrative Film* (White Plains, N.Y.: Longman, 1989).

Lou Cannon, *Ronald Reagan* (New York: G. P. Putnam's Sons, 1982).

Frank Capra, *The Name above the Title* (New York: Bantam, 1972).

Terry Christensen, *Reel Politics: American Movies from Birth of a Nation to Platoon* (New York: Basil Blackwell, 1987).

Michel Ciment, *Kazan on Kazan* (New York: Viking, 1973).

Pam Cook (ed.), *The Cinema Book* (New York: Pantheon, 1985).

Alistair Cooke, *A Generation on Trial* (Baltimore, Md.: Penguin, 1952).

Philip Davies and Brian Neve (eds.), *Cinema, Politics and Society in America* (Manchester, U. K.: Manchester University Press, 1981).

Barbara Deming, *Running Away from Myself: A Dream Portrait of America Drawn from the Films of the Forties* (New York: Grossman Publishers, 1969).

Morris Dickstein, *Gates of Eden: American Culture in the Sixties* (New York: Basic Books, 1977).

Thomas Ferguson and Joel Rogers, *Right Turn: The Decline of the Democrats and the Future of American Politics* (New York: Hill and Wang, 1986).

Frances Fitzgerald, *Fire in the Lake* (New York: Vintage, 1973).

Gerald R. Ford, *A Time to Heal* (New York: Berkeley, 1980).

Hugh Fordin, *The World of Entertainment: Hollywood's Greatest Musicals* (Garden City, N.Y.: Doubleday, 1975).

Brandon French, *On the Verge of Revolt: Women in American Films of the Fifties* (New York: Frederick Ungar, 1978).

Phillip French, *Westerns* (New York: Oxford University Press, 1977).

Neal Gabler, *An Empire of Their Own: How the Jews Invented Hollywood* (New York: Crown, 1988).

Nicholas Garnham, *Samuel Fuller* (New York: Viking, 1971).

Charlie Gillett, *The Sound of the City: The Rise of Rock and Roll*, rev. ed. (New York: Pantheon, 1984).

Eric F. Goldman, *The Crucial Decade—and After, America 1945–1960* (New York: Vintage, 1960).

Walter Goodman, *The Committee: The Extraordinary Career of the House Committee on Un-American Activities* (Baltimore, Md.: Penguin, 1969).

Joseph G. Goulden, *The Best Years, 1945–1950* (New York: Atheneum, 1976).

Gordon Gow, *Hollywood in the Fifties* (New York: A. S. Barnes, 1971).

David Halberstam, *The Best and the Brightest* (New York: Fawcett, 1973).

Stuart Hall and Paddy Whannel, *The Popular Arts* (New York: Pantheon, 1965).

Jon Halliday, *Sirk on Sirk* (New York: Viking, 1972).

Molly Haskell, *From Reverence to Rape: The Treatment of Women in the Movies* (Baltimore, Md.: Penguin, 1974).

Venable Herndon, *James Dean: A Short Life* (New York: Signet, 1974).

Charles Higham and Joel Greenberg, *Hollywood in the Forties* (New York: Paperback Library, 1970).

Godfrey Hodgson, *America in Our Time: From World War II to Nixon, What Happened and Why* (New York: Vintage, 1978).

Diane Jacobs, *Hollywood Renaissance: The New Generation of Filmmakers and Their Works* (New York: Delta, 1980).

Garth Jowett, *Film: The Democratic Art* (Boston: Little, Brown, 1976).

Pauline Kael, *Kiss, Kiss, Bang, Bang,* (New York: Bantam, 1969).

Pauline Kael, *Going Steady* (New York: Bantam, 1971).

Norman Kagan, *The Cinema of Stanley Kubrick* (New York: Grove Press, 1975).

Norman Kagan, *The War Film* (New York: Pyramid Publications, 1974).

Stuart M. Kaminsky, *Don Siegel, Director* (New York: Curtis Books, 1974).

Judith Kass, *Robert Altman: American Innovator* (New York: Popular Library, 1978).

Doris Kearns, *Lyndon B. Johnson and the American Dream* (New York: Signet, 1976).

Siegfried Kracauer, *From Caligari to Hitler: A Psychological History of the German Film*, 3rd ed. (Princeton, N.J.: Princeton University Press, 1970).

William L. Langer, *Political and Social Upheaval, 1832–1852* (New York: Harper and Row, 1969).

Christopher Lasch, *The Culture of Narcissism* (New York: Warner Books, 1979).

Norman Mailer, *Armies of the Night* (New York: Signet, 1968).

Gerald Mast and Marshall Cohen (eds.), *Film Theory and Criticism* (New York: Oxford University Press, 1974).

James Monaco, *American Film Now: The People, the Power, the Money, the Movies* (New York: Oxford University Press, 1979).

Joseph Morgenstern and Stefan Kanfer (eds.), *Film 69/70: An Anthology by the National Society of Film Critics* (New York: Simon and Schuster, 1970).

Victor S. Navasky, *Naming Names* (New York: Viking, 1980).

John E. O'Connor and Martin A. Jackson (eds.), *American History/American Film: Interpreting the Hollywood Image* (New York: Frederick Ungar, 1979).

William L. O'Neill, *Coming Apart: An Informal History of America in the 1960s* (New York: Quadrangle, 1971).

Sidney Poitier, *This Life* (New York: Ballantine, 1980).

Gerald Pratley, *The Cinema of John Frankenheimer* (Cranbury, N.J.: A. S. Barnes, 1969).

Barbara Koenig Quart, *Women Directors: The Emergence of a New Cinema* (New York: Praeger, 1988).

Peter Roffman and Jim Purdy, *The Hollywood Social Problem Film* (Bloomington, Ind.: Indiana University Press, 1981).

Deborah Silverton Rosenfelt (ed.), *Salt of the Earth* (Old Westbury, N.Y.: Feminist Press, 1978).

Robert A. Rosenstone, *Romantic Revolutionary: A Biography of John Reed* (New York: Alfred A. Knopf, 1975).

Richard Rovere, *Senator Joseph McCarthy*, rev. ed. (New York: Harper and Row, 1973).

Michael Ryan and Douglas Kellner, *Camera Politica: The Politics and Ideology of Contemporary Hollywood Film* (Bloomington, Ind.: Indiana University Press, 1988).

Kirkpatrick Sale, *SDS* (New York: Vintage, 1974).

Nora Sayre, *Running Time: Films of the Cold War* (New York: Dial Press, 1982).

Thomas Schatz, *The Genius of the System: Hollywood Filmmaking in the Studio Era* (New York: Pantheon, 1988).

Jonathan Schell, *The Time of Illusion* (New York: Alfred A. Knopf, 1976).

Frederick F. Siegel, *Troubled Journey: From Pearl Harbor to Ronald Reagan* (New York: Hill and Wang, 1984).

Robert Sklar, *Movie Made America: A Cultural History of American Movies* (New York: Vintage, 1975).

Susan Sontag, *Against Interpretation* (New York: Dell, 1969).

Donald Spoto, *Stanley Kramer: Filmmaker* (New York: G. P. Putnam's Sons, 1978).

Diana Trilling, *We Must March, My Darlings* (New York: Harcourt Brace Jovanovich, 1977).

Irwin Unger, *These United States: The Questions of Our Past*, vol. 2, *Since 1865* (Englewood Cliffs, N.J.: Prentice-Hall, 1989).

Robert Warshow, *The Immediate Experience* (Garden City, N.Y.: Anchor, 1964).

Edmund White, *The Beautiful Room Is Empty* (New York: Ballantine, 1988).

Theodore H. White, *Breach of Faith* (New York: Dell, 1980).

Raymond Williams, *Communications*, 3rd ed. (London: Pelican, 1976).

Garry Wills, *Reagan's America: With a New Chapter on the Legacy of the Reagan Era* (New York: Penguin, 1987).

William Julius Wilson, *The Truly Disadvantaged: The Inner City, The Underclass, and Public Policy* (Chicago: University of Chicago Press, 1987).

Michael Wood, *America in the Movies: or, "Santa Maria, It Had Slipped My Mind!"* (New York: Basic Books, 1975).

Robin Wood, *Arthur Penn* (New York: Praeger, 1969).

James Wooten, *Dasher* (New York: Signet, 1978).

INDEX

ABOUT THE AUTHORS

LEONARD QUART is Associate Professor of Cinema Studies at the College of Staten Island/CUNY and co-author of *How the War Was Remembered: Hollywood and Vietnam* (Praeger, 1988). He is an editor of *Cineaste* magazine and a contributor to a wide variety of film and general magazines and newspapers.

ALBERT AUSTER teaches in the communication department of the State University of New York at New Paltz. He is author of *Actresses and Suffragists: Women in the American Theater, 1890–1920* (Praeger, 1984) and co-author of *How the War Was Remembered: Hollywood and Vietnam* (Praeger, 1988). He contributes regularly to *Television Quarterly* and *Journal of Popular Film and Television*.